*Creating Dynamic Multimedia Presentations Using Microsoft PowerPoint,* 2e
Carol M. Lehman

**Editor-in-Chief:**
Jack W. Calhoun

**Team Leader:**
Melissa S. Acuña

**Acquisitions Editor:**
Jennifer L. Codner

**Developmental Editor:**
Taney H. Wilkins

**Marketing Manager:**
Larry Qualls

**Production Editors:**
Heather Mann, Daniel C. Plofchan

**Manufacturing Coordinator:**
Diane Lohman

**Production House/Compositor:**
DPS Associates, Inc.

**Printer:**
West Group
Eagan, MN

**Design Project Manager:**
B. Casey Gilbertson

**Internal and Cover Design:**
B. Casey Gilbertson

**Cover Image:**
Photodisc, Inc.

Library of Congress Cataloging-in-Publication Data
Lehman, Carol M.
Creating dynamic multimedia presentations : using Microsoft PowerPoint / Carol M. Lehman.—2nd ed.
p.cm.
Includes index.
ISBN: 0-324-18767-X
1. Business presentations—Graphic methods—Computer programs.
2. Microsoft PowerPoint (Computer file)
3. Multimedia systems in business presentations.  I. Title.

HF5718.22 .L44 2002
658.4'5'028566869—dc21  2002074315

# creating dynamic
# multimedia
## presentations

## Using Microsoft PowerPoint®

**THOMSON**

**SOUTH-WESTERN**

Australia · Canada · Mexico · Singapore · Spain · United Kingdom · United States

# LEARNING OBJECTIVES FOR:

## *USING VISUAL AIDS*

The objectives for *Using Visual Aids* are listed below. They have been developed to guide you, the reader, to the core issues covered in this book.

### Objectives

❑ 1) **To explain the use of seven types of visual media**

❑ 2) **To show how to organize and create visuals**

❑ 3) **To provide tips and advise about pitfalls in the use of visual aids**

### Assessing Your Progress

In addition to the learning objectives, Crisp Learning has developed an **assessment** that covers the fundamental information presented in this book. A 25-item, multiple-choice and true-false questionnaire allows the reader to evaluate his or her comprehension of the subject matter. To learn how to obtain a copy of this assessment, please call **1-800-442-7477** and ask to speak with a Customer Service Representative.

*Assessments should not be used in any employee selection process.*

# ABOUT THIS BOOK

The first edition of this book, *Visual Aids in Business,* was published in 1989. Trainers and presenters found it practical, helpful, and comprehensive. It has been a steady seller for five years. We felt, though, that it was ready for an overhaul. We wanted to arrange it more simply and logically, to add a section of simple designs for readers to use, and to change the format to make it a sourcebook for presenters. We also wanted to broaden the readership. The first book was written specifically for the businessperson. We've realized there are all sorts of people who need the information in this book—teachers, educators, trainers, workshop and conference presenters, meeting facilitators and leaders.

You will find the book has changed considerably. The new title reflects a broader readership, and the examples throughout the book come from a broad spectrum of presentation scenarios. We think you will find The Toolbox (pages 75 through 80) to be invaluable. It is a collection of simple sketches—basic shapes, adaptations and combinations of shapes and designs—which you can use on flipcharts and other visual aids. Each page of this new edition is meant to be a source of ideas for you; you can thumb through and find different kinds of bullets, handdrawn symbols, simple drawings, unusual designs, and imaginative layouts which will serve as inspiration for finding creative ways to add pizzazz to your presentations.

# ABOUT THE AUTHORS

Claire Raines is a speaker, consultant, and author. Her book, *Twentysomething: Managing and Motivating Today's New Work Force,* was named one of the thirty best business books of 1992 by Executive Book Summaries. She receives rave reviews for her multimedia presentations on "Generation X," which help audiences better understand today's entry-level workers.

Linda Williamson brings over two decades of experience to her work as a trainer, speaker and corporate consultant in classrooms, boardrooms, wilderness environments and trainings throughout the United States, Australia, Singapore, Hong Kong, India, Korea and England. Her contributions to this book are the result of her experiences leading personal and organizational transformation, team building and management effectiveness seminars.

We welcome your comments, questions and inquiries about presentation skills and visual aids workshops. We can be reached through The Springer Group, P.O. Box 5226, Eugene, Oregon 97405 USA, (503) 342-3083.

# CONTENTS

# TO THE READER

We live in a world of words. We are bombarded by information. Picture your desk at this very moment. If you are typical of other busy people, there are stacks of notes and lists, papers, letters, memos, articles, and brochures—all competing for a few moments of your attention.

When you stand up to speak in front of a group, you need to do more than contribute to this constant barrage of words. You need to present your information so that it is powerful, clear, convincing, straightforward, and believable. Good visuals are mental shorthand. They can communicate your ideas imaginatively—without adding more words. Well-planned graphics and visuals will literally help your audience to "see what you mean." A set of common symbols, shapes, and strokes acts like a basic visual alphabet, becoming an interactive language between you and your audience.

When you use high quality visuals, people enjoy taking notes on your presentations. And, when you speak to diverse groups of people from a variety of backgrounds, visuals are especially important since you can use symbols and drawings that are universally recognized and applicable to humans worldwide.

We hope you will find lots of ideas here that will make your presentations more successful. But, most important, we hope you will have more fun with your next presentation!

Best wishes,

*Claire Raines*     *Linda Williamson*

Claire Raines & Linda Williamson

# PART I

## When and Why to Use Visual Aids

# SELF EVALUATION

To improve your effectiveness in planning and using visual aids, it will be helpful to take a look at the expertise you have now. This evaluation will help you identify your strengths and weaknesses. Please read each statement and then circle the number that best describes you. The focus is to be highly effective while *simple* and *professional* in your presentation.

|  | Never | | | Always |
|---|---|---|---|---|

1. I carefully analyze the audience for my presentation before planning the visuals I will use.
    1   2   3   4   5

2. I spent far more time planning and organizing my presentation than worrying about it.
    1   2   3   4   5

3. During my presentations, I notice my successes later, I focus on how to learn from the mistakes.
    1   2   3   4   5

4. When my visuals contain text, there are no more than 36 words.
    1   2   3   4   5

5. My visuals contain only the information that I am presenting in my presentation.
    1   2   3   4   5

6. I am familiar with the basic principles of design and keep them in mind when planning visuals.
    1   2   3   4   5

7. Everything on my visuals can be seen clearly from the back row.
    1   2   3   4   5

8. I remember to have fun and enjoy giving my presentation.
    1   2   3   4   5

9. I use a simple, easy-to-read typeface.
    1   2   3   4   5

10. I have a logical plan for where and how to use the visual aids in the presentation so they have maximum impact.
    1   2   3   4   5

11. I arrive early and check out the equipment until intimately familiar with the on/off switch, location of an extra bulb, focus, and other adjustments.
    1   2   3   4   5

12. I locate my visual aids in an effective position in the room where I'm presenting.
    1   2   3   4   5

| | Never | | | | Always |
|---|---|---|---|---|---|

13. I carefully avoid getting caught between the visual aids and the audience.  1  2  3  4  5

14. I am skilled at maintaining eye contact and facing the audience while using visuals.  1  2  3  4  5

15. I avoid reading from my visuals. Instead, my visuals act as a back-up to my presentation.  1  2  3  4  5

16. I clear away visuals when they no longer apply to the subject I'm presenting. I turn off or black out the screen when it is not in use.  1  2  3  4  5

17. I take care that visuals are support—not the focal point—for my presentations.  1  2  3  4  5

18. To avoid detracting from my presentation, I limit the number of visual aids I use.  1  2  3  4  5

19. When using overhead transparencies, I put them in frames with centering marks.  1  2  3  4  5

20. I congratulate myself on a job well done!     Total score  _____

---

If you scored between *90* and *100*, you plan to use visual aids very effectively and are probably known as an excellent and persuasive speaker.

If your total score was between *80* and *90*, you have the basic expertise to become highly adept at planning and using dynamic visual aids.

If your score was between *30* and *80*, this book has all sorts of information that will move you into one of the top two categories.

If your score was below *30*, you have lots of opportunities to improve your presentation. It takes some work and it can be done. Stick with it.

**Concentrate on the statements you marked 1, 2 or 3. Those are the areas you will want to give the most time to as you work through this book.**

# WHEN TO USE VISUAL AIDS

## Use a visual to:

☆ Clarify a point.

☆ Emphasize a point.

☆ Add variety.

☆ Change focus.

☆ Record the main points of a meeting or presentation.

☆ Enhance your professional image.

☆ Mark off your presentation as special.

## Avoid using a visual when it:

☆ Distracts or detracts from the focus of your presentation.

☆ Is poor quality.

☆ Is irrelevant (even though it is interesting).

☆ Is solely a time-filler.

☆ Is outdated.

☆ Does not suit your purpose.

☆ Does not fit your audience.

# WHY TO USE VISUAL AIDS

- **Visual aids make you more persuasive**

  The Wharton School at the University of Pennsylvania found that presenters using visuals conduct meetings in 28 percent less time, increase audience retention as much as five times, and get proposals approved twice as often.

- **People can grasp more information.**

  A recent study at Harvard University showed that people comprehend about 7 percent of information delivered verbally. They comprehend 87 percent when the information is delivered both verbally and visually.

- **Visual aids add variety and emphasis to your presentation.**

- **Your message is presented both orally and visually.**

  Some people process information best orally (by hearing it); others process it best visually (by seeing it). When you use visual aids with a presentation, you communicate with both types of people.

- **Visuals help organize your presentation.**

  When you plan visuals, you are forced to order and sequence the material you will present.

- **Visuals help you to be concise.**

  When you plan visuals, you are forced to distill your ideas down to their essence.

- **Visuals can help to facilitate meetings.**

  A chart or graphic on a flipchart, for example, can capture individual and collective thoughts in a dynamic way.

# PART II

# VISUAL MEDIA

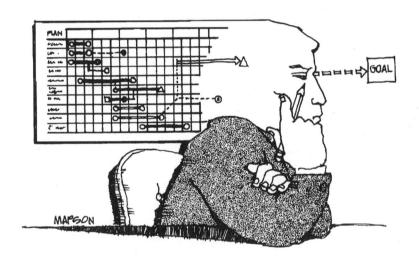

# WHAT'S YOUR MEDIUM?

> Choose the medium in which you can produce the most professional visual given your resources—it's better, for instance, when the audience is small, to have neatly lettered flipcharts than amateurish slides.
>
> Marya Holcombe and Judith Stein
> *Presentations for Decision Makers*

In a typical year, most professional people give a variety of presentations.

For example, Alice is the president of the local parent-teacher association. Last year, she gave over twenty presentations. They included a talk to the school board introducing an intra-district computer directory, a tribute to a retiring volunteer in front of an entire high school student body, a budget debate to the city council, and a topical speech at a national professional association.

In the space below, write four examples of presentations you've given in the past year. (If you've given fewer than four presentations, include some presentations you'd *like* to give.)

_____

_____

_____

_____

_____

_____

# VISUAL AIDS INVENTORY

Now let's take a look at the visual aids you used for the presentations you just wrote down. For each medium, check column A if that medium is appropriate for one or more of the presentations you gave. Check column B if you feel comfortable using that medium. And check column C if you used that medium where appropriate in your presentations.

| | A<br>This medium is appropriate for one or more of the presentations I gave. | B<br>I feel fairly comfortable with this medium. | C<br>I used this medium where appropriate. |
|---|---|---|---|
| • **Overhead Projector** | ☐ | ☐ | ☐ |
| • **35-mm Slide Projector** | ☐ | ☐ | ☐ |
| • **Flipchart** | ☐ | ☐ | ☐ |
| • **Posters** | ☐ | ☐ | ☐ |
| • **Movies/Videotapes** | ☐ | ☐ | ☐ |
| • **Models** | ☐ | ☐ | ☐ |

Ask yourself these two questions:

☐ Have I checked column A for any medium (the medium is appropriate) but left column C blank?

If so, you missed an opportunity to be a more successful presenter.

☐ Is there a medium which might be appropriate (column A), but I'm not comfortable with it (column C)?

You'll give your career a boost by learning about the medium in this section, and practicing with that medium until you feel comfortable with it.

# OVERHEAD PROJECTOR

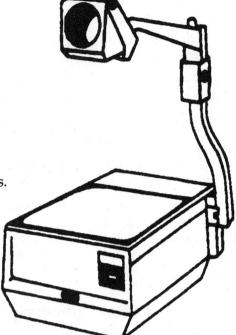

Also known as a viewgraph. The transparencies may be called flimsies or foils.

## ADVANTAGES

- The overhead projector is good for small groups. It can even be used with large groups—up to about 200 people—if the room is arranged properly.

- When you use the overhead projector in a presentation, you don't have to dim the lights.

- Overhead projectors are relatively inexpensive.

- Nearly every organization has at least one.

- Overhead projectors have a low Murphy's Law rating. They don't have many moving parts, and they tend to hold up.

- Transparencies travel well.

- Transparencies are versatile. It just takes a moment to rearrange them. At the front of the room, you can find one quickly in response to a question.

## DISADVANTAGES

- Photos don't reproduce well on overhead transparencies.

- The motor hums.

- The quality of the projected image is not as good as with the slide projector.

# Designing Transparencies

- Letters should be at least $^1/_4$ inch high (at least 30 points).

- If you're using clear transparencies with black images, add a few touches of color with transparency pens.

- For a standard size transparency, your image area should be $7^1/_2$ by 9 inches. This will leave room for borders.

- The standard exterior dimension of a framed transparency is 10 by 12 inches.

### Horizontal Vs. Vertical

Transparencies can be either horizontal or vertical:

**Horizontal**                                    **Vertical**

**OZONE**
...a form of oxygen;
...a major agent in the
formation of smog

**OZONE**
- a form of
oxygen;
- a major agent
in the
formation
of smog

Audiovisual vendors generally produce horizontal transparencies, but you can use either kind. **However, switching transparency directions is very disruptive; it is best in one presentation to have all horizontal or all vertical transparencies.**

## Transparency Frames

Always use frames on your transparencies. Not framing transparencies is a little like having your shirttail out—it's not the end of the world, but it makes you look sloppy in front of the audience. Frames also make transparencies much easier to handle. A stack of unframed transparencies develops static electricity and the transparencies take on a life of their own, sticking together and floating across the projector when laid on the glass stage.

Standard cardboard frames work well. The authors prefer the plastic "flip frame" made by 3M (Reorder Number 78-6969-7128-8). They fold up to $8^{1}/2$ by 11 inches and can be slipped into a briefcase. They're punched to fit into a three-ring binder.

You can write notes on the frame of the transparency. Many professional speakers do this.

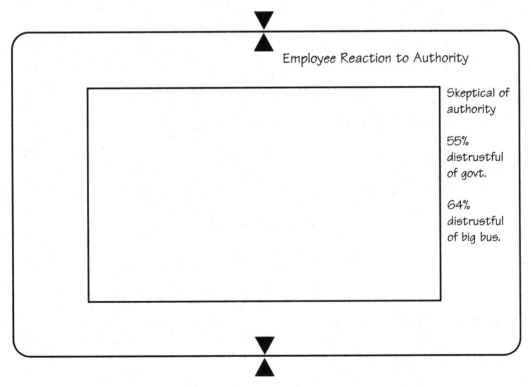

**TIP:** Mark transparency center on top and bottom of frame. When you are testing the projector, center frame on projector screen, then mark center top and bottom of platform with tape. During the presentation, you simply line up each frame mark with the platform mark.

## Setting Up The Room

### ✱ The Projector

Arrive early and get to know the projector. Have you seen speakers in the midst of their presentations searching awkwardly for the on/off switch, or putting transparencies on the stage upside down and inside out? (Transparencies go on the stage exactly as you would place them for yourself if you were going to read from them.)

Set up the projector in the most advantageous place:
• where you, its operator, can be seen by the most possible people
• where its image fills the whole screen
• where the projected image is a suitable size for your audience

Make sure the projector doesn't obstruct anyone's view. Sometimes the best way to remedy this problem is to put the projector on a low stand.

Sometimes light "leaks" around the edge of your framed transparency, projecting a distracting bright line around your projected image. You can remedy this by laying a piece of masking tape right on the glass of the projector's "stage"—the platform where you lay your transparencies.

### ✱ The Screen

The bottom of the screen should be at least four feet above the floor.

Consider putting the screen in the corner and angling it towards the center of the room.

When an overhead projected image is thrown onto a flat screen, there is a keystone effect. It means a rectangular transparency looks like this:

The further the projector is from the screen, and the larger the image, the more distortion there will be. If keystoning bothers you, you can buy a metal extender from your local audiovisual supplier that holds the top of the screen out, reducing keystoning.

## Delivery Techniques

Get the transparency all settled on the projector before you turn the lamp on.

Coordinate the audio and the visual. In other words, <u>turn the light on at precisely the moment you introduce the concept verbally,</u> so that the image and your words coincide.

Maintain eye contact with your audience.

Avoid reading from the transparency. However, you can use the transparency frame for your notes (see example on page 13).

Turn the projector off when you're not using it-or black out the screen.

> Consider making a special transparency with the title of your presentation and other important information. You can display it on the screen while the audience arrives and gets settled. This information gives the audience a clue about whether or not they are in the right room for the right presentation!

**WELCOME!**
**FALL**
**FUNDRAISING**
**SYMPOSIUM**

## Using Pointers

There are four major types of pointers. They are:

### ☆ A 40-inch wooden pointer with a black rubber tip

If you use this type of pointer, here are some guidelines:

• Hold the pointer in the hand nearest the screen. This will allow you to face the audience and maintain eye contact.

• Put the pointer down when you're not using it. You look like a disciplinarian if you hold the pointer with one hand and bounce it up and down in the palm of the other.

### ☆ The collapsible metal pointer

This looks like a pen in your pocket and a bit like a radio antenna when extended. If you use one of these, follow the two tips listed above for the wooden pointer, plus:

• Avoid pushing the pointer in and out when you're not using it. Audiences find this extremely distracting.

### ☆ The swizzle stick

Next time you are on an airplane or in a cocktail lounge, check out their swizzle sticks. They're often ideal pointers for the overhead projector. The best swizzle sticks are little plastic arrows with flat sides. They are good because they won't roll around on the projector. You can lay them directly on the transparency to indicate the point you're discussing.

## ☆ The laser pointer

Audiovisual suppliers now stock a slick little penlight that projects a laser point of light on the screen.

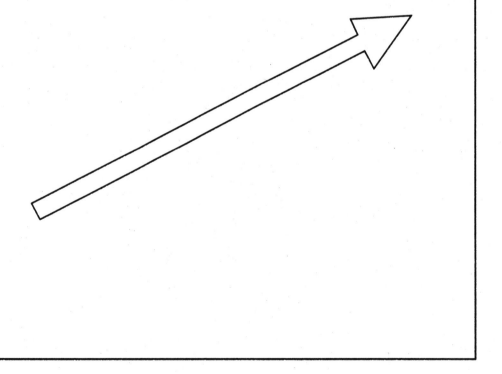

**If you opted for the arrow swizzle stick, but you can't find one, make your own. Use the outline below to cut one from a piece of file folder. Perhaps make several at one time and put them in an envelope in your presentation materials folder.**

## Pens and Markers

You can buy permanent, water-soluble, or dry-erase markers for use with overhead transparencies.

Remember you can do some creative and fun things with colored markers "live" during a presentation, such as:

Checking off items as you discuss them.

Circling numbers as you talk about them.

Underlining components as you discuss a chart.

*See Toolbox (page 78) for more shapes, symbols, and drawings.*

If you use water-soluble or dry-erase markers, you'll be able to reuse the transparency.

Most dry-erase markers don't leave a strong, bold mark and they are difficult to clean off. One idea is to use water-soluble markers on transparencies that are framed with 3M plastic flip frames. It is easy to wash them under running water and dry them with a paper towel, making them ready for your next presentation.

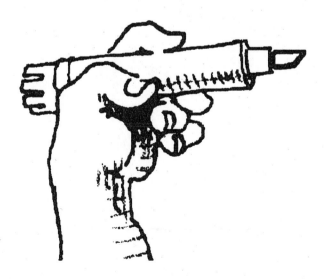

# Advanced Delivery Techniques Using An Overhead Projector

## ☆ Revelation

For this technique, cover everything but the headline, and switch the projector on when you introduce the topic. Then uncover each item as you discuss it.

Half of a file folder makes a great mask for revelation because it is a good weight. Put the mask between the transparency and the glass on the projector. This will make it less likely to fall off when you get near the bottom of the transparency.

A lot of audiences don't like revelation. It makes them feel that the speaker has a secret that will be revealed a little at a time. Revelation, however, keeps the audience focused. (If you are quite nervous and your hands are shaky, this technique is not the best one for you to use).

## ☆ Masking

This technique is the reverse of revelation. It works best when you have a model or diagram and you plan to discuss its components.

Begin by showing your audience the whole transparency and discussing it. Then, when you are ready to focus on one component, cover everything else with a mask.

## ☆ Overlays

You can make overlays by producing transparencies that, when laid on top of the previous transparency, add information.

Overlays have the same effect as revelation—you are able to show the audience only the material you're discussing at that moment.

## ☆ Adding to an acronym

Make a transparency with the first letters of an acronym. Then, as you discuss each letter, write out the word it stands for. This can add a little pizazz to your presentation.

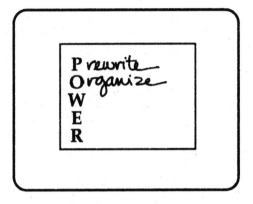

## ☆ Two projectors

Do you have a bilingual audience? Or would you like to show key points and a series of subpoints together?

You can run two overhead projectors and project the images side by side. It is helpful to have someone help you if the presentation is long; it will also be essential to have a practice run with your assistant before the presentation.

## ☆ Dissolve effect

This allows you to change from one transparency to the next, instead of turning the projector off and then right back on again.

Put the new transparency into the light beam above the glass stage while removing the old one. It takes some practice, but creates a slick effect.

# 35-mm SLIDE PROJECTOR

## ADVANTAGES

• The 35-mm slide projector works well for large groups. With the proper screen and room arrangement, you can use slides with as many as 600 people. With rear projection and a large screen, slides are effective with audiences of thousands.

• Well-designed, professionally produced slides create a polished, formal image.

• Photos reproduce beautifully on slides.

• The slide projector requires only that you push the button—unlike the overhead projector, where you need to get everything on straight and lined up properly before you turn on the light.

• Slides are more flexible than videotapes and movies because you can pull out outdated slides or reorganize the order of your visuals.

• Laser-enhanced color graphics look powerful and authoritative.

## DISADVANTAGES

• Your slides have maximum impact when the room is completely dark. The darkness diminishes your eye contact, prohibits you from being able to monitor your audience's reaction, and contributes to audience drowsiness.

• A carousel of slides is bulky for travel.

• Slide projectors have a higher Murphy's Law rating than overhead projectors. Slides can jam. The remote can break. The bulb can burn out.

## Designing Slides

- Decide if your slides will be horizontal or vertical and then stick with one format throughout the presentation.

- Design your slides for the back row.

- When you use photographs of people, plan to depict a pluralistic workforce ( a representative mixture of sexes, ethnicities, ages, disabilities).

- The space between lines of type should be at least the height of a capital letter.

- Number or label all slides so they can be easily reorganized.

- Once a set of slides is arranged properly in a slide tray, mark the upper right hand corner of each slide with a red pen. Then you will never have to worry about putting a slide in backwards or upside down because all of the red corners go together.

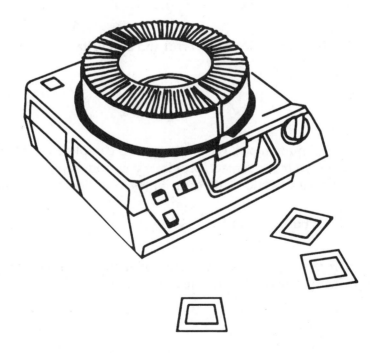

# Setting Up The Room

Arrive early. Set up the projector so you get the largest possible image. If you have both horizontal and vertical slides, make sure they both fit onto the screen. The best possible set-up puts the projector far enough from the screen that the image fills the entire screen and high enough that it projects above the heads of your audience without interfering with anyone's view.

You will be most effective standing in front of your audience, connected to the projector by a remote control. The best equipment includes a wireless remote. If one is not available, make sure you have enough extensions to connect you at the front of the room to your projector in its ideal location. You can stand to the side of the projected image and continue facing the audience.

One major problem when using visual aids is that speakers often give their presentation to the visuals, and not to the audience. This problem can be corrected easily if the speaker remembers to keep shoulder orientation toward the audience at all times as illustrated in Figure 1. Figure 2 shows what happens when your shoulders turn toward the visuals.

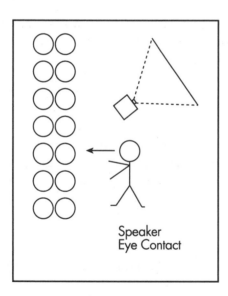

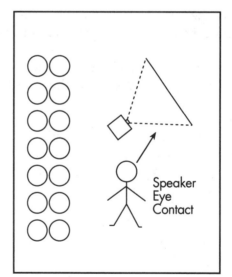

Always have an extra lamp for the projector. If you rent a projector, an extra lamp should be part of the package. But make sure to check on it.

## Delivery Techniques

1. After you've set up the room satisfactorily, do a quick run-through. Go through every slide you'll be using, and check:

   • Can every word and image on your slides be seen clearly from the back of the room?

   • Is the image in focus?

   • Are the slides in the right order?

   • Does the image fill the screen?

   • If, for some reason, you are forced to use both horizontal and vertical slides, do they both fit on the screen?

   • If your audience needs to take notes, can you leave some lights on and still get a clear image on the screen?

2. Mark the forward button on the remote control with a piece of tape so that you don't get confused mid-presentation and turn back to the previous slide.

3. You may wish to begin with a black slide. This will allow you to have the projector up and running without a slide on the screen when you begin your presentation.

4. As a general rule, allow at least ten to twenty seconds per slide. It is best to vary your pace. If you have a one-word slide that drives home a point, you may leave it on the screen for just a few seconds. If another slide requires a detailed explanation, it may stay up for four to five minutes. Avoid an even pace; it can be monotonous.

5. If you're going to venture away from your slides for a few minutes to discuss another matter, insert a black slide so you don't have a distracting visual on the screen.

## Should You Use the Overhead or Slide Projector?

Probably the most common dilemma for speakers preparing visuals for a presentation is whether to use the overhead projector or the 35-mm slide projector. Your decision will be based on the overall image you want to project, your audience size, the room itself, your budget, and the equipment available.

Here is an overview of each medium to help you with your decision:

---

**THE OVERHEAD PROJECTOR:**

☆ less formal

☆ generally not suitable for more than 200 people

☆ best when you need to make last-minute changes in the order

☆ can be used effectively in a fully-lighted room

☆ better if you want to encourage audience participation

---

### OR

---

**THE 35-MM SLIDE PROJECTOR:**

☆ slicker, snazzier

☆ best for projecting photos

☆ the more authoritative medium

☆ usually not appropriate for very small audiences (2–15 people)

☆ makes it hard to monitor audience reaction

---

# CHARTS AND GRAPHS

Do you have an issue that can be simplified for your audience by showing it graphically? Charts and graphs help to clarify complex concepts and show relationships between numbers.

*Four Tips for Planning Charts and Graphs*

- Make sure your headlines are clear and comprehensive.

- Label every element of a chart or graph clearly.

- Remember some people in your audience won't relate to charts and graphs. Even if you think it's perfectly obvious, plan to explain thoroughly:
  —what the chart shows
  —what each of the elements is
  —what any abbreviations or symbols stand for
  —what relationships are represented

- Don't overload your presentation with charts and graphs.

Following are examples of different charts and graphs.

☆ **Bar Charts**

Bar charts emphasize relationships and show how items compare.

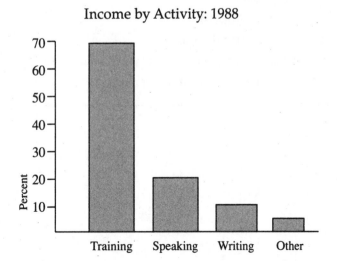

Income by Activity: 1988

### ☆ Flow Charts

Flow charts clarify complex relationships.

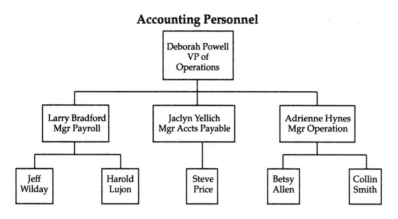

### ☆ Line Graphs

Line graphs illustrate trends, relationships, comparisons. They are good when you're trying to illustrate time-frequency distributions.

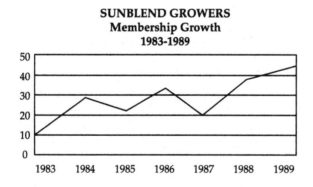

### ☆ Pie Charts

Pie charts help convey percentage relationships. They show proportions well. The entire chart always represents 100 percent or the total number.

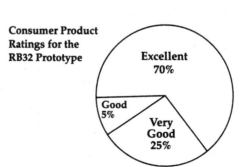

# FLIPCHARTS

## ADVANTAGES

- Flipcharts are inexpensive and adaptable to a variety of situations.
- They make a great medium for facilitating meetings. By graphically catching ideas, suggestions, and complaints on paper, you can lead shorter meetings in which people feel they are heard.
- They can be produced on the spot.

## DISADVANTAGES

- Flipcharts are rather informal.
- They require good handwriting.
- They don't handle large amounts of wording well.
- They do not work well for more than about forty people… and those forty must be well arranged so they can all see the flipchart clearly.

## ☆ Paper

You can buy unlined, lined, or gridded paper. Unless you're a flipchart pro, you will probably want the lined or gridded paper. These have light blue horizontal lines or a checkerboard that help you keep things lined up.

> If you need to transport a tablet of flipchart paper, it will be easier if:
> - you keep it in the box it came in
> - you fasten a bungee cord around the flipchart stand and paper to keep unruly pages together

## ☆ Pens

Mr. Sketch™ pens are good because of their quality for the price. They won't stain your clothes and they're non-toxic. Many permanent markers bleed through to the next page.

## Flipchart Design Tips:

1. Choose bold colors. Avoid pastels...except for highlighting.

2. Your lettering should be one inch tall for each fifteen feet between the flipchart and the back row.

3. Use the fat side of the pen's tip when you write. Lots of flipchart lettering we see is tall enough, but it is not bold enough because the presenter uses the skinny part of the pen.

4. If you prepare your flipchart before your presentation, leave a page or two (whatever it takes to completely cover the message on the next page) in front of each page. Then you can turn to a blank sheet after each point—and the audience won't be able to see through to what's behind.

5. You can use correction fluid to cover a glitch.

6. Make light pencil notes to yourself at the top left corner of the flipchart. Then, as you're speaking, you have reminders of important names and numbers.

7. You can use the overhead projector to size an object for the flipchart. If you want to magnify a small drawing or chart, make a transparency on your office copier. Then project it onto the flipchart in the correct size and draw it with markers.

8. Flipchart sheets have unity and impact when you add a border:

 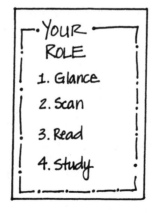

## Lettering

You can produce nice-looking flipchart printing—even if your handwriting is atrocious. It just takes practice. Honest. The most consistent you are with each of the basic strokes, the more readable your writing will be.

These are the basic strokes for lettering flipcharts:

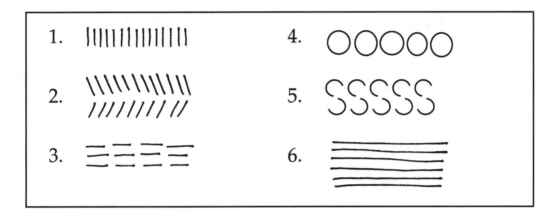

Fill a half page of a flipchart—with each of these six strokes. Change colors every two or three lines. Here are a few helpful pointers:

- When you write, move only your thumb and first finger…not your whole arm. Flex your wrist; you're faster this way.

- For long horizontals, move your whole body without bouncing.

- For long verticals, bend your knees and drop you body straight down.

Now, <u>stand back</u> and critique:

☐ Did you use the broadest part of the tip of your pen?

☐ Are your left margins straight?

☐ Is your lettering straight horizontally…or does it run uphill or down?

☐ Are your straight lines straight and your circles round?

☐ Which colors work best? Which color combinations do you like?

If your efforts were less than satisfactory, keep practicing. That's all it takes.

> No flipcharts around? Turn a table on end and tape paper to it.

## Lettering Techniques

- **USE BRIGHT, BOLD COLORS AND ALL CAPS FOR HEADLINES**

- **use lowercase for details**

- *use italics for variety*

- print neatly and clearly

- change colors for variety

- use bullets

★ add stars on key points

- consider rules between elements

- <u>underline for emphasis</u>

- highlight with boxes

LETTERING STYLES

**BLOCK**

OVERLAPPING

*cursive*

PUFFY

shaded

In the space below, practice writing your name and "The quick brown fox jumps over the lazy dog" in each of these lettering styles.

## Cartoons

True, cartoons are rather informal. However, even powerful executives can use a touch of levity now and then. And a cartoon on a flipchart at just the right moment can add emphasis in a unique way.

No, you don't have to be a talented illustrator. With practice, anyone can master a few basic cartoons. If you've got a few in your repertoire, you're almost certain to find the right place for them on a flipchart.

Here are five simple cartoons:

Choose three of these to practice and master. In the space below, practice each one several times. Once you've mastered them—and anyone can (a long airplane trip is a great time to practice)—you can quickly add them to a flipchart and impress your audience with your creativity.

## Delivery Techniques

**1.** Stand to the side of the flipchart as you speak; make sure you don't block your audience's view.

**2.** If you must face the flipchart and talk at the same time, double the volume of your voice. It has to project off the flipchart and back to your audience.

**3.** Use symbols and abbreviations. Keep all of your wording as simple as possible.

**4.** Get help from the audience. When you're facilitating a meeting and using a flipchart, you can get others to tape the last sheet on the wall while you're putting a headline on the next one.

**5.** You can come across as a real artist in a presentation if you lightly pencil in a diagram or picture before your presentation, then trace it with a marker during your presentation.

**6.** If there's one particular page you'll be referring to a lot during your presentation, put a masking tape tab on it so you can flip to it quickly.

**7.** If you want it to appear that you're producing a written sheet spontaneously: lightly pencil in the upper corner the main points you will discuss. Make a small mark with your marker so you don't accidently write anything else on that sheet during your presentation. Using your pencil notes, write down your main points and expand on each.

# POSTERS

**Posters can be used in a variety of ways.**

A task force committee chairperson puts a poster showing the goals for the coming year as she introduces the agenda for the evening meeting. Without ever having to spell out the connection, she establishes the link between the evening focus and the annual goals.

A salesman takes a poster with a photograph of a new pump into a presentation for a prospective buyer. The salesman is able to stand directly behind the poster for his introduction and point to the poster during the question and answer session.

In a seminar, the trainer posts a short quotation on the importance of supervisory training. The poster is displayed prominently during the training and reveals its important message throughout the four-day program.

## ADVANTAGES

- Posters can be used to present a piece of equipment that would be too unwieldy to bring to the presentation.
- Posters can summarize key concepts or "advertise" a slogan and can be left permanently in high-visibility areas.

## DISADVANTAGES

- Posters are not very portable. They easily get tattered with use.
- As a front-of-the-room visual aid, posters do not work well for groups of over fifteen.

# Delivery Techniques

1. Make sure you position the poster so that it can be seen clearly by everyone. A flipchart easel sometimes works nicely.
2. Avoid passing the poster around among the participants. This distracts from you—the featured presenter. If you must move the poster around the group, carry it to strategic places throughout the audience as you talk.

# MOVIES AND VIDEOTAPES

## ADVANTAGES

- Of all the media, movies and videotapes have the highest potential impact. They are attention-getting and persuasive.

- Movies and videos can make a point quickly.

- They can dramatize problems.

- They can change attitudes.

- For situations like employee orientation, a movie or video can provide standardization.

## DISADVANTAGES

- Producing your own film or videotape is more expensive than any other medium we've considered.

- People are increasingly sophisticated viewers because of exposure to television and movies. If you produce a film or videotape that is not 100 percent professional, your audience will turn into a bunch of rabid critics.

- Film projectors have the highest Murphy's Law factor of virtually any audiovisual equipment.

- Packaged products rarely deliver precisely the message you want to give your audience.

## Questions To Consider

**Before you rent, purchase, or produce a movie or videotape, ask yourself:**

✓ Does a movie or video fit my objectives?

✓ Is it appropriate for this specific group of people and this occasion?

✓ What does it accomplish that couldn't be accomplished by another medium?

✓ Are the people and situations depicted realistically? Are they relevant to the work my participants do?

✓ Are the dialogues natural and believable?

✓ Does the movie or video cover a "digestible" amount of material?

✓ Does it portray a pluralistic workforce (a representative mixture of sexes, ethnicities, ages, disabilities)?

✓ Is the technical quality good?
  • sound and picture clear?
  • colors true?
  • music mixed well?

✓ Is it cost-effective? (Most film and video is expensive—sometimes it's worth the money. You will have to decide if this is one of those times.)

# Delivery Techniques

1. Lights are generally best at half-mast…dark enough for a good picture, light enough for you to watch audience reaction and for people to jot down notes.

2. Before you use a film with a group, watch it at least three times so you know it inside and out.

3. Here's an idea to consider if the visual part works well, but the sound track isn't right for the audience, purpose, or occasion. Develop your own narrative and turn the sound off. Practice your narrative over and over again until you're comfortable with the content and your delivery is natural and conversational.

4. If you hope to involve the audience in a discussion after the film or video, this will require some special planning. Film and video audiences tend to become very passive. Some open-ended questions like these may help to get them active again:

   • Is there anything in the film you're unclear about?

   • Are there any points you'd like me to expand on?

   • Have any of you experienced a situation similar to the one in the video?

   • How does the problem posed in this videotape apply to the kind of work you're doing?

   • Was there anything in the video you feel reluctant to accept?

# MODELS

There are times when the best way to demonstrate a new component of a system is to show off the component itself.  Or when the best way to dramatize the announcement of a new product is by unveiling a model.  Or when the best way to instruct a group about the parts of a new tool is to use the actual tool.

## ADVANTAGES

• Models, since they are tangible, can make your points and instructions seem more realistic.

• When used appropriately, models can add a touch of drama to a presentation.

• Models can give a client "hands-on" knowledge of your product.

## DISADVANTAGES

• Models generally aren't a suitable visual aid for groups larger than fifteen.

• If you pass around a model during your presentation, it is likely to be distracting to everyone.

# Delivery Techniques

1. Keep the model behind the podium, in a box, or covered until you introduce it. This will prevent distraction during your presentation, and will add impact to the moment when you introduce the model.

2. Put the model away when you're no longer talking about it.

3. Avoid passing objects around.  If everyone can't see it, move with it through your audience.

# PART III

## ORGANIZING AND CREATING VISUALS

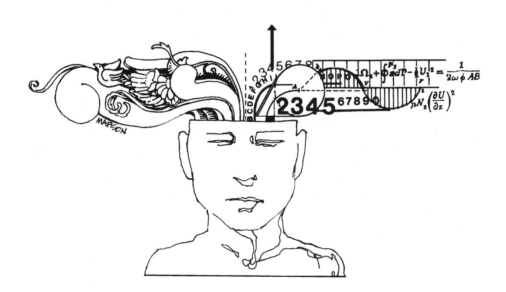

## CONCEPT

When your visuals are produced by professionals and in-house art departments, you are still the DIRECTOR. You have more expertise about your audience and the presentation itself than anyone else. And a basic knowledge of design can only add to your final product: a set of visual aids that enhance your presentation.

When planning visual aids for a presentation—before you do anything else—you should do a quick profile of your audience.

## Audience Profile

Who is the audience for this presentation?

Sometimes presenters don't know who will be in the audience. If they don't, they can still take an educated guess. For example, if a presenter delivers seminars in several cities, they will not know from day to day who will be in the audience. All they can do is make some suppositions such as: college-educated, typically 35 to 55 years old, equal mix of men and women, employees and managers in business, education, non-profit agencies, public and private organizations, representative mix of ethnicities, interested in practical techniques they can take back to the office and put to work the next day.

Think of a presentation you will be giving soon. If you are not scheduled for an upcoming presentation, picture a typical presentation or one you would like to give.

Write the name of your presentation here: _____

# CONCEPT (continued)

**Make notes about your target audience:**

Name of group:

_____

Average age:

_____

Level of education:

_____

Sex, ethnic mixture:

_____

Knowledge of topic:

_____

Attitudes about topic:

_____

Captive or voluntary audience:

_____

Time of day (and do you follow a lively keynote speaker?):

_____

Other comments:

_____

_____

_____

## The Overall Look

Next, based on your audience and purpose, you should decide the overall look of your visual presentation. Also ask yourself how the visual presentation of this topic will tie in with your corporate look, if there is one. Then pick three or four adjectives (clean, sophisticated, professional, classy, confidence-building, friendly, trendy trustworthy, formal, approachable, funny) that describe the look you want the visuals to have.

Define the overall look you want to achieve:

_____

_____

## Thumbnail Sketches

The next step in planning your visual aids is to make some thumbnail sketches—rough drawings (absolutely no need to be artistic)—approximately 2 inches by 3 inches in which you explore some of the possibilities for the layout of each visual.

For example, let's say you have three components to include in a 35-mm slide: a headline, five lines of type, and a drawing of a computer. On your thumbnail sketch, you might show the three components like this:

Headline

Five lines of type

Drawing of a computer

## ☆ Try Some Thumbnails

Suppose you will be giving a presentation, and your first slide will include a headline, five lines of type, and a drawing of a computer. There are lots of ways those three elements could be arranged on a slide. Sketch out the first arrangement that comes to your mind here:

Congratulations. You've just produced a thumbnail sketch! It doesn't matter if it looks great or not…artistic inclination isn't important. The thumbnail simply gives you a chance to experiment with different ways of laying out information on a visual.

Now sketch the same three elements in a different arrangement:

## ☆ More Thumbnails

Continue experimenting with the three elements:
- Try using a border on at least one of your sketches and one or two rules (straight lines) on another.
- Experiment with making some of the elements larger or smaller.

You definitely don't need to be a Picasso to produce a good set of thumbnail sketches. Thumbnails help you to see the possibilities for a visual. Since they're small, they distill the elements so you see them as shapes, giving you a designer's perspective. After you've chosen the best thumbnail, it acts as a "blueprint" for you, or whoever makes the final product.

## Storyboards

A storyboard is an excellent way for you to plan the sequence and organize slides or transparencies for a presentation. It is also the easiest way to communicate with the audio visual department when you are ready to order the production of your visuals. (Lots of professional audiovisual producers will give you free tablets set up for storyboards.)

A storyboard is simply a set of thumbnails—with readable words—for all your slides or transparencies. A glance at the storyboard will help you see:

• if your material is sequenced logically

• if your visuals are consistent

On the next page is a miniature version of part of a storyboard developed a few years ago for a set of slides for an employee benefit consulting firm. The slides were used with a presentation on a life insurance program for public employees. The storyboard helped in planning the slide presentation as a slide sorter would after the slides were produced. It helps to see the flow of visuals so they can be organized logically. But a storyboard is **most** helpful for communicating to those responsible for producing the final slides.

# A SAMPLE STORYBOARD

No. 1
Run copy below
Sunburst

*Group Life Insurance from PERA*

No. 2
PERA logo over
photo of
business people

No. 3
Photo 132 with
hairline

No. 4
Run copy below
Sunburst

*(family)*
*Protection in Early Years*

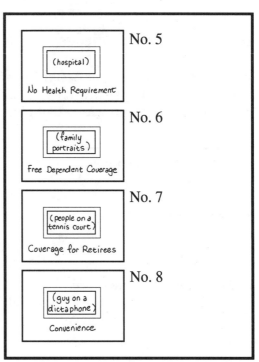

No. 5

*(hospital)*
*No Health Requirement*

No. 6

*(family portraits)*
*Free Dependent Coverage*

No. 7

*(people on a tennis court)*
*Coverage for Retirees*

No. 8

*(guy on a dictaphone)*
*Convenience*

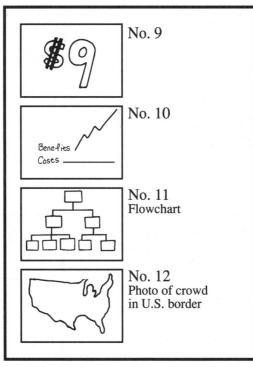

No. 9

No. 10

*Benefits*
*Costs*

No. 11
Flowchart

No. 12
Photo of crowd
in U.S. border

# DESIGN

## Basic Design Principles

A little knowledge of basic design goes a long way when you plan visual aids. You don't have to be an artist or spend a lot of time studying design. As a matter of fact, there are six principles that give you everything you need to know.

| The Six Basic Principles | | Not this: | This: |
| --- | --- | --- | --- |

**1. Keep it simple.**

**2. Leave lots of white space.**
Bunch things together, leaving plenty of unused space around them.

**3. Keep it organized.**
Line things up.

**4. Create a path for the eye.**
You can do this by organizing most important to least important, from left to right and top to bottom (the way English speakers read), using arrows and borders, or overlapping words and other elements.

**5. Make something dominant.**
The audience ought to be able to pick out your most important element immediately, because it is biggest, boldest, or brightest.

**6. Divide space in an interesting way.**

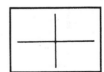 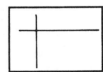

## Applying The Principles

Now select what you consider to be the best of your thumbnail sketches from page 44. Sketch it again here.

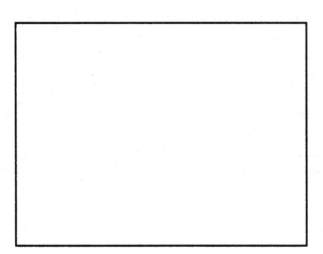

Critique the sketch above in light of each of the six design principles you just read about.

1. Is it **simple**? Is there anything you can do to simplify it? If so, modify it in the space below:

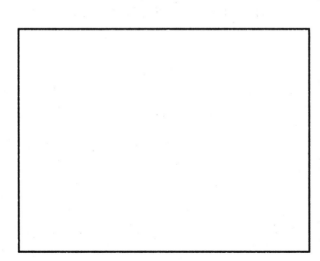

2. Is there **lots of white space**? Can you bunch things up to leave more unused space? If so, modify your design again using this space:

3. Are things **organized** and **lined up**? Can you organize your design better? If so, modify it in this space:

4. Is there a **path for the eye**? If not, see if you can arrange the elements so they flow—probably from top to bottom, left to right:

5. Is **something dominant?**  If not, you can probably make one of your elements larger, bolder, or brighter to give it dominance.  It ought to be the element you want your audience to focus on first.  Modify your design once more:

6. Is the **space divided in an interesting way**?  If not, experiment with a different division of space here:

> The three golden rules of effective visuals:
> 1. Keep it simple.
> 2. Keep it simple.
> 3. Keep it simple.
>
> *Anonymous*

## Design Hints

1. Put a headline on every visual.

2. Each visual should present just one idea.

3. Add interest to a words-only visual with a large first letter.

4. Flop photos and graphics so they face the middle of your visual. You don't want the president of your organization staring off the edge of the screen!

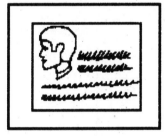 

5. Check carefully for errors.

6. Use a framing device to pull two elements together.

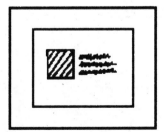 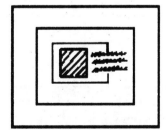

## Adding Pizzazz

Have you got a basic design for your title slide that is just fine, except it lacks snazziness?

Try:

- Turning it.

- Showing it inside out.

- Making it bigger—or smaller.

- Making it shorter—or taller.

- Making it round—or square.

- Making it longer.

- Making it darker—or lighter.

- Making it glow.

- Making it sparkle.

- Making it heavier.

- Repeating it.

- Coloring it.

- Making it transparent.

- Making it look wet.

- Projecting it.

- Sharpening it—or softening it.

- Making it look more comfortable.

- Adding human interest.

Post this suggestion list above your desk. When you are designing something and get stuck, it will help!

## COLOR

In-house art departments and outside producers use color when they make visual aids. People who create visual aids infrequently often don't think of this and use standard clear overhead transparencies printed in black, without any color. When you don't use color on visuals, you are missing a great opportunity to add emphasis, interest, and power.

## Using Color

Try it. You're presenting the design for a component revision in a communications system. You've reproduced an overhead transparency with the basic system design. It looks like this:

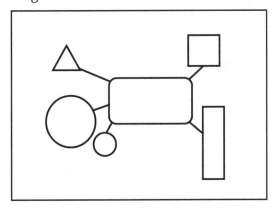

Your presentation will focus on the revised component represented by the small square in the upper right quadrant of the transparency. Find a colored marker, flairtip pen, pencil, or crayon and color in the square:

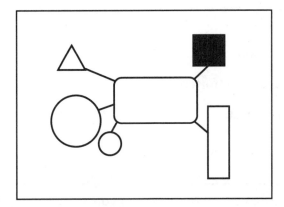

Do you agree that **one touch** of color makes a significant difference?

In just five minutes, it is possible to go through a set of transparencies to add touches of color with transparency pens. The impact is worth every minute of preparation.

You may also want to consider using the following three techniques in front of your group:

☆ Color part of a diagram, model or chart **in front of the group.** It adds active, visual interest to your presentation.

☆ With a colored marker, circle, underline or box in an important figure or concept **as you discuss it.**

☆ When you have a list of items on a visual, check each off with a colored marker **as you discuss it.**

These techniques take almost no effort or practice, yet they will add significantly to your presentation.

## Color Psychology

When you choose colors for a visual aid, remember that people associate feelings and concepts with each color:

☆ **Green** can signify growth and movement.

☆ **Blue,** the most universally liked color, can convey calm. On the other hand, it can look institutional. Blue also fades faster than any other color.

☆ **Red** can stand for power, energy, or danger. Keep in mind that red means debit spending to accountants—and that on a flipchart, it is difficult to see from a distance.

☆ **Yellow** is usually thought of as positive, and so works well for highlighting something against a dark background. If you're thinking of using it as a background color, though, you should know that more people dislike yellow than any other color.

☆ **Purple** has spiritual meaning for some people.

One, two or three colors are plenty. Watch your temptation to overdo it. When in doubt, stop at two colors.

## Color Contrasts

The chart shown below will be helpful if you're planning visual aids and need to know which foreground colors contrast most with which background colors. The colors listed are rank-ordered, with the highest contrast on top.

---

**With a dark background, use these colors for the foreground:**

| | |
|---|---|
| 1. White | 5. Red |
| 2. Yellow | 6. Blue |
| 3. Orange | 7. Violet |
| 4. Green | |

**With a light background, use these colors for the foreground:**

| | |
|---|---|
| 1. Black | 5. Blue |
| 2. Red | 6. Violet |
| 3. Orange | 7. Yellow |
| 4. Green | |

Shades of the same color can illustrate minor change.

---

# USE OF TEXT

Seventy-five percent of all visual aids consist of 35-mm slides or overhead transparencies that show words alone.  A visual aid almost always includes some words.

## What to Include

How do you decide just which words to include on a visual?

- When you get ready to choose the words, think of yourself as a **headline writer.**

- Distill your message to its **absolute essence.**

- Use the **fewest words** possible.

Example:
Let's say you want to discuss the following information in your presentation:

---

What do consumers complain about most?  Last year, the Better Business Bureau received its greatest number of complaints—72,000—about phone purchases.  Mail orders placed second at 69,000 complaints.  Next highest were home remodeling problems (47,000 complaints) followed by auto repair problems (28,000 complaints).

---

Your first draft might look like this:

---

WHAT CONSUMERS COMPLAIN ABOUT MOST

1. Phone purchases (72,000 complaints)
2. Mail orders (69,000 complaints)
3. Home remodeling repairs (47,000 complaints)
4. Auto repair problems (28,000 complaints)

Better Business Bureau, 19xx

---

This is a good start, but it still has too much information on it.  Visuals are best when they're **very simple.**  A good final version of the visual might be one of the two samples on the next page.

# USE OF TEXT (continued)

**2 Possible Final Versions: Consumer Complaints Visual**

| **Consumer Complaints** | **Consumer Complaints** |
| --- | --- |
| 1. Phones | * phones |
| 2. Mail orders | * mail orders |
| 3. Home remodeling | * home remodeling |
| 4. Car repairs | * car repairs |

Agreed, the above visuals don't make a lot of sense by themselves. But they are ideal because they are simple and contain only the main ideas. You can give your audience the actual numbers—and tell them they came from the Better Business Bureau.

*Remember that visuals are only aids. The words you say are the essence of the presentation!*

When you are deciding how much to include on a visual:

☆ Write the message with a marker on an 8 1/2 x 11-inch paper and see how it looks. If there's too much, edit first, or use a second visual if necessary.

☆ Put items in the order you will cover them.

☆ Eliminate anything you won't be talking about.

☆ A note about numbers: Avoid putting all the numbers into your visual. Include only:
    the totals
    the numbers you will talk about
    the numbers your audience cares about

# The Rule of Six

**Thou Shalt Not Use More Than Six Lines,
and
Thou Shalt Not Use More Than Six Words Per Line.**

This is a good rule. It is based on reading research that attempted to answer the question, "How much information can a person absorb visually at one time?" The conclusion of the study was six lines of six words each.

## ☆ Headlines

Your headlines should be set in a larger and/or bolder type for emphasis. They should be set apart by at least three spaces above and two spaces below.

Subheads should be smaller and/or less bold. They do not need to be separated from the words that follow them.

Have a headline/subhead text plan, and follow it consistently.

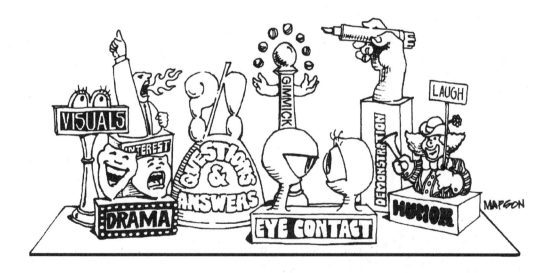

## Exercise—You Try It

Imagine for this exercise you are chairing the Board of Directors of a non-profit organization that takes a stand about an issue you care deeply about. You have been asked to give a presentation to a group of twelve potential contributors. You will be using an overhead projector. You've decided to use a transparency to support your introduction. This section of your presentation is supposed to give your audience a basic understanding of the primary objectives of the organization.

Decide what words you would include on a single overhead transparency.

1) Jot them down:

2) Now rewrite them more briefly:

3) Finally, rewrite once more, if you can, even more briefly:

**Checklist**

☐ Did you include a headline?

☐ Have you used the *fewest* words possible? Positively the fewest? Are there ANY words you can do without?

☐ Have you limited yourself to six lines with six words per line?

# Lettering Size

## How large should the words be?

Unfortunately, there is no simple answer, but here are a few guidelines:

☆ **For flipcharts, white/blackboards, and posters**
Letters should be 1 inch tall for each 15 feet between the visual and the back row.

☆ **For overhead transparencies**
In general, letters should be at least 30 points (about $^1/4$ inch). But test a transparency in a room which is the same size as the one you'll be using. Make sure the words can be seen clearly from the back row.

☆ **For slides**
This will vary according to the size of your audience. Letters should be clear and readable from the back row.

# TYPOGRAPHY

Here are some general guidelines about the use of type.

1. Use a simple, straightforward, easy-to-read typeface. Lots of beautiful typefaces are almost impossible to read; they detract from your presentation.

   Two typefaces that always work are Helvetica, which is called sans-serif—without "feet"—and looks like

   > This

   and Times Roman, which is called a serif—with "feet"—and looks like

   > This

2. Use upper and lower case.

   > DON'T USE ALL CAPS FOR LARGE BLOCKS OF TYPE. READERS READ FASTEST WHEN SENTENCES ARE PRINTED IN UPPER AND LOWER CASE—THE WAY THEY NORMALLY ARE SEEN IN PRINT. HEADLINES ARE SET IN ALL CAPS BECAUSE THEY REQUIRE THE READER TO SLOW DOWN, GIVING EMPHASIS TO A FEW WORDS. WASN'T THIS BLOCK OF ALL CAPS DIFFICULT TO READ?

   Compare:

   > Don't use all caps for large blocks of type. Readers read fastest when sentences are printed in upper and lower case—the way they normally are seen in print. Headlines are set in all caps because they require the reader to slow down, giving emphasis to a few words. Wasn't this better?

3. Check, recheck, and get someone else to check correctness of numbers, grammar, punctuation, spelling.

4. Limit yourself to one or two typefaces consistently throughout your presentation.

5. *Italics are least likely to be read. Save them for disclaimers (The Surgeon General has determined…)* Don't use them for emphasis because they don't give it.

6. Don't use more than three type sizes on one visual. Reserve the largest size for emphasis.

7. Do you want numbers or bullets?

   Numbers send these messages:
   1. order of importance.
   2. chronological order.

   Bullets are more generic:
   • they give each item equal importance.
   • they don't distract from the words that follow them.

> *The only thing more damaging to credibility than a visual with a misspelled word is a visual with numbers that don't add up.*
>
> Eugene Fetteroll

## THINGS TO REMEMBER

√...Include a headline.

√...Turn photos of people so they face toward the center of visuals.

√...Add a touch of color.

√...Use only six words per line, six lines per visual.

√...Include only essential words.

√...Make the words large enough to read.

√...Use upper and lower case for large blocks of type.

√...On the visual, include only those items you will talk about.

√...Check and recheck your spelling and numbers.

> **Avoid "Data Dump."*** Crowding your presentation with too many visuals and/or too much information will reduce their effectiveness and you will lose impact. Usually the fewer, the better!

*Reprinted from *Effective Presentation Skills*, Steve Mandel. You can order this title using the form in the back of this book.

# PART IV

## TIPS AND CHECKLISTS

# PRESENTATION TECHNIQUES

*HINTS TO KEEP IN MIND NO MATTER WHICH MEDIUM YOU USE:*

## 1. When in doubt, do without.

You're better off with too few visual aids than too many.

## 2. Coordinate audio and visual.

At the precise moment you say, "Our company has three goals for the spring quarter," switch on the overhead projector with the transparency that says: "Spring Quarter Goals."

## 3. Remove the visuals <u>immediately</u> after you're finished talking about them.

If you've used a flipchart to illustrate a new design concept and then gone on to talk about the budget on another project, the illustration on the flipchart will distract your audience. It interferes with your current focus and competes with you for the audience's attention.

## 4. When the light goes on, there is drama.

Test this yourself by observing any audience. The moment the light from an overhead or 35-mm projector flashes on the screen, every eye in the audience goes there. If you turn on the projector with no visual, you are not using the medium effectively. If you leave the light on during your entire presentation, you're missing the opportunity to capitalize on the moment of drama.

## 5. Face your audience and maintain eye contact.

You have probably watched the backs of presenters' heads in countless second-rate presentations. If you use a pointer, hold it with the hand closest to the visual, keep your body open to your audience, and focus on your listeners.

## 6. Remember that visuals are aids; you're the main attraction.

One of the worst things you can do is read your visuals to the group! They can read. They came to hear what *you* have to say.

# FIVE WINNING TIPS

## 1. ORDER EARLY.

Give yourself plenty of time to plan, produce, and revise your visuals. Most visual aids producers charge extra for rush work.

## 2. USE DUPLICATES.

If you are going to repeat your presentation, use duplicates. Then if they are lost (by an airline, for example), you can arrange to have a back-up set sent. Or to be safer, take your essential materials on the plane in a carry-on bag.

## 3. CARRY EXTRAS.

* extension cords
* cables
* projector bulbs
* chalk
* scissors
* 3-prong adapters
* remotes
* lamps
* pens/markers

## 4. CARRY MASKING TAPE.

Tape down cords so you and your audience won't have to worry about tripping. Tape off a frame on the overhead projector if your transparencies are unframed. Tape up a sign on the door if necessary. You can get yourself out of all sorts of jams with some paper, pens, and tape.

## 5. HAVE A BACKUP PLAN.

Think through the worst-case scenario. Have a Plan B strategy.

If you arrive at the client's and there is no overhead projector even though they have promised you over and over again there will be one...

YOU NEED A BACKUP PLAN.

If you get midway through the presentation to the school board and the slide projector jams...

YOU NEED A BACKUP PLAN.

If your flipchart is locked in the closet because the janitor is out sick...

YOU NEED A BACKUP PLAN.

# VISUAL AIDS CHECKLISTS

Here are checklists you can photocopy* and post on your wall. Use them as you prepare for your presentations! They will help you create and give a brilliant performance!

BEFORE YOUR
PRESENTATION

☐ 1. Profile your audience: In/out organization? Age? Education? Gender, ethnic mixture? Knowledge of topic? Captive/volunteer audience? Time of day/order of presentation? (page 41)

☐ 2. Select your medium by evaluating: audience, purpose, available equipment, room (capacity, permanent fixtures, etc.), time of day.

☐ 3. Plan the general layout of your visuals by doing some thumbnail sketches. (page 43)

☐ 4. Keep your visuals simple, clean (lots of white space), organized, logical.

☐ 5. Have a concise headline for every visual.

☐ 6. Limit yourself to one idea per visual.

☐ 7. Add some color and pizzazz! (page 53)

---

*Permission to photocopy for personal use only, not for classes or other uses.

# VISUAL AIDS CHECKLISTS
# (continued)

☐   8.   Follow the rule of six: no more than six words per line six lines per visual.

☐   9.   Use the fewest words possible.

☐ 10.   Use a simple typeface.

☐ 11.   Use upper and lower case.

☐ 12.   Include only items you will talk about.

☐ 13.   Stick to one or two typefaces.

☐ 14.   Label every element of charts and graphs.

☐ 15.   Design visuals for the back row.

☐ 16.   If you're not sure a visual is necessary, don't use it.

☐ 17.   Coordinate the audio (your words) and the visual.

☐ 18.   *PRACTICE, PRACTICE, PRACTICE!*

WHEN YOU
ARRIVE

☐ 1. Meet the facility coordinator (if there is one), go over requests and agreements, and find out about meetings being held in adjacent rooms (in case, for example, there is a meeting that is using loud sound equipment).

☐ 2. Set up the room so:
  • everyone can see the screen.
  • the image is the right size for the audience.
  • you won't block the audience's view.

☐ 3. Adjust the lighting to avoid a light shining directly on screen.

☐ 4. Know your equipment.  Practice several times before you start.

☐ 5. Know where the lights are located.

☐ 6. Carry extra supplies:
  • extension cords
  • cables
  • projector bulbs
  • chalk
  • scissors
  • masking tape
  • 3-prong adaptors
  • remotes
  • lamps
  • pens/markers
  • blank paper
  • name tags
  • name tag cards
  • sign in sheet
  • blank transparencies

# VISUAL AIDS CHECKLISTS (continued)

**DURING YOUR PRESENTATION**

☐ 1. Position yourself so everyone in the room can see and hear you.

☐ 2. Face your audience and maintain eye contact when you use visuals. Speak to the back row.

☐ 3. Remember that you're the presentation; the visuals are aids.

☐ 4. When using the overhead projector, get the transparency settled on the projector before you turn the light on.

☐ 5. Remember to experiment with doing some "live" creative things with colored markers on transparencies.

☐ 6. Avoid reading aloud from your visuals.

☐ 7. If you use the flipchart::
  - use bold colors
  - use caps for headlines
  - print neatly and clearly
  - highlight with boxes
  - write with the fattest part of the marker
  - use lowercase for details
  - underline for emphasis
  - change colors for variety

☐ 8. Lettering on flipcharts needs to be one inch tall for each fifteen feet between the flipchart and the back row.

☐ 9. Make light pencil notes to yourself at the top left corner of the flipchart.

☐ 10. During your presentation, you can write problems in black, hot issues in red and positive comments in blue.

☐ 11. If you speak and write at the same time, stand to one side of the flipchart...or write, then speak.

☐ 12. Remember to breathe!

☐ 13. Ask someone you know to keep notes on your presentation (continuity of information, presentation techniques, eye contact, voice), and to coach you at the end of your presentation.

# PART V

## RESOURCES

# TOOLBOX: SHAPES, DESIGNS, IDEAS

The purpose of the **The Toolbox** is to provide ideas, samples, and inspiration for individuals who need to design their own graphics.

The categories in **The Toolbox** are:

- Basic Shapes

- Variations of Basic Shapes

- Combinations of Basic Shapes

- Flipchart Ideas

# BASIC SHAPES

Circle, square, rectangle, triangle, line, dot, spiral

# VARIATIONS OF BASIC SHAPES

Circle, square

# COMBINATIONS OF BASIC SHAPES

# FLIPCHART IDEAS

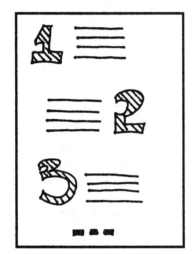

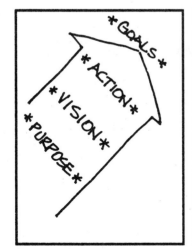

# *BIBLIOGRAPHY*

Ailes, R. *You Are The Message*. Homewood, Illinois: Dow Jones-Irwin, 1988.

*130 Alphabets and Other Signs*. Boston: Shambhala, 1993.

Anderson, J. B. *Speaking to Groups Eyeball to Eyeball*. Vienna, Va: Wyndmoor Press, 1989.

Amstutz, Walter. *Japanese Emblems and Designs*. New York: Dover Publications, 1970.

*Book of Art Deco Alphabets*. New York: Sterling Publication Company, 1990.

Davis, Susan. *59 More Studio Secrets for the Graphic Artist*. Ohio: Northlight Books, 1989.

Edwards, Betty. *Drawing on the Right Side of the Brain*. New York: G.P. Putnam Sons, 1989.

Holmes, Nigil. *Designing Pictorial Symbols*. New York: Watson-Guptill, 1985.

Sibbett, David. *I See What You Mean!* San Francisco: Sibbet and Associates, 1981.

Sibbett, David. *Fundamentals of Graphic Language*. San Francisco: Graphic Guides, Inc., 1991.

Smith, T.C. *Making Successful Presentations: A Self-Teaching Guide*. New York: John Wiley and Sons Inc, 1984.

Solo, Dan. *Decorative Display Alphabets*. New York: Dover Publications, 1990.

NOTES

# NOTES

# NOTES

# NOTES

# Now Available From

# CRISP.
# Learning™

## Books•Videos•CD-ROMs•Computer-Based Training Products

## Subject Areas Include:

*Management*

*Human Resources*

*Communication Skills*

*Personal Development*

*Marketing/Sales*

*Organizational Development*

*Customer Service/Quality*

*Computer Skills*

*Small Business and Entrepreneurship*

*Adult Literacy and Learning*

*Life Planning and Retirement*

VERK

# CRISP WORLDWIDE DISTRIBUTION

English language books are distributed worldwide. Major international distributors include:

## ASIA/PACIFIC

*Australia/New Zealand:* In Learning, PO Box 1051, Springwood QLD, Brisbane, Australia 4127   Tel: 61-7-3-841-2286, Facsimile: 61-7-3-841-1580 ATTN: Messrs. Richard/Robert Gordon

*Malaysia, Philippines, Singapore:* Epsys Pte Ltd., 540 Sims Ave #04-01, Sims Avenue Centre, 387603, Singapore   Tel: 65-747-1964, Facsimile: 65-747-0162 ATTN: Mr. Jack Chin

*Hong Kong/Mainland China:* Crisp Learning Solutions, 18/F Honest Motors Building 9-11 Leighton Rd., Causeway Bay, Hong Kong   Tel: 852-2915-7119, Facsimile: 852-2865-2815 ATTN: Ms. Grace Lee

*Japan:* Phoenix Associates, Believe Mita Bldg., 8th Floor 3-43-16 Shiba, Minato-ku, Tokyo 105-0014, Japan   Tel: 81-3-5427-6231,  Facsimile: 81-3-5427-6232 ATTN: Mr. Peter Owans

## CANADA

Crisp Learning Canada, 60 Briarwood Avenue, Mississauga, ON L5G 3N6 Canada Tel: 905-274-5678, Facsimile: 905-278-2801 ATTN: Mr. Steve Connolly

## EUROPEAN UNION

*England:* Flex Learning Media, Ltd., 9-15 Hitchin Street, Baldock, Hertfordshire, SG7 6AL, England Tel: 44-1-46-289-6000, Facsimile: 44-1-46-289-2417   ATTN: Mr. David Willetts

## INDIA

Multi-Media HRD, Pvt. Ltd., National House, Floor 1 6 Tulloch Road, Appolo Bunder, Bombay, India 400-039 Tel: 91-22-204-2281, Facsimile: 91-22-283-6478 ATTN: Messrs. Ajay Aggarwal/ C.L. Aggarwal

## SOUTH AMERICA

*Mexico:* Grupo Editorial Iberoamerica, Nebraska 199, Col. Napoles, 03810 Mexico, D.F. Tel: 525-523-0994, Facsimile: 525-543-1173   ATTN: Señor Nicholas Grepe

## SOUTH AFRICA

*Bookstores*: Alternative Books, PO Box 1345, Ferndale 2160, South Africa Tel: 27-11-792-7730, Facsimile: 27-11-792-7787   ATTN: Mr. Vernon de Haas

*Corporate*: Learning Resources, P.O. Box 2806, Parklands, Johannesburg 2121, South Africa, Tel: 27-21-531-2923, Facsimile: 27-21-531-2944 ATTN: Mr. Ricky Robinson

## MIDDLE EAST

Edutech Middle East, L.L.C., PO Box 52334, Dubai U.A.E. Tel: 971-4-359-1222, Facsimile: 971-4-359-6500   ATTN: Mr. A.S.F. Karim

# USING VISUAL AIDS
## The Effective Use of Type, Color, and Graphics

**Claire Raines**
**Linda Williamson**

**CREDITS**
Editor: **Tony Hicks**
Managing Editor: **Kathleen Barcos**
Typesetting: **Interface Studio**
Cover Design: **Carol Harris**
Artwork: **Ralph Mapson**

© 1995 by Crisp Publications, Inc.
Printed in the United States of America by Von Hoffmann Graphics, Inc.

CrispLearning.com

04 05  10 9 8 7 6 5 4

Library of Congress Catalog Card Number 94-80034
Raines, Claire
Williamson, Linda
Using Visual Aids
ISBN 1-56052-326-3

# USING VISUAL AIDS

## The Effective Use of Type, Color, and Graphics

**Claire Raines**

**Linda Williamson**

# A FIFTY-MINUTE™ SERIES BOOK

This Fifty-Minute™ book is designed to be "read with a pencil." It is an excellent workbook for self-study as well as classroom learning. All material is copyright-protected and cannot be duplicated without permission from the publisher. *Therefore, be sure to order a copy for every training participant by contacting:*

**CRISP.**
**Learning**
Menlo Park, California

1-800-442-7477
CrispLearning.com

1-05

Throughout your career, you will be judged by the effectiveness with which you communicate in your daily activities. You might make a presentation to your peers in committee work, to subordinates as a part of a training or information program, or a formal presentation to senior management or a client. In each case your reputation is on the line. When you are effective, you gain status and earn respect. You find managing others easier, and you become promotable to increasingly higher levels.

The basics of preparing an effective presentation have not changed with the advent of computer graphics and multimedia software packages. No innovative technological tool can substitute for the ability to determine a purpose that meets an audience's needs, relate ideas clearly and effectively, and be sincere and responsive to the audience. Today's managers must focus on fundamental communication skills while using technology to enhance each phase of the presentation process: developing crisp, well-organized content; designing top-notch support tools (overhead transparencies, electronic or Web presentations, and audience handouts); and delivering the presentation smoothly and professionally.

For these reasons, *Creating Dynamic Multimedia Presentations* goes beyond the simple how-to manual for learning to create simple PowerPoint presentations using standard presentation designs and consisting of dense, countless bulleted lists and other bland, dull designs. In ten short projects, you will

- Master the full functionality of Microsoft PowerPoint 2002®.

- Apply presentation design guidelines that will empower you to build high-impact presentations that enhance your delivery and credibility without robbing you of precious preparation time—determining exactly what your audience needs and wants to know; developing logical, compelling content; and rehearsing for a smooth delivery.

- Acquire skillful delivery techniques that reduce the distance technology often places between the speaker and the audience.

*Creating Dynamic Multimedia Presentations* expedites your mastery of these powerful skills. Rather than spend too much of your valuable time creating basic slides, you will critique slides a novice might create and then build enhanced slides that correct violations in basic slide design guidelines and, more importantly, ensure communication effectiveness. While completing these ten brief projects and the reinforcement activities new to this edition, you will quickly enhance your proficiency in the following exciting ways:

- Creating a basic presentation including a title and bulleted lists with simple clip art, slide transitions, and custom animation.

- Adding impact and appeal with (a) dynamic and relevant images and sound; (b) creative animation techniques that target the audience's attention for higher impact; (c) compelling tables and graphs that clarify and reinforce potentially overwhelming numerical data; and (d) hidden slides and hyperlinks that add flexibility and interaction to the delivery of the slide show.

- Showcasing your organizational structure and cinching seamless delivery by
    - Incorporating agenda and divider slides that transition the audience smoothly through the sections of the presentation.
    - Recording and analyzing rehearsal timings to identify a variety of content and delivery improvements.
    - Using the Speller and Style Checker to eliminate embarrassing errors on your slides.
    - Creating useful speaker's notes and professional audience handouts that enhance your credibility and extend the usefulness presentation.
- Designing a custom template that fits the needs of a specific audience or topic and reflects your company's professional image and unique corporate identity.
- Taking your presentation design and delivery expertise to the next level by designing an electronic presentation specifically for posting to the Web for access by remote audiences.

While applying numerous creative design techniques, you will encounter feature boxes that provide supplemental information related to four important presentation areas:

- **Designer's Pointers**—basic slide design guidelines that lead to the development of compelling slides that communicate ideas effectively and involve the audience in the message.

- **Presenter's Tips**—suggestions for using a specific PowerPoint feature and design technique to deliver a presentation effectively.

- **FYI**—tidbits of information related to multimedia development that reach beyond the operation of PowerPoint.

- **Troubleshooting Tips**—detailed assistance with PowerPoint or Windows-related operations, problems the author has anticipated as a result of extensive training experience.

The time devoted to completing this textbook will yield positive results as you seek to become an effective speaker in today's highly competitive workplace. You will gain expertise in designing dynamic PowerPoint presentations that focus on timeless communication skills that allow you to connect with your audience and achieve the goals you have established for that group—regardless of the presentation media you choose. Take the time to incorporate design features that assist you in delivering a slide show in an effortless, seamless manner and practice until the technology is virtually transparent, positioned in the background to serve as your supporting cast. Assume your important role as the presentation star, and you will reap the benefits gained from honing your presentation skills to meet the high expectations of today's audiences.

# PROJECT 1

## Learning Objectives

- Start PowerPoint and understand the parts of the PowerPoint screen.

- Apply a template to a new and an existing presentation.

- Create a title slide and a bulleted list using an AutoLayout.

- Save a presentation.

- Move within a presentation and manipulate slides (copy, delete, and change order).

## Understanding PowerPoint

PowerPoint is a graphics software program that allows you to create compelling presentation visuals for a variety of purposes. A PowerPoint presentation is developed by adding individual slides related to the same topic to a single file. A slide is comparable to pages in a word processing document or sheets in a worksheet. The slides can be projected on a screen using projection equipment, printed as transparencies, or posted to a Web page or broadcast for viewing by a broad audience in diverse locations.

### Starting PowerPoint

1. Double-click the PowerPoint icon (or click **Start**, **Programs**, **Office XP**, **PowerPoint**). The startup dialog box appears.

2. Note the options for creating a new presentation using a blank presentation, a design template, or a wizard, and for opening an existing presentation.

3. Click **From Design Template** to start PowerPoint. You will now review the PowerPoint window before designing your first slide.

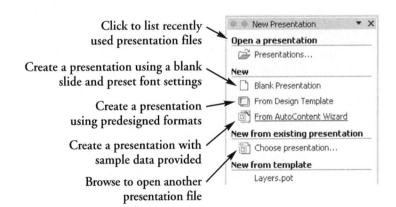

Click to list recently used presentation files

Create a presentation using a blank slide and preset font settings

Create a presentation using predesigned formats

Create a presentation with sample data provided

Browse to open another presentation file

## Understanding the PowerPoint Window

Study the following diagram and terms that identify and explain the various elements of the PowerPoint screen and presentation window.

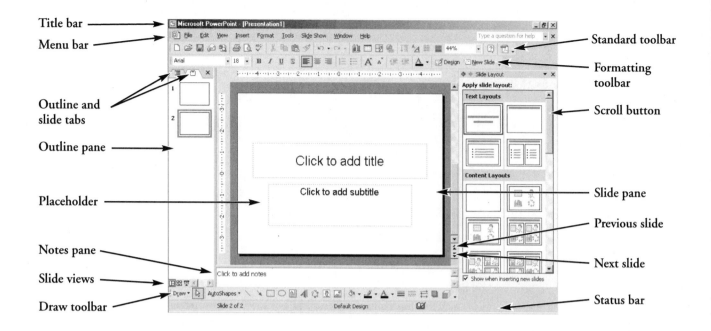

*Screen Parts*

**Title bar**                   Identifies that PowerPoint is running and displays
                               the file name.

**Menu bar**                    Provides pop-down menus from which features can
                               be accessed.

**Standard toolbar**            Gives quick access to the most frequently used file
                               functions.

**Formatting toolbar**          Provides buttons for changing fonts, sizes, attrib-
                               utes, and color.

**Draw toolbar**                Provides buttons for inserting text or quick graphics.

*Presentation Window*

**Slide**                       Displays placeholders for text and graphics to be
                               inserted.

**Placeholder**                 Dotted-line boxes that designate the location on a
                               slide in which titles, text, art, graphics, charts, and
                               other objects are placed.

**Text object**                 A term used to describe text in a text box (often a
                               graphic object).

**View buttons**                Control the number of slides displayed and the
                               display layout (normal, slide sorter, and slide
                               show).

**Status bar**                  Contains the slide number and the template selected.

**Previous slide**              Displays the previous slide.

**Next slide**                  Displays the next slide.

**Horizontal and vertical       Moves the text in the window up, down, left, or right.
scroll buttons**

# Understanding Design Templates

PowerPoint provides an extensive library of predesigned templates created by professional graphic artists. These templates include formatting for color, fonts, bullets, graphics, and other formatting that makes creating a basic presentation simple.

## Selecting a Design Template

1. Click **From Design Template** (from the opening menu).
   *Note:* You completed this step already to allow you to review the PowerPoint window.

2. Click the **Design Templates** option. Scroll to view available options displayed at the right of the slide and click to apply a design template of your choice.

3. Click the **Color Schemes** tab and scroll to view the various color variations in the template you selected. Click to select a color scheme for your presentation.

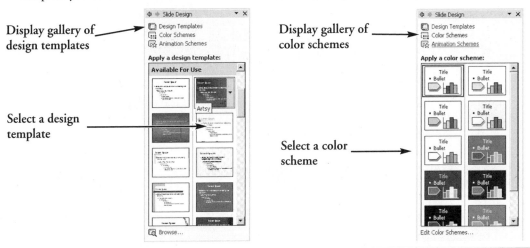

Display gallery of design templates

Select a design template

Display gallery of color schemes

Select a color scheme

Select a presentation type and the wizard will create a sample presentation

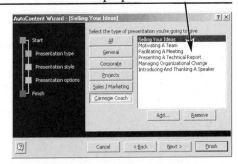

FYI

Become familiar with sources of other presentation designs (templates) that will create exactly the mood you wish to convey.

- Click **Help**, **Office on the Web** and download presentation designs from Microsoft's Web site. New templates are added to this site regularly.

- Open a content template that includes all the elements of a design template, a suggested outline, and text suggestions for your presentation. You simply edit your choices with your own information.

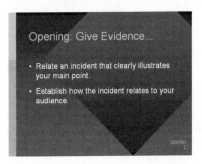

**Sample slide created from an Autocontent Wizard**

## Applying a Design Template to an Existing Presentation

You will select a different presentation design template for the presentation you've just opened. Note you can apply different design templates to specific slides in a single presentation; however, limiting design choices and applying them consistently throughout a presentation will result in a simple, uncluttered, appealing design.

1. Click **Format**, **Slide Design** (or click the Design button on the Formatting toolbar and Design Templates).

2. Scroll to view the design templates displayed at the right of the slide and click to apply the template to your presentation.

3. Proceed to the next section.

# Creating a Title Slide and Simple Bulleted Lists

PowerPoint provides the basic structure for numerous slide layouts, allowing you to simply click in the designated area (placeholder) and input text and graphics. These standard layouts (called *AutoLayouts*) allow you to create a slide show with a consistent, professional appearance that can be customized when needed to fit your content.

## Creating a Title Slide

*Directions:* Follow the instructions to build the title slide as shown in the model.

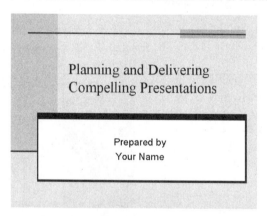

1. Click **Insert**, **New Slide** (or click New Slide on the Formatting toolbar). The available slide layouts (text and contents) are displayed at the right. Pointing to the layout reveals a brief description of the layout; graphics provide visual cues to the nature of each layout. Scroll down to reveal all layout categories.

2. Select the Title Slide layout from the Text Layouts category. This layout is surrounded by a border and includes shaded lines depicting positions for a title and subtitle.

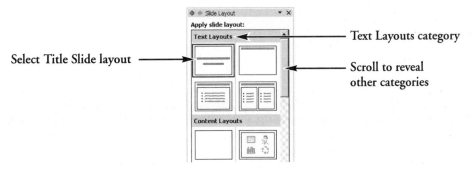

Select Title Slide layout ⟶

Text Layouts category ⟶

Scroll to reveal other categories ⟶

3. Click in the title placeholder. Note that a selection rectangle surrounds the placeholder with the cursor positioned ready for inputting text. Key the title.

4. Click in the subtitle placeholder and key the subtitle.

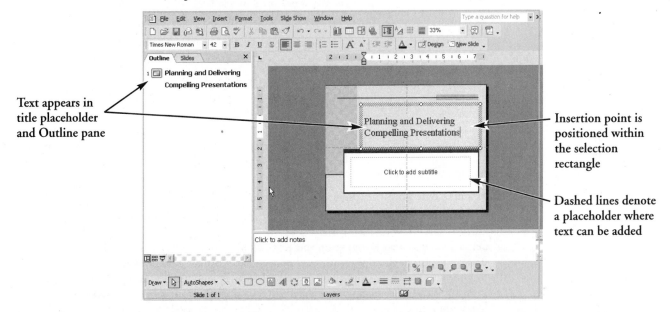

Text appears in title placeholder and Outline pane

Insertion point is positioned within the selection rectangle

Dashed lines denote a placeholder where text can be added

## Creating a Simple Bulleted List

*Directions:* Follow the instructions to build the slide shown in the model.

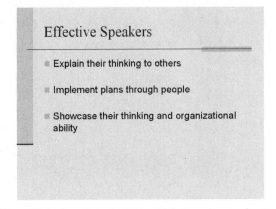

Effective Speakers

- Explain their thinking to others
- Implement plans through people
- Showcase their thinking and organizational ability

1. Click **Insert, New Slide** (or click the New Slide button on the Formatting toolbar).

2. Select the Title and Text layout from the Text Layouts category.

3. Click the title placeholder and key the slide title.

4. Click the bulleted list placeholder and key the text for the first bulleted item.

5. Press **Enter**.

6. Key the remaining bulleted items.

## Creating a Bulleted List from the Outline Pane

*Directions:* Follow the instructions to build the slide shown in the model.

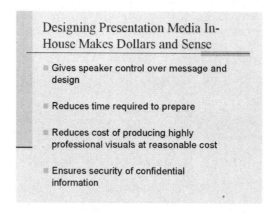

1. Be certain the Outline tab is selected.

2. Insert a new slide from the Outline tab:

   a) Click to the right of the last icon for Slide 2 or after the last word of the slide.
   b) Click **Insert**, **New Slide** (or press Ctl-D).
   c) Select Title and Text layout from the Text Layouts category. If the slide layout box doesn't display to the right of the slide pane, click Format, Slide Layout.
   d) Key the title to the right of the new icon designating a new slide and press **Enter**. Press the **Tab** key to begin the bulleted list and **Enter** to continue to the next bulleted item.

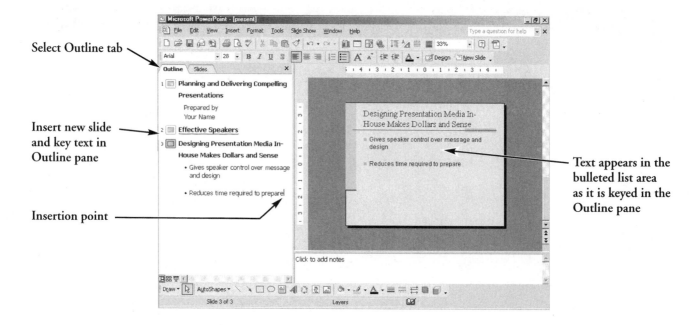

## Designer's Pointer ——————————————————

Follow these capitalization rules when building slides:

1. **Use initial caps in slide titles.** Lowercase words are easier to read than UPPERCASE WORDS. Uppercase was used to emphasize ideas in the age of the typewriter, but today emphasis is added with a variety of techniques—bold and shadow effects, changes to font face, size, and color, etc.

2. **Capitalize only the first word in bulleted lists.** This style allows viewers to scan a line of text and comprehend ideas quickly. A viewer's eyes move up and down with initial caps (first word and important words capitalized), a movement that creates a wave effect that is distracting and decreases readability.

# Saving and Closing a Presentation and Exiting PowerPoint

Save your presentation to the hard drive or a disk so you can open and edit the file at a later time. Plan to save after you have created each slide to prevent losing data if power to your computer is interrupted. Save more often when building slides that require a great deal of time and effort.

1. Click **File**, **Save As**.

2. Click in the **Save in** box and key a drive designation (e.g., a: drive).

3. Click in the **File name** box and key **Present** as the file name.

4. Click **Save**.

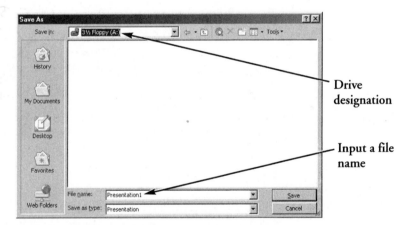

Drive designation

Input a file name

## Closing a Presentation

1. Click **File**, **Close**. The file is no longer in your computer's memory but can be reopened for later use.

## Exiting PowerPoint

1. Click **File**, **Exit**.

The huge size of PowerPoint files containing graphics, sound, and animation has posed a challenge to users needing to transport files between computers. Trading in our floppy disks for ZIP disks, writable CD-ROMs, and other removable memory drives has certainly simplified this process.

In the event you get that dreaded "insufficient disk space" message, PowerPoint's Pack and Go Wizard could be a handy option for compressing the file to fit your storage media—your ZIP disk, floppies, or even your hard drive. Simply click **File**, **Pack and Go**, and the wizard will walk you through the process of compressing the files and fonts used in the presentation together on as many disks as necessary. Later, when you wish to view the packaged file in its new location, click on the packaged file in Windows Explorer to execute the unpacking process that reassembles the files. If you plan to run the packaged presentation on a computer that does not have Microsoft PowerPoint installed, be sure to include the Microsoft PowerPoint Viewer in the package.

# Opening an Existing Presentation

You can open and revise a presentation that has been saved on the hard drive or a disk.

1. Restart PowerPoint (click **Start**, **Programs**, **Office XP**, **PowerPoint**).

2. Click **Presentations** from the startup dialog box. The File, Open dialog box is displayed automatically so you can browse and open an existing file.

3. Open the file **Present** and continue to the next section.

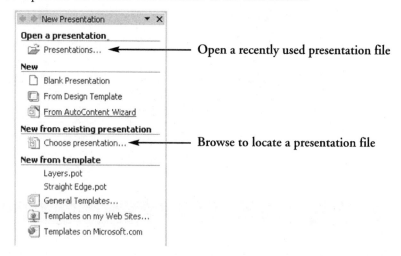

# Viewing a Presentation

View buttons control the number of slides displayed and the display layout. The View buttons (normal, slide sorter, and slide show) are located at the bottom left side of the screen, as shown in the following illustration.

## Normal View

The normal view includes the outline, slide, and notes panes so you can view these sections of your presentation all at once. You can adjust the size of different panes by dragging the borders.

- **Outline pane**: Displays (a) the title and body text for slides or (b) a thumbnail (miniature version) of the complete slide. This view facilitates organizing ideas in a presentation and is the most efficient view for entering text for numerous slides.

- **Slide pane**: Displays a single slide with text and graphics and is useful for entering text and graphics.

- **Notes pane**:   Provides space below the slide pane where text and graphics can be inserted. The pane can be used for (a) inputting notes to prompt the speaker's next point, (b) inputting cues to aid a projectionist advancing the slide show for a speaker, and (c) recording ideas for further slide design. Project 8 focuses on creating useful notes pages using this pane.

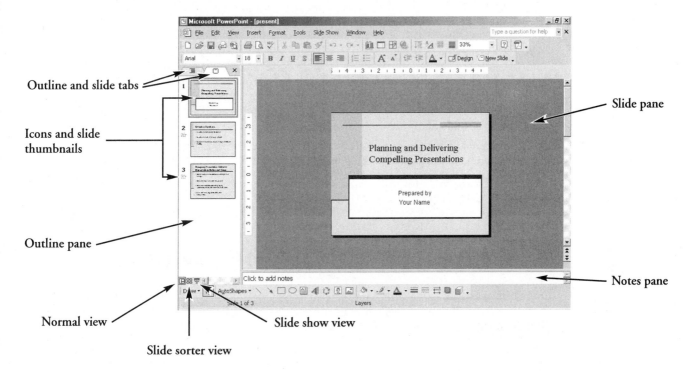

## Slide Sorter View

The Slide Sorter view, illustrated on the next page, displays a thumbnail of each slide in the file similar to the way one would arrange 35mm slides on a light table. This view is convenient for adding, deleting, and moving slides, and adding slide transitions.

To switch to the Slide Sorter view:

1. Click the **Slide Sorter view** button (or click View, Slide Sorter).

2. Click **Zoom** (right side of the Standard toolbar) and select **33%** to view the slides without scrolling. As you become familiar with PowerPoint, select a Zoom setting of your choice (large enough that you can recognize the content of the slides but small enough to minimize scrolling to locate a specific slide).

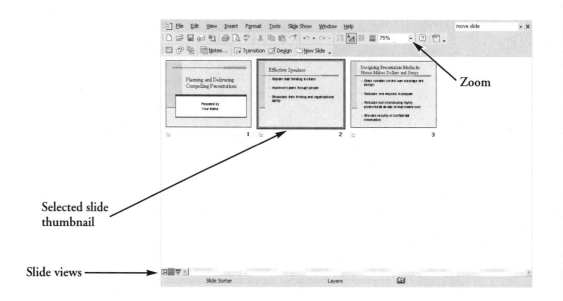

Zoom

Selected slide
thumbnail

Slide views

## Slide Show View

The Slide Show view is used to run a full-screen presentation for preview on your monitor, or to project the slide show while a speaker is presenting.

To switch to Slide Show view:

1. Click **View**, **Slide Show** or click the Slide Show view button. The slide selected when the command is executed is displayed.

2. Press **Escape** to return to the presentation window.

# Presenter's Tip

To deliver a presentation with professional style and high impact, you must remain in slide show view at all times—even when an audience member asks you to return to a previous slide. You'll learn to run your presentation like a polished professional in Project 2.

# Manipulating Slides and Inputting Text

Learning to move within a presentation and to copy, delete, and change the sequence of slides will increase your efficiency in designing an effective slide show. Explore the various methods for completing these functions and adopt the one(s) you think works best for you.

## Moving Within a Presentation

Explore various methods for moving within a presentation:

1. Be certain the file is open in Normal view (click the **Normal view** button from the status line at the bottom of the screen or click View, Normal).

2. Choose a method for moving within the presentation:

- **Slide Pane:** Use the next slide and previous slide buttons, the arrow keys, or the scroll bar at the far right of the screen to move from one slide to another.

- **Outline Pane:** Click the numbered icon in the Outline pane to move to a specific slide (displays the slide in the Slide pane for editing). Scroll to reveal all slides in the Outline pane.

## Deleting Slides

Slides can be deleted from Normal or Slide Sorter views.

### Normal View

1. Switch to Normal view (click the Slide Sorter view button from the status line at the bottom of the screen or click View, Normal).

2. Click to select the title slide in the Outline pane (a shaded border or highlighted text appears to indicate the slide has been selected).

3. Press **Delete**.

Alternatively, right-click and click Cut.
*Note:* Click the **Undo** curved left arrow on the standard toolbar to restore the deleted slide.

### Slide Sorter

1. Switch to the Slide Sorter view (click the Slide Sorter view button from the status line at the bottom of the screen or click View, Slide Sorter).

2. Select the title slide by pointing to the slide and clicking (a shaded border surrounds the selected slide).

3. Press **Delete**. *Note:* Click **Undo** (curved left arrow on the standard toolbar) to restore the deleted slide.

To select multiple slides to be moved or deleted, select the first slide and hold down the Shift key as you click additional slides. A border will surround each selected slide. If you click without holding down the Shift key, only the last slide you click will be selected.

## Changing Slide Order

The order of slides can be changed in the Normal or Slide Sorter views.

### Normal View

1. Click the numbered icon or thumbnail of any slide in the Outline pane.

2. Hold the left mouse button as you drag this slide to a position of your choice.

3. Release the mouse to drop the slide when a vertical line marker appears indicating the slide can be dropped. This procedure is referred to as *drag and drop*.

### Slide Sorter View

1. Click a slide thumbnail of any slide.

2. Hold the left mouse button as you drag this slide to a position of your choice.

3. When a vertical line marker appears indicating that the slide can be dropped, release the left mouse button to drop the slide. This process is illustrated on the following page.

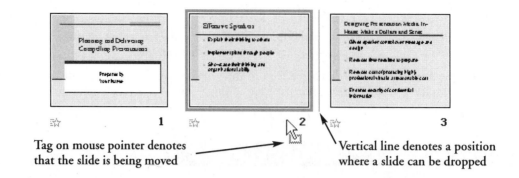

Tag on mouse pointer denotes
that the slide is being moved

Vertical line denotes a position
where a slide can be dropped

## Copying a Slide

Slides can be copied in the Normal or Slide Sorter views.

### Normal View

1. Click the numbered icon of the title slide in the Outline pane and click **Copy**.

2. Move the cursor to the point where you wish to insert the copied slide. A vertical line marker appears to indicate a position where a slide can be inserted.

3. Click **Paste**.

Alternatively, click Edit, Duplicate (or Ctl-D). A slide appears below the original slide and can then be moved to the desired position.

### Slide Sorter View

1. Select the slide thumbnail of the title slide and click **Copy**.

2. Move the cursor to the point where you wish to insert the copied slide. A vertical line marker appears to indicate a position where a slide can be inserted.

3. Click **Paste**.

Alternatively, click Edit, Duplicate (or Ctl-D). A slide appears to the right of the original slide and can then be moved to the desired position.

## Copying and Moving a Slide

1. Select a slide in either Normal or Slide Sorter view.

2. Hold down the Control key as you drag it to a new position. Note an icon with a plus sign at the top appears as you drag the slide indicating an object is being moved and copied. Release the mouse button to drop the copied slide into its desired location.

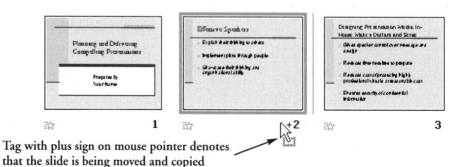

Tag with plus sign on mouse pointer denotes
that the slide is being moved and copied

## Moving Slides Between Presentation Files

Often you will find it useful to copy slides from a presentation you developed previously into a presentation you are currently developing.

1. Open the file Present.

2. Click **File**, **New** to create another presentation file. Select a presentation design template different from the one you used in the Present file. Insert a title slide and provide a title of your choice. Save the file as **Newpresentation**.

3. Click **Window** and **Present** to make the Present file the active presentation on your desktop.

**Check mark denotes the active presentation**

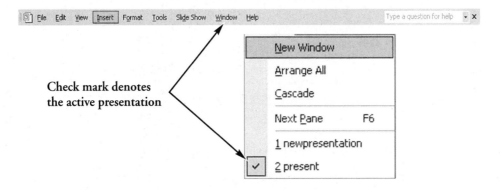

4. Select Slides 2–3 and click **Copy**.

5. Click **Window** and **New Presentation** to make this new file the active presentation.

6. Click below the title slide in the Outline pane and click **Paste**. Slides 2–3 are inserted and reformatted using the presentation design of the new presentation. You can also paste slides in the Slide Sorter view.

## Designer's Pointer ————————

Make a duplicate of slides when creating a slide with similar design elements to ensure consistency and save time. When experimenting with a design enhancement, editing a duplicate slide rather than the original will allow you to return to the original design without reformatting the slide. Simply delete the duplicate slide containing your trial format and resume formatting the original slide.

# Reinforcement Activities

Add the following slides to the file Present for added reinforcement of the PowerPoint features you learned in this project. Position the slides as shown in the table at the end of this project.

## Activity 1

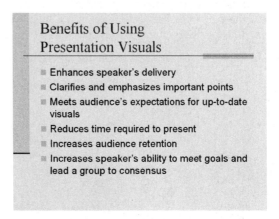

Build the slide as shown in the model using the Title and Text layout.

## Activity 2

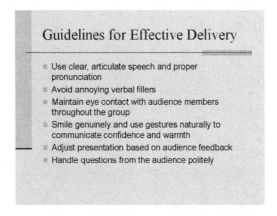

Build the slide as shown in the model using the Title and Text layout.

## Slide Order

Sequence the slides in the file Present as follows:

1. Title Slide

2. Effective Speakers

3. Designing Presentation Media In-house Makes Dollars and Sense

4. Benefits of Using Presentation Visuals

5. Guidelines for Effective Delivery

# PROJECT 2

## Learning Objectives

- Create bulleted lists with multiple levels and two columns.

- Add relevant, engaging clip art to bulleted lists by searching the Microsoft Clip Gallery and the Microsoft Clip Art Design Gallery Live Web site.

- Customize PowerPoint's autolayouts by adding new placeholders.

- Add slide transitions and custom animation effects to add impact and to target the audience's attention.

- Print a presentation in various formats: slides, handouts, notes pages, and outline view.

- Run a presentation in a seamless, professional manner during a presentation.

## Creating Bulleted Lists with Multiple Levels

You will learn to promote and demote text in a bulleted list to show the relative importance of each item (e.g., major or minor point within an outline).

### Promoting and Demoting Text in a Bulleted List

*Directions:* Follow the instructions to build the slide shown in the model.

**Demands Changing World Places on Speakers**

- Meet audience's expectations of high-quality visual support including advanced technologies:
  - Alternative presentation delivery methods (distance and team)
  - Non-linear Web designs that allow audiences flexibility in viewing presentations
- Adapt to faster pace and shorter attention spans
- Face diversity challenges

1. Create a new slide using the Title and Text layout from the Text Layouts category.

2. Key the slide title and the first-level point ("Meet audience's . . . ") Press **Enter**.

3. Click the **Demote** button (right arrow on the Formatting toolbar or press Tab) to begin the second-level (minor) point of this bulleted item.

4. Click the **Promote** button (left arrow on the Formatting toolbar or press Shift+Tab) to move back to key a first-level point.

5. Complete the bulleted list.

**Click Promote and Demote icons to denote the level of points in a bulleted list**

## Creating a Two-Column Bulleted List

*Directions:* Follow the instructions to build the slide shown in the model.

1. Create a new slide with the Title and 2-Column Text layout from the Text Layouts category.

2. Key the slide title.

3. Click the left column bulleted list placeholder. Key the text using the Promote and Demote buttons to create the list with major and minor points.

4. Click the right column bulleted list placeholder and key the text.

### Considerations Affecting Presentation Media Choice

- Audience's preferences
- Speaker's purpose
- Audience size
- Degree of formality
- Available resources
  - Time and money
  - Equipment
  - Facilities
- Simplicity of use
- Risk of failure
- Transportability

# Adding Clip Art to a Slide

Including clip art on a slide can engage the audience's attention, reinforce an important point, and help the audience visualize a complex idea. Clip art can be selected easily from the Microsoft Clip Gallery or Microsoft's Clip Art Design Gallery Live Web site. Once inserted, the clip art can be sized and positioned to achieve a desired effect.

## Selecting Clip Art from the Microsoft Clip Gallery

You will select clip art from the Microsoft Clip Gallery.

*Directions:* Follow the instructions to revise the "Effective Speakers" slide in the file Present.

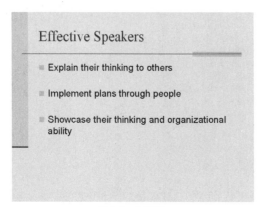

**Original Slide**

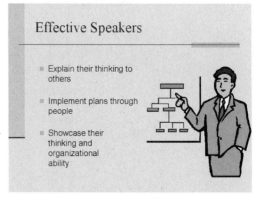

**Enhanced Slide**

1. Display the "Effective Speakers" slide in Normal view.

2. Click **Format**, **Slide Layout** to display the slide layouts.

3. Scroll to display the Text and Content Layouts category and select Title, Text, and Contents. Note the bulleted list is reformatted and a placeholder for contents is added. Point to each icon and note the prompt that describes the content that may be inserted.

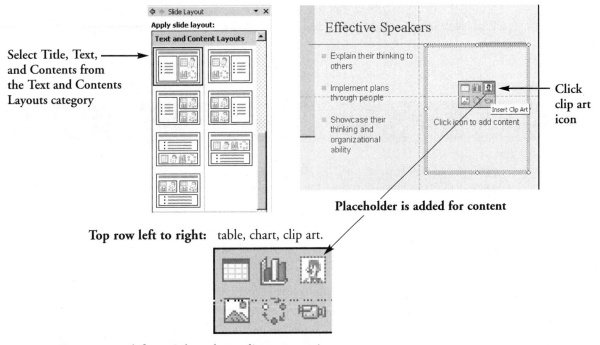

Select Title, Text, and Contents from the Text and Contents Layouts category

Click clip art icon

**Placeholder is added for content**

**Top row left to right:**   table, chart, clip art.

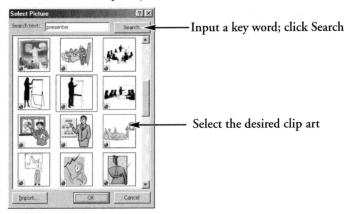

**Bottom row left to right:**   photo, diagram, movie.

4. Click the icon to add clip art. The Select Picture section of the Microsoft Clip Gallery appears.

5. Input a keyword in the keyword box (e.g., presenter) and click **Search**. A gallery of clip art images matching the keyword appears.

6. Click to select the clip art you wish to insert and click **OK**.

Input a key word; click Search

Select the desired clip art

7. Select the clip art (sizing handles appear). Point to a corner handle and hold down the Shift key as you drag outward to enlarge the clip art slightly.

8. Point to the center of the clip art and drag it down near the bottom right quadrant of the slide. This position provides a realistic perspective and avoids the impression that the presenter is floating on the page.

# Designer's Pointer

Research shows that people notice graphics second only to headings. Optimum placement of a graphic (clip art or chart) supporting text is the lower right quadrant of the slide. Your graphic acts as a "draw" to pull the viewer's eye from the title area, through the text area, to focus on the graphic.

## Importing Clip Art from Microsoft's Design Gallery Live Web Site

An abundance of clip art, photographs, video clips, and sound files is available to help a speaker illustrate key concepts or points. Commercial software, public domain, and shareware clip art galleries are available. Multimedia files can be downloaded from Internet sites such as the Microsoft Design Gallery Live you will use in this project.

*Directions:* Follow instructions to build the slide shown in the model.

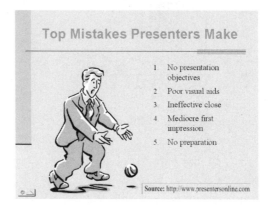

1. Create a new slide using the Title and Text layout from the Text Layouts category.

2. Key the slide title and the bulleted list.

3. Click **Insert**, **Picture**, **Clip Art** (or click the Clip Art button on the Draw toolbar). A search dialog box appears.

Clip Art

4. Click **Clips Online**. Wait while your browser connects to the Microsoft Design Gallery Live Web site.

5. Input a keyword in the keyword box (e.g., mistakes) and click **Go**. A gallery of clip art images matching the keyword appears.

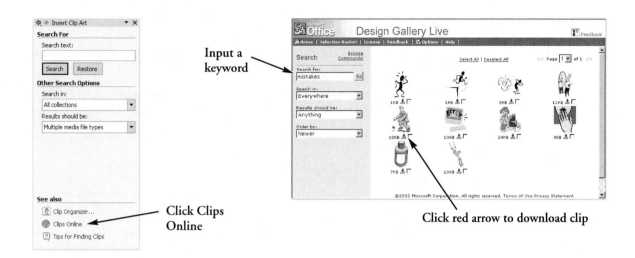

Input a keyword

Click Clips Online

Click red arrow to download clip

6. Click the red down arrow below the image to download. The image is inserted in the Downloaded Clips section of the Microsoft Clip Organizer for easy insertion on a PowerPoint slide.

7. Click the down arrow to the right of the image and click **Copy**. Note the commands for organizing the clip within the Microsoft Clip Organizer.

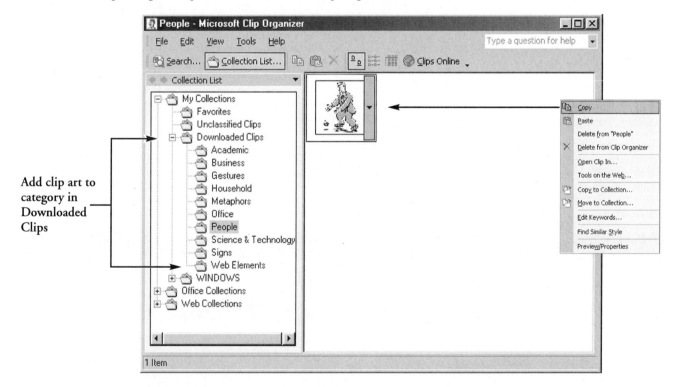

Add clip art to category in Downloaded Clips

8. Return to your PowerPoint slide and click **Paste**.

9. Select the clip art (sizing handles appear). Point to a corner handle and hold down the Shift key as you drag outward to enlarge the clip art slightly. Point to the center of the clip art to move it into the desired position at the left of the slide and adjust the bulleted list for balance with the clip art.

## Designer's Pointer

Too much text and too many meaningless images clutter a visual. An audience will ignore an image perceived to be complicated or concentrate on deciphering the slide and not listen to the speaker. Keep your audience's attention by designing clean, uncluttered slides. To avoid clutter,

- Leave 60 to 70 percent of the slide blank.

- Follow the 7 × 7 rule: Limit text to 7 lines per slide and 7 words per line.

# Working with New Placeholders

Any autolayout can be modified to fit the specific content of a presentation. In this section, you will add a placeholder for a source note on a slide. A placeholder not included as a part of the standard design of the template is referred to as a *specimen*, a one-of-a-kind in a presentation. This specimen format for source notes can be copied to other slides containing source notes for consistency and efficiency.

*Directions:* Follow the instructions for revising the slide shown in the model.

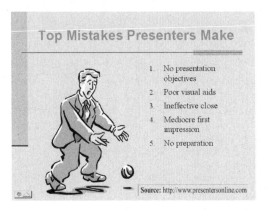

## Creating a New Placeholder

1. Click the **Text** button on the Draw Toolbar.

Text

2. Position the mouse pointer anywhere on the slide. Click and hold the left mouse button as you drag down and to the right. A selection rectangle with diagonal lines and a series of sizing boxes [handles] surround the placeholder. The insertion point indicates text can be keyed.

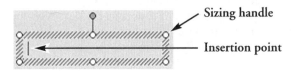

Sizing handle

Insertion point

3. Key the text in the placeholder: Source: **http://www.presentersonline.com**

Hold down the Shift key and drag a corner sizing handle to change the width and height proportionally. This technique is especially useful when resizing clip art, photos, and charts.

**FYI**

## Repositioning a Placeholder

4. Select the placeholder by clicking the placeholder once to display the selection rectangle with diagonal lines and a second time to display a shaded border between the sizing handles.

5. Move the mouse pointer directly between any two handles until the mouse pointer turns into a four-headed arrow. Drag the placeholder to its new location at the bottom right of the slide. Note the icon attached to the mouse pointer indicates text is being moved.

6 Release the mouse button when the placeholder is in position.

7. Click anywhere outside the placeholder to deselect the placeholder.

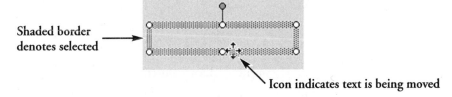

Shaded border denotes selected

Icon indicates text is being moved

## Troubleshooting Tip

If you are having trouble moving a placeholder, check to see if the cut and copy icons on the Standard toolbar are dimmed. If so, you'll also note the placeholder you're trying to move is not selected. Click the selection rectangle again. The diagonal lines between the sizing handles will be replaced with the shaded border, and the cut and copy icons will be active.

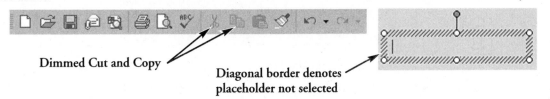

Dimmed Cut and Copy

Diagonal border denotes placeholder not selected

## Resizing a Placeholder

8. Point to the *sizing handle* on the right side of the placeholder and drag to the right until the text fits on one line.

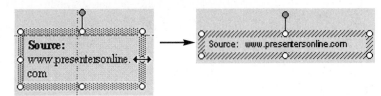

Source: www.presentersonline.com

## Deleting a Placeholder

9. Select the placeholder containing the source note you just created.

10. Press Delete.

11. Click the **Undo** button (curved left arrow) on the Standard toolbar to restore the placeholder.

Undo

## Editing Text in a Placeholder

As you edit the appearance of the text in the specimen placeholder, you will become familiar with the numerous ways text can be enhanced to produce a creative design. In Project 4 you will learn to edit the Master Slide to change the appearance of standard design elements such as the slide title and bulleted lists. An edit made on the Master Slide will change the appearance of all slides, eliminating the need to edit each slide individually.

12. Highlight the text to be edited (http://www.presentersonline.com). Click the **Bold** button on the Formatting toolbar.

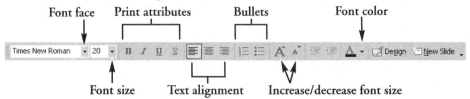

13. Highlight the text to be edited. Click **Format**, **Font**.

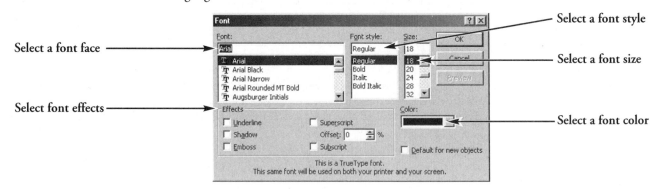

14. Select a new font in the Font box.

15. Change the font size to **14 points** by selecting or keying a number in the Size box.

16. Change the text color by clicking the down arrow in the Color box and selecting a color from the menu.

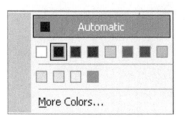

Select a color that is complementary with your template background and that the audience can read easily. For easy readability, the contrast between the background color and foreground color (text) must be high. For example:

*High contrast:* blue background with yellow text
*Low contrast:* light blue background with white text

17. Study other changes that can be made from the Font dialog box (shown above).

18. Make the following changes by clicking icons on the Draw toolbar:
    a) Add a one-point-wide border around the placeholder that is a dashed line.
    b) Select a line color complementary with your design template background.

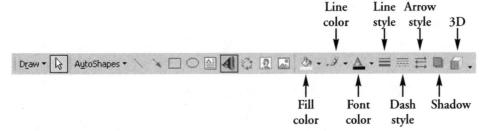

19. Study other changes that can be made from the Draw toolbar.
    - **Font color:** Color of text. Several colors that are complementary with the template chosen are displayed. For example, click **More Fill Colors** to select a different color.
    - **Fill color:** Solid color behind the placeholder.
    - **Line color:** Line around the placeholder.
    - **Line style:** Width of line around the placeholder.
    - **Dash style:** Style of line around the placeholder (solid, dashed, dotted, etc.).
    - **Arrow style:** Style of arrow.
    - **Shadow:** Several shadow effects.
    - **3D effect:** Several 3D effects.

# Troubleshooting Tip

Click **View**, **Toolbars** to display a list of toolbars. Checkmarks appear before toolbars that are currently displayed. For example, click in front of Picture to remove the checkmark and remove the toolbar from the screen. Click **View Toolbars**, **Picture** again to redisplay the toolbar.

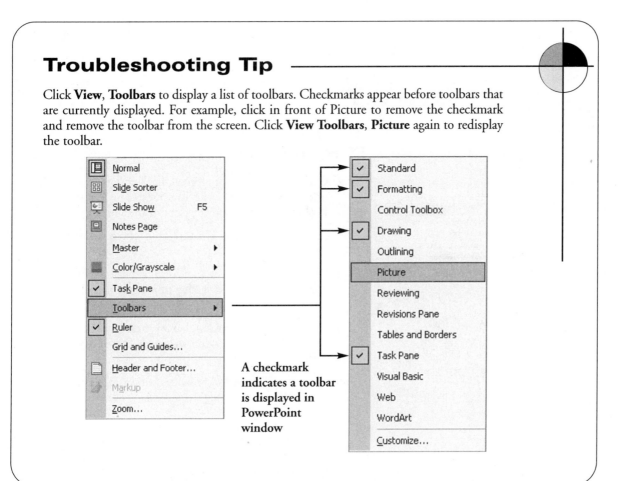

A checkmark indicates a toolbar is displayed in PowerPoint window

# Adding Slide Transitions

Slide transitions add impact to the way one slide replaces another when the presentation is run. Transition effects include blinds, horizontal or vertical; box in or out; cover or uncover; push; split; shapes (circle, diamond, wheel, plus); wipe; etc. Guidelines for applying transitions effectively are provided in the Presenter's Tip on page 25.

*Directions:* Add slide to the slides in the file Present as directed.

1. Display your presentation in Slide Sorter view (click the **Slide Sorter view** button or View, Slide Show). Note that the Slide Sorter toolbar is automatically displayed.

Slide Sorter toolbar ——→

Slide Transition ——→

Icon denoting slide transition effect has been added ——→

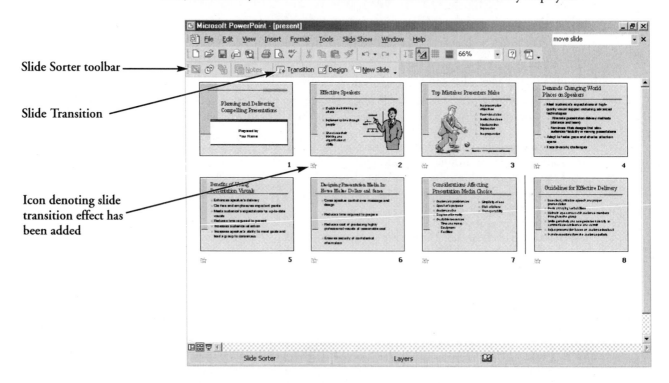

## Add a Transition Effect for All Slides

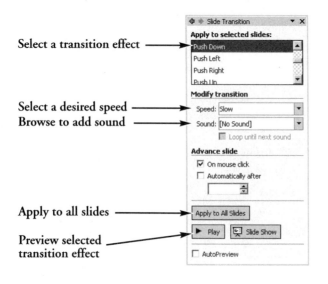

Select a transition effect ——→

Select a desired speed ——→
Browse to add sound ——→

Apply to all slides ——→

Preview selected transition effect ——→

2. Click the **Transition** button on the Slide Sorter toolbar or click Slide Show, Slide Transition. The Transition Dialog box appears to the right of the slide.

3. Select the transition effect of your choice from the list.

4. Select the speed of the transition by clicking Fast or Slow or Medium. Click **Play** to preview the selected effect.

5. Take time to become familiar with each of the transition effects. Then, select the **Push Down** effect at a **Slow** speed setting.

6. Click **Apply to All**. A small transition icon appears below the selected slide to indicate a transition has been set.

## Presenter's Tip

1. Create a systematic pattern for slide transitions. A good practice is to choose two transition effects; one for the slides and one for the divider slides—slides that you add to mark the beginning of each major section of your presentation. For a long presentation, you might choose a different transition for each section to give the audience a change of pace. A transition is not necessary for the first slide if the slide will be displayed prior to a formal introduction.

2. Create a blank slide with no transitions as the last slide; this nondistracting slide may remain on the screen during a question-and-answer period. Alternately, you can change your preferences to end a slide show with a black side as discussed in Project 1 (click Tools, Options, View, End with Black Slide).

### Add a Unique Transition Effect to Selected Slides

7. Click to select Slide 1 (the title slide) in the Slide Sorter view.

8. Click the **No Transition** effect from the Transition dialog box displayed at the right. The icon below Slide 1 is removed.

Two other advanced transition capabilities will be incorporated in later projects:

- **Advancing slides automatically.** Timed settings advance the slides automatically without a mouse click.

- **Adding sound effects.** Sound will play each time the slide show advances to the next slide.

# Enhancing with Custom Animation

Animation effects allow speakers to add impact to a presentation and to direct the audience's attention to important points. Rather than displaying objects when the slide is advanced, the speaker identifies objects to be displayed at his/her discretion in the desired order. Bulleted lists can be displayed all at once or point by point, a letter or word at a time, and with or without a dimming effect on points already discussed depending on the speaker's purpose.

## Inserting Custom Animation

1. Display the "Effective Speakers" slide in Slide view.

2. Click **Slide Show**, **Custom Animation**. The Custom Animation dialog box is displayed in the task pane at the right. (Alternatively, right-click and click Custom Animation).

### Add an Animation Effect to the Clip Art

3. Select the clip art image.

4. Click **Add Effect**, **Entrance**, **Circle**.

5. Click **Play** to preview the selected effect.

## Designer's Pointer

Select a subtle animation effect to apply consistently to all bulleted lists in a presentation. Subtle transitions such as wipe, fade, or expand are especially effective as they discreetly reveal information left to right in the direction an audience reads.

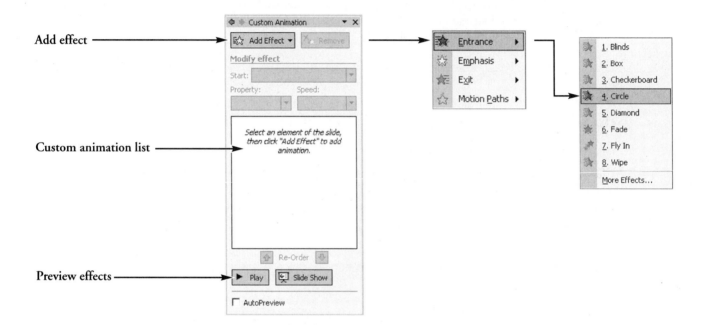

The animated object (the clip art) is added to the Custom Animation list. This list shows the animation sequences for a slide in the order the animations are added. The numbered icons at the beginning of each sequence indicate the timing of the sequence in relation to other animation events. A non-printing numbered tag that correlates to the effects in the list appears on the slide in Slide view but not in Slide Show view. Each of these icons is annotated in the illustration on page 27.

Become familiar with the wide range of animation effects (entrance, emphasis, exit, and motion) and options available for enhancing the effect:

- **Start:** Start an animated object with a mouse click or automatically based on timings.
- **Direction:** Select a direction for the selected effect (circle) from the list by clicking the down arrow.
- **Speed:** Select a speed for the effect from the list (slow, medium, fast) by clicking the down arrow.
- **Remove:** Click **Remove** to eliminate animation; the object is deleted from the animation list and will appear when the slide is displayed.

6. Modify the circle animation effect added to the clip art in Step 5 by editing the options:

a) Retain the default value that starts the clip art On Click.
b) Set the direction of the box effect to **Out**.
c) Set speed of the effect to **Medium**.

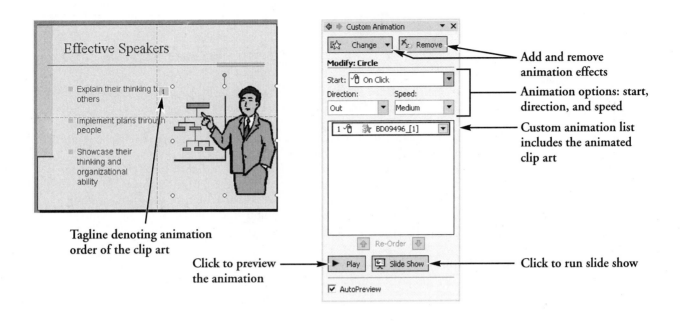

Tagline denoting animation
order of the clip art

Add and remove
animation effects

Animation options: start,
direction, and speed

Custom animation list
includes the animated
clip art

Click to preview
the animation

Click to run slide show

## Add an Animation Effect to the Bulleted List

7. Select the bulleted list.

8. Click **Add Effect**, **Entrance**, **Wipe**.

9. Change the direction to **From Left** and the speed to **Fast**.

## Change the Animation Order

10. Display the clip art first and the bulleted list second:
    a) Select an animation sequence in the Custom Animation list.
    b) Click the up or down arrow to reorder the sequences.

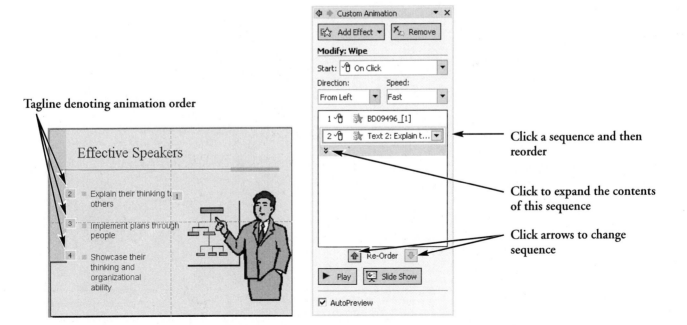

Tagline denoting animation order

Click a sequence and then
reorder

Click to expand the contents
of this sequence

Click arrows to change
sequence

# Presenter's Tip

Items in an animated bulleted list in PowerPoint automatically appear one item at a time until the entire list is built. This build effect, also known as progressive disclosure of information, is comparable to moving a blank sheet of paper down an overhead transparency to uncover points as they are discussed. Disclosing text progressively allows the speaker to control the flow of information for targeted impact.

Bulleted lists discussed as a unit should be displayed without a build effect to avoid the distraction caused by a speaker repeatedly clicking the mouse to display the points one immediately after the next. Examples of slides that should be presented as a unit include an agenda slide previewing the major points in the presentation or a summary slide reviewing a series of slides on a related idea.

## Introducing Text Without a Build Effect

1. Click the arrow below the bulleted list in the Custom Animation list to expand the contents revealing an icon for each bulleted item. Taglines appear before each of the three bulleted items.

2. Edit the Start options to display all items in the bulleted list at once:
   a) Click the down arrow beside the first point and click **Start**.
   b) Choose **On Click**, which requires a mouse click to display this object.
   c) Repeat Steps a and b for all subsequent points and choose **With Previous** to display all the items in the bulleted list at one time.

   *Note:* The taglines on the slide show two items in the animation order: The #1 icon denotes the clip art; and #2, the bulleted list.

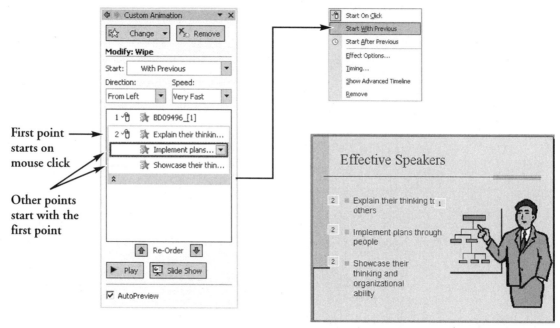

One tagline (#2) for the bulleted list indicates entire list will apprear at once (no build effect)

## Introducing Text With a Build Effect

1. Display the "Top Mistakes Presenters Make" slide in Slide view.

2. Click **Slide Show**, **Custom Animation**.

3. Select the clip art and animate to fade in at fast speed.

4. Select the bulleted list and add an effect of your choice.

5. Expand the contents of the animated object. Note each of the five items is set by default to start with a mouse click; thus, a separate tagline is assigned to each point in the list (#2 through #6).

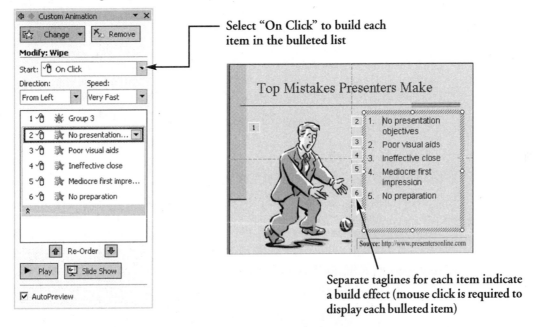

Select "On Click" to build each item in the bulleted list

Separate taglines for each item indicate a build effect (mouse click is required to display each bulleted item)

6. Continue building this slide in the next section.

## Adding a Dimming Effect to Previously Displayed Bulleted Items

1. Select the first point in the bulleted list in the Custom Animation list.

2. Click the down arrow and **Effect Options**.

3. Be sure the Effect tab is selected and click the down arrow beside "After animation."

4. Select a color from the palette or click **More Colors** to display additional color choices for a dimming effect. When you advance past a bulleted item, the previous item appears in the color you selected—preferably a slightly lighter color that can still be read easily by the audience. Click **Preview** to critique color choices.

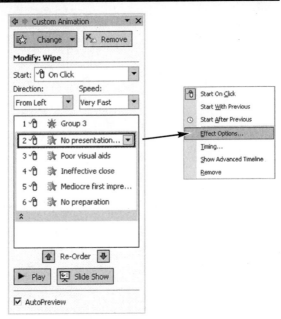

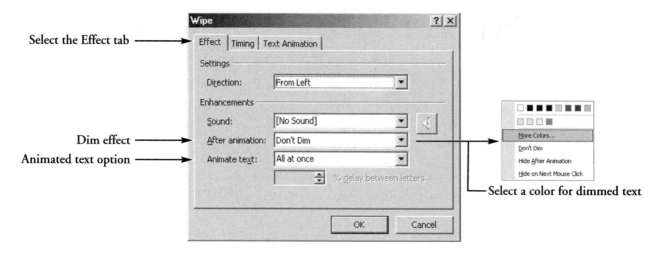

Select the Effect tab

Dim effect

Animated text option

Select a color for dimmed text

5. Click the down arrow beside "Animate text" and note the options for displaying the text in this bulleted list: all at once, by word, and by letter. After previewing several of these options, retain the default value of introducing the text all at once.

6. Repeat Steps 1–5 for the remaining points in the bulleted list.

7. Reorder the animation to display the clip art first and the bulleted list second.

# Printing a Presentation

PowerPoint allows you to print your presentation in several ways. The following section focuses on printing your presentation as slides, handouts, notes pages, and outline view. Project 8 will be devoted to creating highly professional handouts and notes pages. Work through the directions in this section printing only the pages directed by your instructor.

*Directions:* Print the file Present as directed.

1. Click **File**, **Print**. The Print dialog box appears.

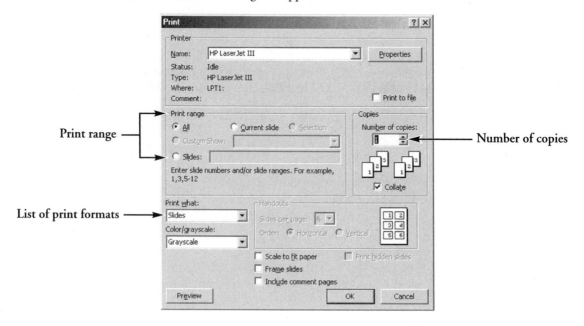

Print range

List of print formats

Number of copies

## Choose the Print Range

2. Note the three print ranges:

*To print all slides:* Select All.

*To print a specific slide:* Select Current Slide. (The slide selected when the Print command is executed prints.)

*To print multiple slides:* Select Slides and input the number of slides in the dialog box to the right (e.g., 2, 3, 5-12).

## Select the Type of Printout

3. Click the down arrow in the Print What list box to view the four types of output that can be produced.

- **Slides:** Prints a full-screen view of the slide. Use this option to print slides directly on transparency acetates to be projected on an overhead projector.

- **Handouts:** Prints slides as an audience handout in various formats:
  - **Number of slides per page:** Choose from 2, 3, or 6.
  - **Order slides are printed:** Choose horizontal or vertical.
  - **Frame slides:** Add an attractive border around each slide.

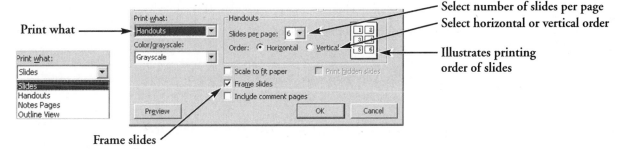

- **Notes pages:** Prints pages with a miniature slide at the top and notes for designers described in Project 1 (See slide views).
- **Outline view:** Prints the slide title and text without graphics.

# Delivering a Presentation

Learning to run your slide show professionally is essential to ensuring a successful presentation. You will learn efficient, foolproof ways of moving around in your slide show that will keep the audience's attention focused on the speaker—not the technology. A Presenter's Tip on page 32 provides additional advice for delivering a seamless presentation.

## Moving Within a Presentation

1. Display Slide 1 (title slide) in Slide view.

2. Click the **Slide Show** button. The slide show starts running in full-screen view beginning with Slide 1, the slide that was selected when you began the show.

3. Complete the following instructions to learn to run your presentation professionally. Try the mouse and the keyboard methods to determine the method most convenient for you.

## Advance to the Next Slide

**Mouse:**    Left mouse click
**Keyboard:**  Enter, space bar, right arrow key, or page down

## Presenter's Tip

To appear polished and professional, keep the slide show in Slide Show view at all times. Your audience should see the full screen view and not the untidy work areas (e.g., Normal or Slide Sorter views). Practice the mouse and keyboard controls to avoid any klutzy moves that will diminish your professional delivery.

### Return to the Previous Slide

**Mouse:**      Right mouse click
**Keyboard:**  Left arrow key or page up

### Move to a Specific Slide

**Mouse:**      Input the slide number using the numerals on the alphanumeric keypad and press **Enter**.

**Keyboard:**  Right-click and experiment with each of the following movements:

1. Select **Next** to move to the next slide.

2. Select **Previous** to move back one slide.

3. Select **Go, Slide Navigator**, and select a slide from the list of slide titles.

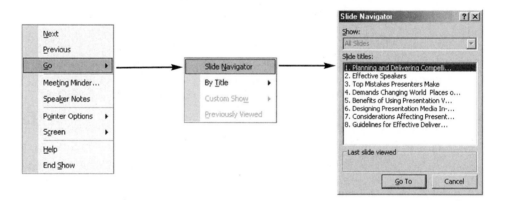

4. Select **Go, By Title**, and select a slide from the list of slide titles.

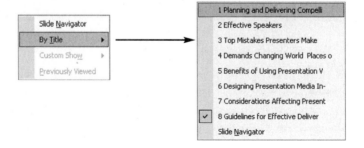

### End a Slide Show

Press **Escape** to exit the slide show view. The Slide view of Slide 1, the active slide when you clicked the Slide Show button, will be displayed.

## Presenter's Tip

Practice these techniques to make your delivery appear virtually invisible and effortlessly executed:

- Set PowerPoint to end the presentation with a black slide so you do not have to be concerned about advancing past the last slide and exiting to one of the other views.

- Use the left arrow key or page up to move to the previous slide. Program the right-click to move backward without displaying a distracting drop-down menu linking to the slide navigator. This process is time consuming and directs attention to the technology and away from the speaker.

- Number the slides on your speaker's notes so you can quickly display a slide needed to answer an audience member's question. There is no need to exit to the Slide Sorter view to locate the correct slide or right-click to display the slide navigator. Just input the specific slide number and move effortlessly back to a previously displayed slide or advance forward to new slides if you believe the question warrants reordering the order of your presentation.

- Use the black and white out technique when an audience member asks a question as you are advancing to a new slide. Removing the new information will keep your audience focused on your answer to the question and will allow you to transition into the new topic as you had planned.

## Additional Techniques to Ensure Professional Delivery

1. Display Slide 1 in Slide view and then click the **Slide Show** button to begin running the presentation.

### Black Out the Screen

2. Press the **B** key on the keyboard. The screen becomes black.

3. Press the **B** key again to return to the slide.

### White Out the Screen

4. Press the **W** key on the keyboard. The screen becomes white.

5. Press the **W** key again to return to the slide.

### End the Presentation with a Black Screen

6. Click **Tools, Options, View**.

7. Click to add a check before **End with black slide**.

8. Run your slide show again and note the black slide that appears at the end. Advance once more to exit the slide show.

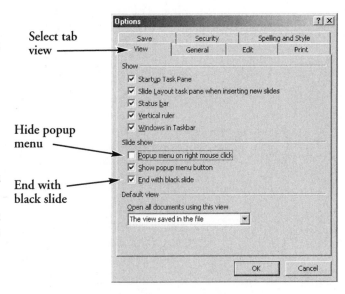

Select tab view →

Hide popup menu →

End with black slide →

### Move to Previous Slide with Right Mouse Click

9. Click **Tools, Options, View**.

10. Click to remove the check before **Popup menu on right mouse click**.

11. Display Slide 2 in Slide View. Right-click to return to the previous slide. The slide moves backward seamlessly without displaying an unattractive menu.

# Reinforcement Activities

Add the following slides to the file Present for added reinforcement of the PowerPoint features you learned in this project. Position the slides as shown in the table at the end of this project.

## Activity 1

1. Display the "Designing Presentation Media In-house Makes Dollars and Sense" slide in Normal view.

2. Select and insert relevant clip art using Microsoft Clip Gallery or Microsoft Design Gallery Live.

Designing Presentation Media In-House Makes Dollars and Sense

- Gives speaker control over message and design
- Reduces time required to prepare
- Reduces cost of producing highly professional visuals at reasonable cost
- Ensures security of confidential information

## Activity 2

1. Create the following slide using the Title, Clip Art, and Text layout from the Other Layouts category. Use the Microsoft Clip Gallery or Microsoft Design Gallery Live to locate relevant clip art.

2. Add custom animation effects:

   **First:** Title enters with slide (no animation).
   **Second:** Speaker starts with a subtle effect of your choice.
   **Third:** Bulleted list starts with wipe from left; build points with no dimming effect.

An Effective Design Is Transparent

- Keeps the speaker as the essence of the presentation
- Supports ideas without allowing the visuals to become the presentation
- Allows speaker to deliver the entire presentation even if problems occur with the visuals

## Activity 3

1. Create the first slide using the Title and 2-column Text layout from the Text Layouts category. Use the Microsoft Clip Gallery or Microsoft Design Gallery Live to locate relevant clip art.

2. Add a new placeholder for the recommendation and format attractively with a complementary fill and line color and shadow effect.

3. Add custom animation effects:

   **First:** Title enters with slide (no animation).
   **Second:** Clip art starts with subtle effects of your choice.

**Third:** Bulleted list on left and then the list on the right with subtle effects of your choice; build points with a dimming effect.
**Fourth:** Recommendation starts with a dramatic effect and a subtle sound effect to bring attention to this summarizing text.

4. Duplicate the slide and edit the content to create the other three slides in an efficient manner that will ensure consistent formatting for these slides that present similar information.

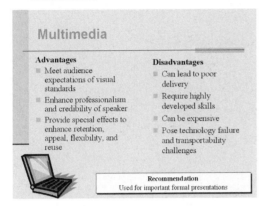

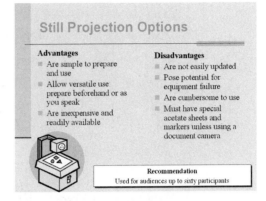

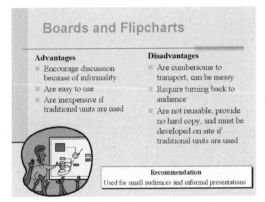

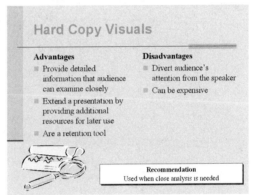

# Activity 4

Add custom animation effects to the remainder of the slides in the file Present as follows:

1. Title Slide—None

2. Designing Presentation Media In-House Makes Dollars and Sense
   **First:** Clip art—dissolve
   **Second:** Bulleted list—wipe from left; build effect

3. Benefits of Using Presentation Media
   Bulleted list—wipe from left; build effect

4. Demands Changing World Places on Speakers
   Bulleted list—wipe from left; no build effect

5. Considerations Affecting Presentation Media Choice
   **First:** Bulleted list (left)—wipe from left
   **Second:** Bulleted list (right)—wipe from left; build with dimming effect

6. Guidelines for Effective Delivery
   Bulleted list (left)—wipe from left; no build effect

## Slide Order

Print a copy of the file Present as an audience handout with six slides per page. Sequence the slides as shown. Your instructor may instruct you to print the slides created or revised in Project 2 only (highlighted slides).

1. Title Slide

2. Effective Speakers **(revised)**

3. **Top Mistakes Presenters Make**

4. **Demands Changing World Places on Speakers**

5. Benefits of Using Presentation Visuals

6. Designing Presentation Media In-house Makes Dollars and Sense **(revised)**

7. **Considerations Affecting Presentation Media Choice**

8. **Multimedia**

9. **Still Projection Options**

10. **Boards and Flipcharts**

11. **Hard Copy Visuals**

12. **An Effective Design Is Transparent**

13. Guidelines for Effective Delivery

# PROJECT 3

## Learning Objectives

- Create drawn objects to enhance slides.
- Ungroup and rotate clip art.
- Use WordArt to add dramatic effects to text.
- Insert photographs as a slide object, slide background, and photo album page.
- Add sound to slide objects and slide transitions.

## Using Drawing Tools to Enhance a Presentation

You will learn to enhance the basic presentation you created in Projects 1 and 2 with drawn objects, enhanced clip art, WordArt, photographs, and sound. First, you will add drawn objects, such as rectangles and ovals, to add a creative flair to a slide and to enhance the appearance of simple clip art. You will explore various ways of enhancing the drawn objects with color, lines, shadows, and other effects.

### Enhancing a Title Slide

*Directions:* Follow the instructions to enhance the original slide as shown.

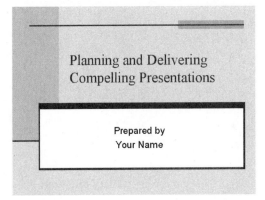 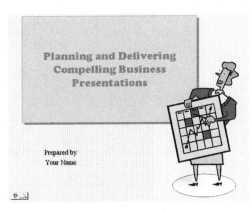

1. Open the file Present and display Slide 1 (title slide) in Normal view.

## Remove the Background Graphic Object

2. Click **Format, Background**.

3. Click to add the check in front of Omit Background Graphics from Master.

4. Click **Apply** to remove the object from the title slide only.

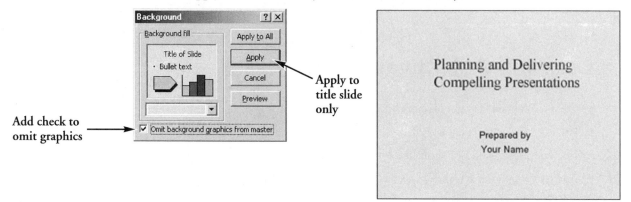

Add check to omit graphics

Apply to title slide only

## Apply a Patterned Background for Added Impact

5. Click **Format, Background**.

6. Click the list arrow to the right of the color bar.

7. Click **Fill Effects**.

Change background color or add fill effects

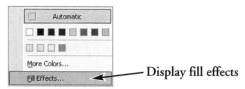

Display fill effects

8. Click the **Pattern** tab and select a pattern from the gallery.

9. Select a foreground and a background color complementary with the template color.

10. Click **Apply.**

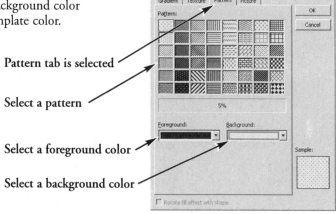

Pattern tab is selected

Select a pattern

Select a foreground color

Select a background color

**Gallery of Pattern Effects**

## Create a Projection Screen to Showcase the Slide Title

11. Click the title placeholder and resize and position to create the perspective of a projection screen behind the speaker.

12. Format the title placeholder using the icons on the Draw toolbar:

   a) Click the list arrow to the right of **Fill Color**. Select an off-white color similar to the color of an actual projection screen or a light color already used in the presentation design template.

   b) Click the list arrow to the right of **Line Color**. Select a color slightly lighter than the background color.

   c) Click **Shadow**.

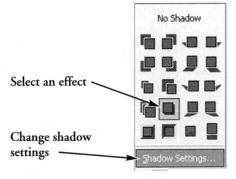

Select an effect

Change shadow settings

- Select the shadow effect shown from the gallery of options available (shadow appears on the bottom and right of the placeholder in the model).
- Click **Shadow** again and **Shadow Settings** to display the Shadow Settings toolbar.
- Click the right arrow next to **Shadow Color** to select the color of the shadow.
- Click the down arrow key two times and the right arrow two times to enlarge the size of the shadow slightly.

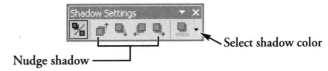

Nudge shadow ─────    Select shadow color

## Format the Title and the Presenter Identification

13. Highlight the title and select a creative font face (e.g., Comic Sans) and font size of at least 48 points to create a dramatic effect.

14. Select a font color for the title that contrasts well with the border fill color.

15. Reposition the placeholder containing the presenter identification to create an appealing balance on the slide.

## Add Relevant Clip Art

16. Insert a clip art image similar to the one shown with the full torso including the legs of a speaker. (**Insert**, **Picture**, **Clip Art** or click the Clip Art button on the Draw toolbar).

17. Size and position the clip art as shown on the model. Note the clip art should be large as you are creating the setting of a presentation. Refer to the Designer's Pointer for tips on anchoring clip art.

## Designer's Pointer ─────────────────────────

Anchor the clip art at the bottom of the slide and make it large enough to create the impression that the audience is involved in this setting rather than that the art is simply "plastered" on the slide.

## Create a Stage for the Speaker

18. Click **AutoShapes**, **Oval** and draw the stage below the clip art of the speaker.

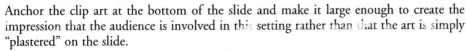

└── Oval tool

## Change the Order of the Objects (Clip Art and Stage)

19. Select the oval AutoShape (stage) and click **Draw**, **Order**, **Send to Back** to send the stage behind the clip art.

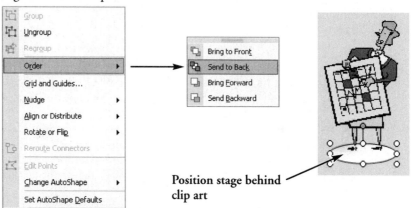

Position stage behind clip art

20. Size and position the stage and the clip art to create the desired effect.

## Format the Shape

21. Add a textured fill:

    a) Click the list arrow beside **Fill Color** on the Draw toolbar.

Change fill color

    b) Click **Fill Effects**, **Texture**.

    c) Select a texture that resembles a floor (brick, hardwood) or a gradient color to add dimension and creative appeal from the gallery.

Texture tab is selected

Select a texture

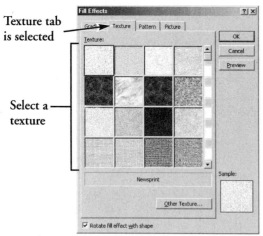

**Gallery of Textured Effects**

Gradient tab is selected

Select the colors to blend

Select the style and variation of the blended colors

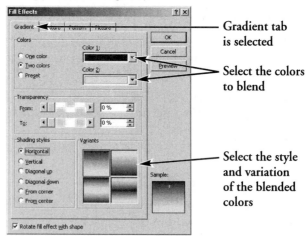

**Gallery of Gradient Effects**

22. Make other format changes to achieve a desired effect: line color, line style, dash style, shadow, or 3D.

Change width of line surrounding fill —⌐     ⌐ Add shadow

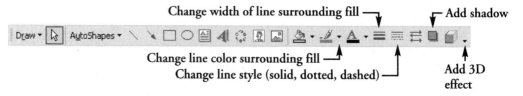

Change line color surrounding fill —⌐

Change line style (solid, dotted, dashed) —⌐    Add 3D effect

## Group the AutoShape and the Clip Art

23. Click the AutoShape (the stage) to select it. Sizing handles will appear.

24. Hold down the Shift key (**Shift + click**) as you click the clip art image. Sizing handles now appear on the screen bean and the AutoShape (as shown in the illustration).

25. Click **Draw**, **Group**.

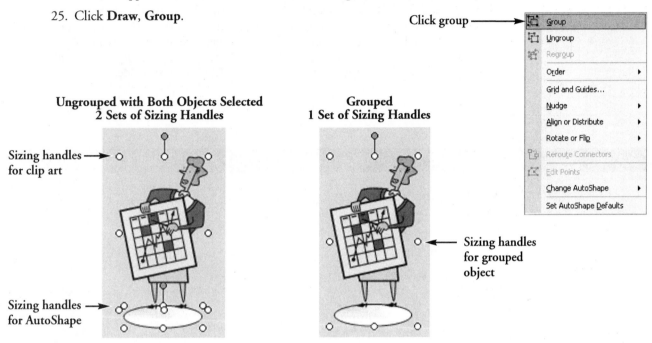

**Ungrouped with Both Objects Selected**
**2 Sets of Sizing Handles**

Sizing handles for clip art

Sizing handles for AutoShape

**Grouped**
**1 Set of Sizing Handles**

Sizing handles for grouped object

Click group

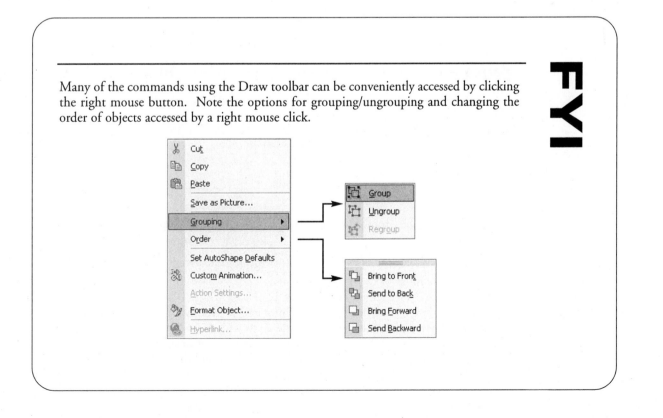

Many of the commands using the Draw toolbar can be conveniently accessed by clicking the right mouse button. Note the options for grouping/ungrouping and changing the order of objects accessed by a right mouse click.

**FYI**

## Troubleshooting Tip

If you are having trouble deleting a placeholder, it is likely not selected. Note whether the cut and copy icons are active or dimmed (not active). If you clicked the placeholder once, you will have a diagonal border between the sizing handles, and the cut and copy icons will be dimmed—a sign you cannot delete or copy this placeholder. Point to the diagonal border and click again. The border will become shaded and the cut and copy icons will be active. The placeholder is selected and you can delete the placeholder.

## Adding an AutoShape to Enhance a Bulleted List Slide

*Directions:* Follow the instructions to enhance the original slide as shown.

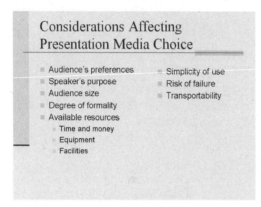

**Original Slide**

**Enhanced Slide**

1. Display the slide shown in the model in Slide view.

## Create a Projection Screen Behind the Bulleted List

2. Select the rectangle AutoShape on the Draw toolbar and draw the projection screen.

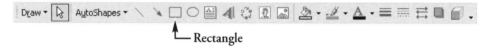

Rectangle

3. Resize and position to create the impression of a projection screen behind the two-column list.

4. Send the AutoShape behind the bulleted lists (Click **Draw**, **Order**, **Send to Back** or use the right click).

5. Format the AutoShape to create the effect of a projection screen:

   a) Change the fill color to an off white color.
   b) Select a pen color and line style.
   c) Add a shadow and adjust the shadow color and the width of the shadow. Refer to the instructions for enhancing the title slide with a shadowed rectangle at the beginning of this project if necessary. Alternately, you may copy the projection screen created for the title slide directly to this slide and then reformat as needed.
   d) Add other creative effects of your choice.

## Add Relevant Clip Art

6. Insert clip art to create the impression of a speaker delivering a presentation.

7. Change the order of the clip art so that the speaker is standing in front of the projection screen.

8. Size and position the clip art to achieve proper balance and perspective.

## Designer's Pointer ————————————

The slides you have created in this project illustrate how changing the order of objects provides the ability to add creative dramatic effects to an otherwise bland, dull slide. Note the effect created by placing the clip art in front of other objects on the slide.

# Working with Clip Art

You can increase the usefulness and appeal of clip art by applying the following techniques: recoloring, ungrouping, rotating, and cropping.

## Recoloring Clip Art

*Directions:*  Follow the instructions to recolor the clip art in the "Effective Speakers" slide.

1. Display the slide "Effective Speakers" in Normal view.

2. Select the clip art and click the **Recolor** button on the Picture toolbar. Click **View**, **Toolbars**, **Picture** to display the toolbar if necessary. The color of each segment of the clip art appears in the original column (e.g., the first color in the list is the speaker's hair; second color, tie; third, suit, etc.).

3. Select the list arrow in the New column beside the segment you wish to change and select a color. Click **Preview** to see the change. *Note:* The checkmark before the "Original" color for the second color in the list indicates a change has been made already. To return to the original color, click the box and remove the check.

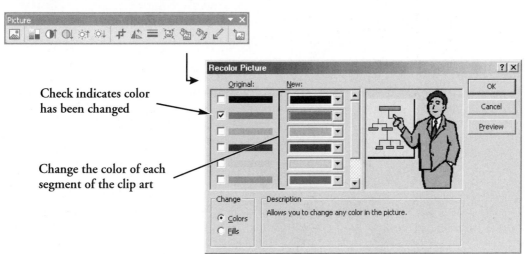

Check indicates color has been changed

Change the color of each segment of the clip art

4. Click **OK** when you have made all the necessary changes.

5. Recolor other clip art images in the file Present as needed to make them complementary with the presentation design template.

## Designer's Pointer

To position objects precisely, select the object, then use the arrow keys to nudge the object up, down, left, or right a short distance.

## Ungrouping Clip Art

The slide at the left illustrates three common errors in slide design: (1) the bulleted list must have at least two bullets, (2) the clip art is too small and thus looks lost and out of place on the slide, and (3) the slide's focus on the source of the survey does not reinforce the speaker's main point that typical business presentations need improvement.

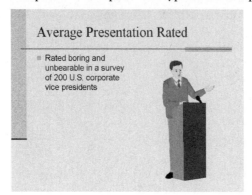

**Ineffective Slide**             **Enhanced Slide**

*Directions:* Follow the instructions to enhance the original slide as shown.

1. Create a new slide using the Title Only layout from the Other Layouts category.

2. Key the title.

## Create the Speaker and Audience

3. Insert the clip art shown by searching "audience" from the Microsoft Clip Gallery.

4. Ungroup the clip art:
   a) Click **Draw**, **Ungroup**.
   b) Click **Yes** to convert the picture to a Microsoft Office drawing object.

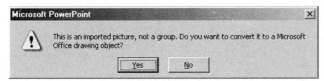

   c) Repeat the Draw, Ungroup command until the clip art cannot be ungrouped further. Sizing handles appear for each segment of the ungrouped clip art.

**Portions of the picture are ungrouped**     **All segments are ungrouped**

   d) Click outside the clip art to deselect all sections of the image.

Regroup the speaker:

5. Draw a rectangle with the left mouse click that encloses all segments of the speaker.

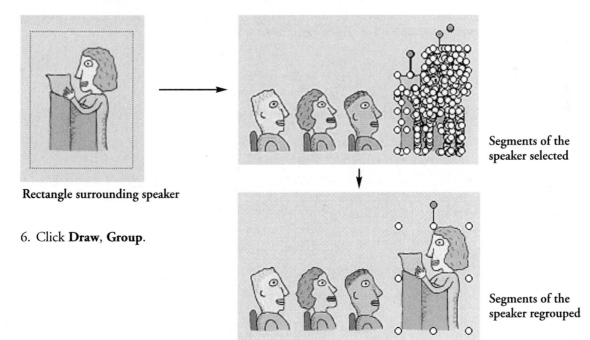

**Rectangle surrounding speaker**

Segments of the
speaker selected

6. Click **Draw**, **Group**.

Segments of the
speaker regrouped

Regroup the audience:

7. Draw a rectangle that encloses all segments of the audience.

8. Click **Draw**, **Group**.

Segments of the audience selected                    Segments of the audience regrouped

9. Resize and position the speaker and audience to achieve the perspective shown in the model.

## Troubleshooting Tip

Selecting all segments of a clip art image that has many small segments is difficult. An easy trick is to left click and drag as you draw a box to surround the entire clip art. When you release the mouse, the sizing handles will appear. If you miss a segment, hold down the Shift key as you point to the unselected segment. Of course, you can click outside the clip art image to deselect the entire image and then redraw the box.

## Create a Dialog Box for the Audience's Comment

10. Click **AutoShapes**, **Callouts** on the Draw toolbar. Select one of the four balloons in the top row.

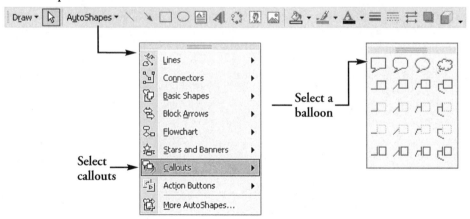

11. Key the following text in the callout box: **Boring and unbearable**.

12. Format the callout box as desired (fill color, line color, line style, shadow, 3D).

13. Format the text as desired (font face, font size, font color, and print attributes such as bold, shadow, etc.).

## Add the Source Note

14. Create a new placeholder and key the text for the source note: **200 U.S. corporate vice presidents surveyed**.

15. Resize the text box to display the text on one line as shown in the model.

16. Position the source note beneath the speaker as shown in the model.

17. Fine tune the size and position of each object (speaker, audience, callout box, and source note) to produce a realistic effect.

## Designer's Pointer

Text in source notes should be at least 14 points for a typical presentation room. This size is large enough for the audience to see. The source provides credibility to the slide but should not assume a prominent point of emphasis on the slide.

## Add Custom Animation and Sound

18. Click **Slide Show**, **Custom Animation**. Refer to Project 2 to review custom animation if necessary.

19. Edit the Custom Animation dialog box to create the following effects in the order shown:

   a) **Unanimated:** Slide title, speaker, and audience (will start with the slide).
   b) **Callout box:** Start on mouse click with an engaging effect (e.g., flip, bounce).
   c) **Source note:** Start with a subtle effect (e.g., expand) on an automatic timing that starts the source note .2 seconds after the callout box appears (the previous event):
      • Click the down arrow to the right of the source note in the Animation List.
      • Click **Timing**.
      • Input **.2 seconds** in the spin box for the Delay selection.

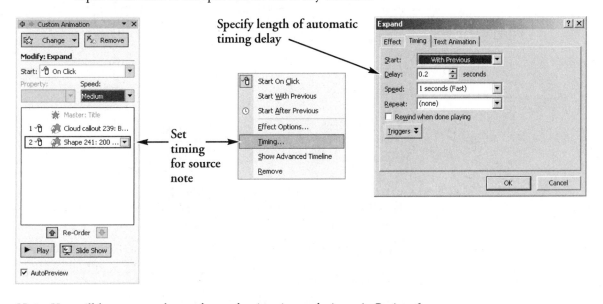

*Note:* You will learn more about advanced animation techniques in Project 6.

An abundance of clip art, photographs, video clips, and sound files is available to help a speaker illustrate key concepts or points. Regular commercial software or public domain or shareware clip art galleries are available, and some multimedia files can be downloaded from the Internet. You are encouraged to locate useful sites and share the addresses with your class and instructor.

When using images downloaded from the Internet, read the copyright agreement carefully to avoid copyright infringement. The licensing agreement of commercial clip art allows you to use the art on one computer at a time and as part of any document or publication you choose to distribute (same stipulation as with other commercial software). You may not share clip art via a network without a site license. Look for public-domain software that is not copyrighted and can be used with little or minimal charge.

## Add a Sound Effect

20. Click the **Clip Art** icon from the Draw toolbar (or click Insert, Clip Art).

21. Click the down arrow beside Multiple media file types and click off all options except Sounds.

22. Search for a sound file of a boring yawn by inputting "Yawn" as the keyword for the search.

23. Click a sound clip. Note that a sound icon is inserted on the slide, and a prompt to animate the sound appears.

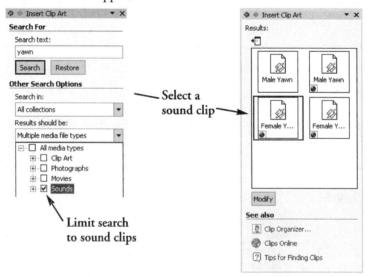

24. Click **Yes** to play the sound clip automatically or click **No** to play the sound clip with a mouse click. If adjustments to the animation of the sound effect are needed, right-click on the sound icon and click **Custom Animation**.

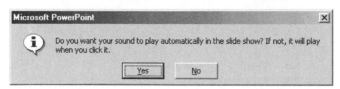

25. Make the sound icon invisible by moving it off the slide.

Position icon off the slide

# Using Photographs to Enhance a Presentation

Photographs are useful in helping the audience visualize actual persons, places, or objects. Photographs can be added as a slide object or as the slide background. Special enhancements can be made easily using photo editing software and modifying the slide as a photo album page.

## Inserting a Photograph as a Slide Object

*Directions:* Follow the instructions to complete the slide as shown.

1. Create a new slide using the Title, Text, and Content layout.

2. Key the title and the bulleted list.

### Select a Photo

3. Select a relevant photo using one of the following methods:
   a) Insert a photo from the Microsoft Clip Gallery or the online clips at Microsoft Design Gallery Live.
   b) Scan a photograph or download a file from an Internet site or a digital camera.

### Add a Creative Border for the Photograph

4. Select the relevant photograph, click **Line Style** on the Draw toolbar, and click **More Lines**.

Line style

5. Be certain the Colors and Lines tab is selected and edit the line to create an appealing border for the photograph:

   a) Select a line color complementary with other colors in the presentation design template.

   b) Increase the line weight to 10 points for a more dramatic effect.

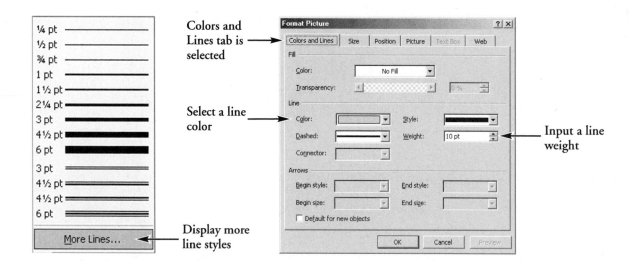

Colors and Lines tab is selected

Select a line color

Input a line weight

Display more line styles

6. Click the **Shadow** button on the Draw toolbar and select a shadow from the gallery. Edit the shadow settings by selecting a much darker shadow color than the line color and extending the shadow for greater effect. Refer to the instructions for editing shadow settings at the beginning of this project if necessary.

7. Animate the slide:

   **Unanimated:** Title (comes in with slide).
        **First:** Photograph—start with a mouse click and a dramatic effect
     **Second:** Bulleted list—start with a mouse click and wipe from left

Generic photographs from Microsoft or other commercial galleries are available but may be inappropriate in a presentation. You can use a scanner to scan photographs taken with a regular camera and convert the photograph to an image that can be imported into your presentation. Additionally, you can use a digital camera to capture the photograph as a computer file that can be imported into a presentation without having to develop film.

## Inserting a Photograph as the Slide Background and Rotating Text

*Directions:* Follow the instructions to complete the slide as shown.

1. Create a new slide using the Blank layout in the Contents layout category.

### Select and Insert the Photo

2. Click **Format**, **Background**.

3. Click **Omit background graphics from master** and click **Apply** to remove the template object from this slide only.

4. Click **Fill Effects**, **Picture**, **Select Picture**.

5. Browse to locate the photo file. Select a photo you wish to use from the Microsoft Clip Gallery or Design Gallery Live, the Internet, or a digital file scanned or captured with a digital camera. Click **OK**.

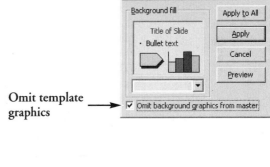

Omit template graphics → Omit background graphics from master

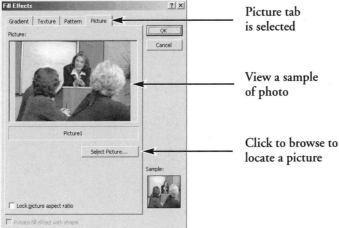

Picture tab is selected

View a sample of photo

Click to browse to locate a picture

### Add and Position a Photo Caption

6. Create a text box that expands across the entire width of the slide and key the text **Personal Connection a Must**.

7. Format the text as desired (font face, font size, font color, and print attributes such as bold, shadow).

8. Format the text box as desired (fill color, line color, line style, shadow, 3D).

9. Click **Draw**, **Rotate or Flip**, and **Rotate Left**. The text box is turned to lie vertically at the left of the slide as shown in the model.

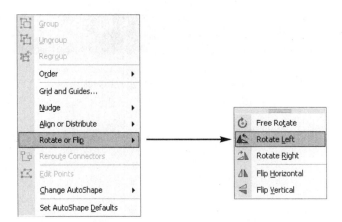

Alternately, you can click the Free Rotate tool (green circle above the top center sizing handle) and drag the text box into the desired position.

**Use the free rotate tool to position the text box**

## Add a Slide Transition

10. Click **Slide Show**, **Slide Transition**.

11. Select **Dissolve** as the slide transition effect at Fast speed.

12. Add a sound effect such as Applause or one of your choice to bring attention to this important concept.

The slide "Personal Connection a Must" can be considered a "specimen slide" because it has a completely different format from the other slides in this presentation. Therefore, a new slide transition (different from the wipe from left used on the other slides) can be used to add to the dramatic effect of this slide.

## Enhancing Photographs with Photo Editing Software

Photo editing software, such as Microsoft Picture It and Microsoft Photo Editor, offer several tools for enhancing a photograph scanned or downloaded from the Internet or a digital camera.

*Directions:* Follow the instructions to enhance the slide.

Ineffective Slide            Enhanced Slide

1. Create a new slide using any layout and insert a photograph from the Microsoft Clip Gallery.

2. Select the photo and right-click. Click **Save as Picture**.

3. Key a file name and designate a drive where you wish to save the file.

4. Delete the slide containing the photograph.

5. Open the photograph file in a photo editing software such as Microsoft Photo Editor or Microsoft Picture It. Clicking on the file in Explorer will automatically open the file in your default software.

6. Experiment as you explore the menu options. Menus will vary depending on software used.

**Effects.** The first group of effects enables you to correct minor imperfections in the photograph. The second group of effects is used to add an artistic filter effect. Select a filter and then adjust controls for intensity, direction, etc.

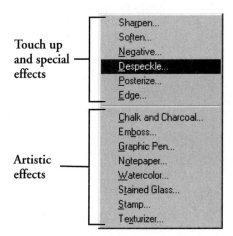

**Image.** Click **AutoBalance** to adjust the brightness and contrast levels of an image automatically or **Balance** to adjust manually. Use options on the crop menu to create attractive mats and oval and rectangular shaped images. Rotate images as desired using the options from the Rotate menu.

Try these simple adjustments to improve the quality and to add an artistic flair to the original photograph shown in the model.

a) Apply the despeckle special effect to reduce a grainy look.

b) Apply the Texturizer, Canvas special effect to add texture and dimension.

c) Save the changes made to the file.

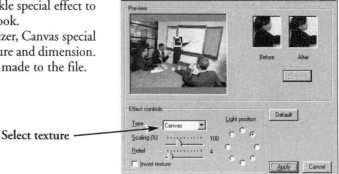

Select texture

7. Continue building this slide in the next activity.

## Creating a Photo Album

The photo album feature, new to PowerPoint 2002, allows you to create a handsome photo album of your favorite photos. You quickly add multiple pictures, choose the layouts and frames, add captions, and then e-mail the file to friends and family or post on the Web. You also can use this powerful and efficient feature to enhance photographs in a presentation file you are delivering.

1. Click **Insert**, **Picture**, **New Photo Album**.

2. Click **Picture** and browse to locate the photo you enhanced in the previous section.

3. Select **1 picture with title** as the picture layout from the drop-down menu.

4. Select **Rounded Rectangle** as the frame shape or an option of your choice from the drop-down menu.

5. Click **Create**.

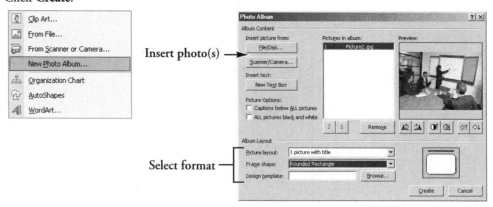

Insert photo(s)

Select format

Note that a new PowerPoint presentation was created with a title page and one slide containing the photo in the format you specified.

6. Copy the photo slide into the file Present:

a) Switch the new presentation (photo album) to Slide Sorter view.

b) Select the slide containing the photo and click **Copy**.

c) Click **Window**, and select **Present** from the list of open presentations.

d) Switch the file Present to Slide Sorter view and click in front of the slide where the photo slide is to be inserted.

e) Click **Paste**. The photo slide is reformatted to match the file Present.

f) Close the new presentation (photo album) without saving.

## Adding WordArt

WordArt displays text creatively using colorful outlines, drop shadows, and a variety of shapes that gives the text a three-dimensional appearance. An eye-catching design using WordArt can help you direct the audience's attention to an important point and add a creative flair to your presentation. Use WordArt images cautiously. Overuse obviously defeats its purpose for emphasis, and the distortion in the WordArt design can make the text difficult to read.

1. Display the "Meeting the Demands of Today's Audiences" slide in Normal view and click anywhere in the slide.

2. Click the **WordArt** button on the Draw toolbar.

L— WordArt

3. Choose a style from the WordArt Gallery.

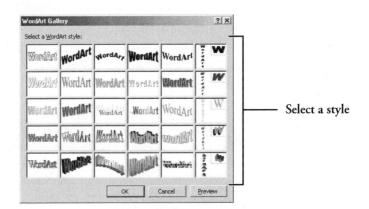

Select a style

4. Make these changes in the Edit WordArt dialog box:

a) Input the text **Make it good and get to the point**.

b) Select a font face and font size.

Select a font face and size

Key text →

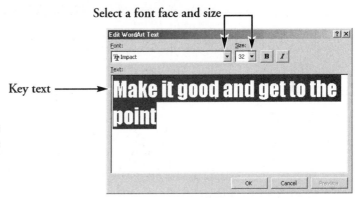

Note that a WordArt toolbar appears on the Draw toolbar after you input text in the WordArt dialog box.

5. Click the **Format WordArt** button and select a fill color and line color complementary with your background.

6. Click the **Change Shape** button and select a shape for the WordArt if you wish to change the default (e.g., can up).

Return to Gallery     Change shape     Changes to vertical text

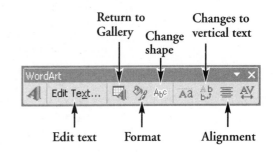

Edit text     Format     Alignment

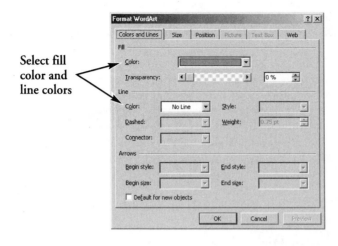

Select fill color and line colors

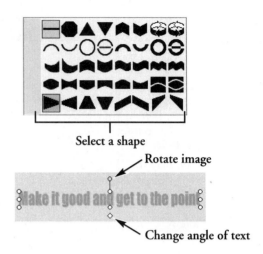

Select a shape

Rotate image

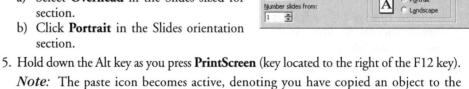

Change angle of text

7. Point to the green circle on the WordArt object and drag to rotate it as you wish.

8. Animate the slide:

   **Unanimated:** Title (comes in with the slide).

   **First:** Photograph—Start with a mouse click with a dramatic effect of your choice.

   **Second:** WordArt—Start automatically with an effect of your choice.

## Creating Screen Captures

*Directions:* Follow the instructions to complete the slide shown in the model.

1. Create a new slide using the Title and Text layout.

2. Key the title and bulleted list.

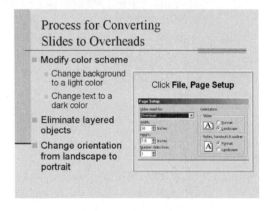

### Capture the Image

3. Display the Page setup dialog box by clicking **File**, **Page Setup**.

4. Edit the Page Setup menu to appear exactly as you wish it captured:

   a) Select **Overhead** in the Slides sized for section.

   b) Click **Portrait** in the Slides orientation section.

5. Hold down the Alt key as you press **PrintScreen** (key located to the right of the F12 key).

   *Note:* The paste icon becomes active, denoting you have copied an object to the clipboard.

6. Click **Cancel** as you are **not** executing the command to change the page setup.

## Insert the Captured Image on the Slide

7. Click in the area on the slide where the screen capture will appear.

8. Click **Paste**.

9. Continue building this slide in the next section.

## Cropping Images

1. Select the screen capture. The Picture toolbar should appear when the image is selected. If not, click **View**, **Toolbars**, **Picture**.

2. Click the cropping tool on the Picture toolbar.

Cropping tool

3. Point to the sizing handle in the right center of the selected object. Drag to the left to crop the image to the right of the arrow shown in the illustration.

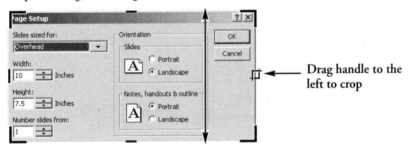

Drag handle to the left to crop

4. Create a text box and key the following text commands: **Click File**, **Page Setup**.

5. Center the text box directly above the screen capture. Format the font face and font size to fit the box attractively.

6. Use the rectangle tool on the Draw toolbar to surround the text box and the screen capture with a showcase box.

7. Select the rectangle and send it behind the screen capture and the text box (**Draw**, **Order**, **Send to Back**).

8. Create an appealing format for the showcase box:
   a) Click **Fill Color** on the Draw toolbar and click **No Fill**.
   b) Select an attractive line color, line style, and shadow effect from the Draw toolbar.
   c) Group the showcase box, text box, and screen capture so the group can be animated to start together.

9. Animate the slides:

   **Unanimated:** Title (come in with the slide)
          **First:** Bulleted list—Wipe from Left with a build effect on the major points
      **Second:** Grouped image—Center Revolve

# Inserting Slide Transitions

*Directions:* Follow the instructions to add slide transitions to the slides created in this project.

1. Display the presentation in Slide Sorter view.

2. Select any slides that do not include a slide transition icon below the slide.

3. Click the Slide Transition button on the Slide Sorter toolbar.

4. Select **Wipe from Left** effect at a Fast speed setting.

5. *Note:* This slide transition effect has been used for all other slides in this presentation except for the slide that contains the photograph as the background, a specimen slide that requires a more dramatic effect.

6. Click **Apply**.

# Reinforcement Activities

Add the following slides to the file Present for added reinforcement of the PowerPoint features you learned in this project. Position the slides as shown in the table at the end of this project.

## Activity 1

1. Complete Project 2, Reinforcement Activity 2, on page 34 if you have not done so already.

2. Revise the clip art:
   a) Recolor the speaker's clothing to complement your presentation design template.
   b) Ungroup the clip art in order to delete the speaker's visual aid. Regroup the clip art and add a subtle animation effect to the speaker.

3. Format the bulleted list text box to create the impression of a projection screen for showcasing the speaker's points: add a fill color, a 10-point line slightly darker than the fill color, and a shadow effect.

4. Add the Wipe from Left slide transition.

Original Slide

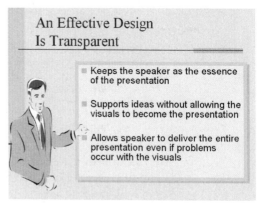

Enhanced Slide

## Activity 2

1. Display the slide in the model from the file Present. Replace the clip art you added in Project 2 by using "speaker" as the keyword to search the Microsoft Clip Gallery.

2. Ungroup the clip art, delete the winding mechanism on the speaker's back, and regroup.

3. Add a subtle animation effect to the speaker.

4. Add the Wipe from Left slide transition.

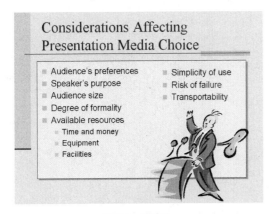 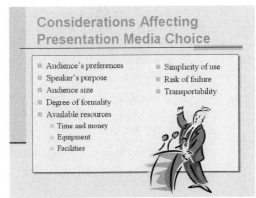

Original Slide                    Enhanced Slide

## Activity 3

1. Create the enhanced slide shown in the model using the Title, Text, and Content layout. Note the improvements over the original slide: a title that clearly describes the slide's purpose, a creative image depicting the reflection on one's audience needed to identify a clear objective, and text reinforcing the exact question to be asked.

2. Use the Microsoft Clip Gallery or Microsoft Design Gallery Live to locate clip art depicting a diverse audience.

3. Add an AutoShape callout cloud and group with the clip art.

4. Add the text box and format the text to bring attention to this key point.

5. Reorder the objects in the custom animation list: (1) title, (2) speaker, (3) callout group, and (4) text box.

6. Animate with effects of your choice.

7. Add the Wipe from Left slide transition.

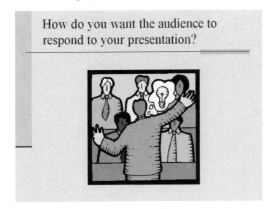 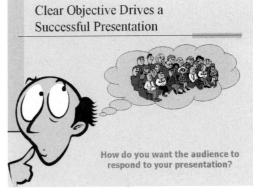

Original Slide                    Enhanced Slide

## Activity 4

1. Create the slide shown in the model.

2. Create a photo album using a photograph of yourself that you scanned or captured with a digital camera. Enhance the photo using photo editing software to create an effect of your choice.

3. Copy the slide into the file Present. Add a text box and supply your own contact information.

4. Animate the objects as desired and reorder in the custom animation list: (1) title, (2) speaker, and (3) contact information starting on an automatic timing immediately after the photograph.

5. Add the Wipe from Left slide transition.

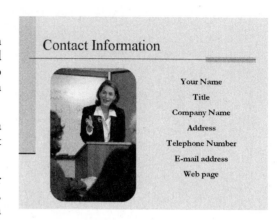

## Activity 5

1. Create the slide shown in the model using the Title, Text, and Contents layout.

2. Omit the bullet and format the text for emphasis and appeal (**Format**, **Bullets and Numbering**, **None**).

3. Locate a photograph from the Microsoft Clip Gallery or Design Gallery Live and format attractively.

4. Add an attractive text box for displaying the source: **Source: H. Dennis Beaver, "Visual aids: How much is too much?"** *ABA Banking Journal*.

5. Animate the objects as desired and reorder in the custom animation list: (1) title, (2) photograph, (3) quote, and (4) source starting on an automatic timing immediately after the quote.

6. Add the Wipe from Left slide transition.

## Activity 6

Locate a quotation related to planning and delivering compelling presentations and design your own slide similar to the model in Activity 5. Position the slide with related content in the file Present.

## Activity 7

1. Create the slide shown in the model.

2. Omit the graphics from the background to allow more space for the screen capture.

3. Create a screen capture of a useful Web site for presenters (e.g., http://www.presentations.com; or http://www.powerpointers.com). Crop the image to omit the browser toolbars.

4. Add an attractive text box for displaying the Internet address.

5. Animate the objects as desired and reorder in the custom animation list: (1) title, (2) screen capture, and (3) Web address starting automatically .2 seconds after photograph.

6. Add the Wipe from Left slide transition.

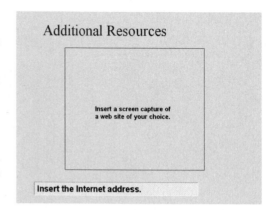

## Slide Order

Print a copy of the file Present as an audience handout with six slides per page. Sequence the slides as shown. Your instructor may instruct you to print the slides created or revised in Project 3 only (highlighted slides).

1. Title Slide

2. Effective Speakers (*revised*)

3. **Average Presentation Rated**

4. Top Mistakes Presenters Make

5. Demands Changing World Places on Speakers

6. **Adapting Speaking Style to Today's Fast Pace**

7. **Meeting the Demands of Today's Audiences**

8. **Personal Connection a Must**

9. **A Speech Is a Gift**

10. **Clear Presentation Objective Drives a Successful Presentation**

11. Benefits of Using Presentation Visuals

12. Designing Presentation Media In-house Makes Dollars and Sense (*revised*)

13. Considerations Affecting Presentation Media Choice (*revised*)

14. Multimedia (optional)

15. Still Projection Options (optional)

16. Boards and Flipcharts

17. Hard Copy Visuals

18. **Process for Converting Slides to Overheads**

19. An Effective Design Is Transparent (*revised*)

20. Guidelines for Effective Delivery

21. **Contact Information**

22. **Additional Resources**

23. **Project 3, Activity 6 (*position in file will vary*)**

# PROJECT 4

## Learning Objectives

- Edit the master slide to modify standard design elements consistently and efficiently.

- Modify the color scheme of a standard presentation design to fit a topic and the needs of a specific audience.

- Create a custom template for a company that reflects its corporate identity and displays a high standard of quality and originality.

## Customizing PowerPoint

Customizing PowerPoint allows the designer to adjust the standard design elements of a presentation design consistently and efficiently. Additionally, PowerPoint slides can be easily formatted to produce professional overhead transparencies.

Changes you will make in this project include (a) editing the slide master, (b) modifying the color scheme of a standard presentation design, and (c) creating a custom presentation design for a specific topic and a company.

### Editing the Slide Master

A slide master controls the standard elements displayed in the title slide, all other slide formats, and handouts. Any format change you input on the slide master automatically reformats each slide in the presentation. Inputting a change to the slide master rather than revising each slide individually ensures consistency in all slide elements, and naturally increases your efficiency as you make the change only once. A designer typically edits the master slide before developing the majority of the slides. However, you will modify the file Present in this activity to illustrate the efficiency of using the slide master to make universal changes.

*Directions:* Follow these instructions to modify the slide master for the file Present. You will change the font face, size, and color; select a new bullet and change color and size for the first and second bullet levels; and enhance the title placeholder.

**Effective Speakers**

- Explain their thinking to others
- Implement plans through people
- Showcase their thinking and organizational ability

1. Be sure the file Present is open.

2. Click **View**, **Master**, **Slide Master**.

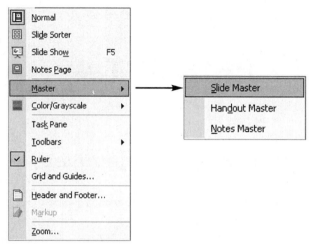

3. Select the **Insert New Slide Master** button.

Click to insert new Slide Master and new Title Master

## Revise the Title Placeholder

4. Click in the Title placeholder and make the following changes.

   a) Select a sturdy font that can be read easily from a distance (e.g., Arial). Add bold and a shadow effect. Refer to the Designer's Pointer related to font selection and size on page 65.

   b) Change the text alignment of your presentation design's current setting. Click the desired alignment from the Alignment buttons on the Formatting toolbar or click Format, Alignment, and the desired format: left, center, or right align.

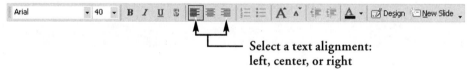

Select a text alignment:
left, center, or right

   c) Enhance the placeholder to draw the audience's attention to the title first. (The title should reveal the key point being made in an engaging manner.) Follow these suggestions or develop ideas of your own:

     • Change the fill color of the placeholder to a shade slightly lighter than the slide background or add a special fill effect (gradient, patterned, or texture).

     • Add a narrow border in a subtle color and/or add a shadowing effect.

     • Resize the placeholder to extend the full width of the slide.

Click to edit title

Click to edit bulleted list

Click to add footer text
on each slide

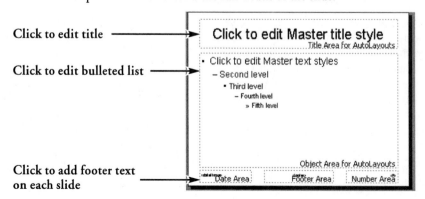

# Designer's Pointer

Follow these general guidelines for making font choices that (a) an audience can easily read on a projected visual, (b) are fresh and interesting, and (c) clearly define the importance of the various sections of text (slide title, text, source notes, etc.):

1. Limit the number of fonts within a single presentation to at least two but no more than three to prevent a cluttered and confusing look.

2. Choose interesting fonts that convey the mood of a presentation and are a fresh change from the most commonly used (e.g., **Times New Roman** and **Helvetica**). For example, for a less formal presentation, consider informal fonts such as **Comic Sans MS** and **Tahoma**.

3. Choose sturdy font faces that can be easily read from a distance, perhaps in a dark room. Avoid delicate fonts with narrow strokes that wash out, especially when displayed in color. Likewise, avoid italic, decorative fonts, and condensed fonts (letters are close together) that are difficult to read. Examples of poor choices include *Times New Roman, Italic,* ALGERIAN (decorative) and **Abadi MT Condensed**. Good choices are illustrated below.

4. Use fonts large enough for the audience to read. General guidelines for slides projected in a typical presentation room (approximately 30 participants) appear in the table below, but font sizes must be adjusted for larger rooms. Larger fonts are also needed when transmitting via videoconference; the fuzziness resulting from compressed video makes text smaller than 44 points difficult to read.

5. Create a hierarchy of importance among the standard elements (slide title, bulleted lists, and source notes) by varying the font size and the font face.

   a) Use different size fonts for the slide title, bulleted list, and other text on the slide to enable the audience to recognize differences in the importance of these items. The slide title should be keyed in the largest font to draw the audience's attention to the title, followed by the bulleted list, and then other text on the slide (source notes, text within AutoShapes, etc.).

   b) Use a sturdy sans serif font for the slide title and a serif font for bulleted text to further distinguish the slide from other text. When presenting by videoconference, use all sans serif font as these plain, simple fonts are easier to read with the fuzziness of compressed video.

### Recommendations for Font Faces and Sizes

| Slide Element | Recommended Font Type | Recommended Font Size | Examples |
|---|---|---|---|
| Slide Title | **Sans Serif** A font without cross-strokes, known as serifs. (Sans means without.) Has simple, blocky look that is appropriate for displaying text, as in the slide title or headlines of a newspaper. | 24 to 36 points | **Arial** **Univers** **Century Gothic** **Arial Black** |
| Bulleted List | **Serif** A font with short cross-strokes that project from the top and bottom of the main stroke of a letter—the type that typically is read as the main print in textbooks and newspapers. | 18 to 24 points | **CG Times** **Times New Roman** |
| Other Text | **Serif** | No smaller than 14 point | See serif examples. |

## Modify a Bullet

5. Click **Click to edit Master text styles** in the bulleted list placeholder.

6. Change the font face and font size for the first level to a selection of your choice.

7. Click **Format**, **Bullet**.

8. Be sure the Bulleted tab is selected. The Numbered tab allows you to select a numbering style, which is used to indicate a required sequence (1, 2, 3 . . . ).

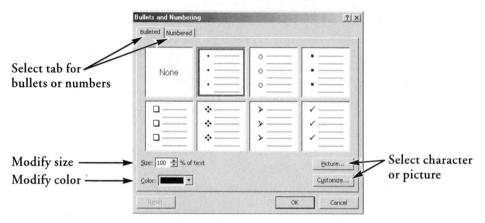

9. Click **Customize** to select a new bullet.

   a) Explore the various categories and available bullets for each category by clicking the drop-down list.
   b) Select the Monotype Sorts category and click the bullet shown or one of your choice.

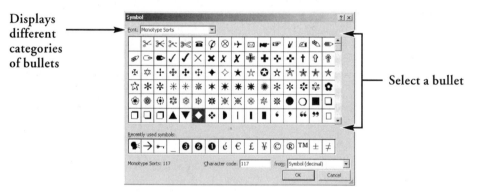

10. Click **OK** to return to the Bullets and Numbering Dialog box and change the appearance of the bullet.

    a) Increase the bullet size by double-clicking in the Size text box and inputting a number larger than 100 percent (e.g., 120).
    b) Select a new bullet color by clicking the Color list arrow and selecting a color complementary with the presentation design.

11. Click **OK** to return to the slide master.

12. Click **Second Level** and modify the appearance of the second-level bulleted items following the same process (Steps 8–11).

## Preview Changes to the Slide Master and Print Selected Slides

13. Click **Close Master View** to exit the slide master and return to Normal or Slide Sorter view (the view you were using when you accessed the slide master).

Letters are measured from the top of the highest extender to the bottom of the lowest extender. A letter measuring one inch is 72 points.

# 72pts. = 1 in.
## 48pts. 36pts. 24pts. 14pts.

**FYI**

14. Advance through the presentation noting the modifications made to the slide master that are now reflected in each slide.

15. Save the file using the file name **Present-new**.

16. Print Slides 1–3 as an audience handout, three slides per page if directed by your instructor.

## Modifying the Color Scheme of a Presentation Design

Changes in the slide master allow designers to customize the format of text and template objects. Changes to the color scheme of a standard presentation design can help a speaker use the power of color to convey a particular mood, to associate the presentation with a company or concept, or to simply give an original look to a familiar PowerPoint presentation design.

*Directions:* You will apply a new color scheme to the standard presentation design you applied to the file Present-new in the previous activity.

1. Be sure the Present-new file is open.

2. Read the Designer's Pointer on page 69 related to guidelines for effective color selection.

## Apply a Standard Presentation Design

3. Click **Format**, **Slide Design** (or click Design on the Formatting toolbar).

4. Click **Color Schemes** and preview samples of the available standard color schemes for the presentation design template applied to the file Present. The colors used for each standard design element (background, text colors, fills, shadows, etc.) are illustrated in the thumbnail.

5. Click a color scheme and click **Apply to All Slides** to convert all slides in the file to the new standard color scheme.

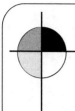

## Troubleshooting Tip

Changes that have been input on individual slides will not update to reflect modifications made on the slide master. Thus, avoid the temptation to modify slides as you build. Instead, make changes in standard design elements on the slide master first.

6. Advance through the slide show evaluating the appeal of the new color scheme. Select other standard color schemes until you are satisfied with a specific color scheme.

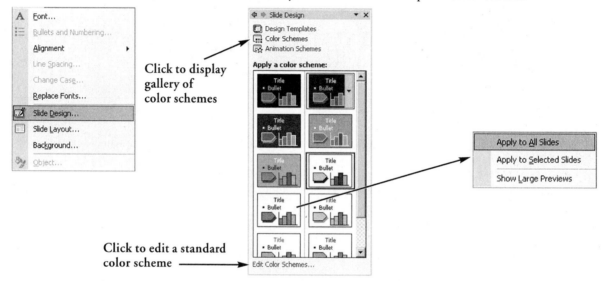

## Modify a Standard Presentation Design

7. Display the gallery of standard presentation designs as you did in Steps 3–4.

8. Click **Edit Color Schemes** (option below the gallery of designs). Refer to the illustration above.

9. Select the Custom tab and note the color of each element in the color scheme as shown in the list and the thumbnail.

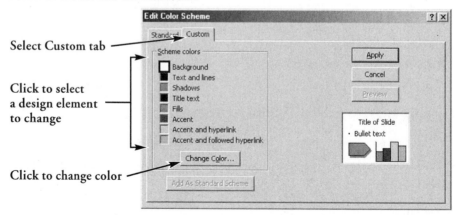

10. Click the color thumbnail for the Background and click **Change Color**.

11. Select the Standard tab and select a color for the slide background from the standard color wheel that is displayed.

## Designer's Pointer

Several important factors affect your choice of an effective color in a presentation:

**Formality and Effect:** Conservative colors (blue) add formality; brighter colors (yellow) lend a less formal and perhaps trendy look. Also, blues and greens create a more relaxed and receptive environment than warm colors such as red, orange, or yellow.

**Association:** An audience naturally associates colors with certain ideas; e.g., green for money or go; yellow for caution; red for stop, danger, or financial loss; school colors, and company and product colors. Because red is naturally associated with financial loss, red should not be used in a table of numbers or a graph depicting growth or a healthy financial condition.

**Differentiation:** Color helps the audience distinguish between different design elements. For example, create a hierarchy indicating level of importance by selecting one color for the slide title and a different, less prominent color for the text (e.g., yellow for title and white for ⋯ blue background).

**Output** ⋯ color scheme that will be legible with the output me⋯ ⋯ the method you will use for producing ⋯

- D⋯ ⋯ best in a dark room (slides o⋯

- ⋯ well-lit room (color trans-

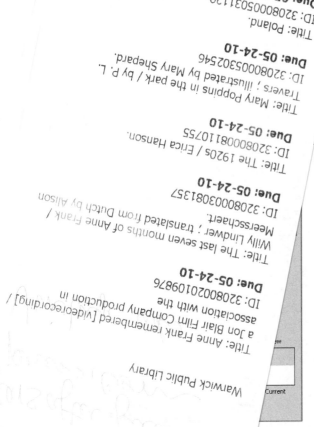

⋯ evaluate the appeal of the new ⋯ other standard color schemes

⋯ ct the **Custom** tab to mix a color ⋯ lor wheel. Refer to Steps 3–4.

⋯ lighten the color, comparing the ⋯ with various choices.

⋯ kground color applied to the slides. ⋯ until you are satisfied with it.

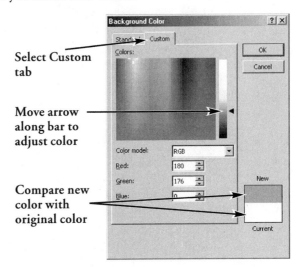

Select Custom tab

Move arrow along bar to adjust color

Compare new color with original color

16. Change the color of other design elements in the color scheme as required. There should be high contrast between the new background color and the text colors to allow for easy readability (e.g., change text and lines and title text from the list).

17. Print Slides 1–3 as an audience handout, three slides per page if directed by your instructor.

# Designing a Custom Presentation Design

Use of stock presentation designs that provide no association with a company and/or the topic gives the impression that a speaker is unprepared, pays little attention to details, and perhaps leads to the logical conclusion that the company this speaker represents is incompetent as well.

## Reinforcing a Presentation Topic

Presenters who want to set themselves apart devote the time and energy to develop powerful, creative designs that reinforce the topic being discussed. Creative templates are easily developed to reinforce presentations that utilize vivid word imagery, such as those developed around creative analogies. For example, developing a creative template is simple for one effective speech that compares principles of effective speaking to the four keys to a successful ski jump, as used in a powerful speech by Andrew Wilson entitled "Ache for the Impact: Four Steps to Powerful Oratory." In the following activity, you will see how lively, upbeat fonts and colors and related template images (diverse group of people participating in an exercise program) reinforce the speaker's message extolling the benefits of facilitating employees' efforts to maintain a healthy lifestyle.

***Directions:*** Follow the instructions to create a custom template that a team of consultants might develop for a presentation recommending that a client company establish a corporate wellness program.

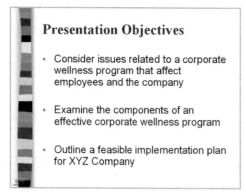

Original Slide: Standard PowerPoint Template

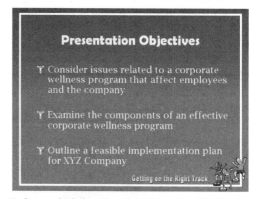

Enhanced Slide: Custom Template Reflecting the Presentation Topic

## Designer's Pointer

Follow this systematic process when selecting the color scheme of a custom presentation:

**Choose the background color first because this area displays the largest amount of color.** Consider the issues affecting color discussed in a previous Designer's Pointer: formality, mood, association, differentiation, and output media.

**Choose foreground colors—a color for the slide title and a second color for the text—with high contrast with the background for easy readability.** Black text against a white background has the greatest contrast. A blue background with yellow text contrasts well, but white text would be difficult to read because of the low contrast.

**Evaluate the readability of the fonts with the color scheme you have selected.** Colored text tends to wash out when projected; therefore, be certain the fonts are sturdy enough and large enough to be read easily.

**Choose accent colors that complement the color scheme.** Accent colors are used in small doses to draw attention to key elements; e.g., bullet markers, bars and slices in charts, fills, and specimen text.

**Project your presentation ahead of time in the room where you are to present so you can adjust the color scheme.** This process is necessary because colors display differently on computer monitors than projection devices. You can also double-check the readability of the text in the actual room and proofread for errors. Your goal is to ensure that everyone in the room, including the person seated in the last row, can see your presentation.

## Develop the Custom Design

1. Open a new presentation by clicking **File**, **New**. A Title slide using the default presentation design (blank) is displayed.

Open blank presentation with no color or graphics →

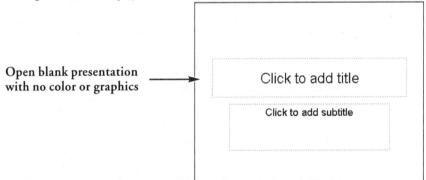

## Select the Color Scheme

2. Read the Designer's Pointer above to review the systematic process for developing a new color scheme.

3. Select the color scheme for each standard design element in the presentation using the following recommendations or your own preferences:
   - **Background:** Gradient blue using a horizontal variant with dark medium blue at the top and a slightly lighter shade at the bottom
   - **Title text:** Yellow
   - **Text for Level 1 of bulleted list:** White
   - **Fills:** Medium green

## Edit the Master Slide

4. Review the design principles for selecting fonts presented in the Designer's Pointer on page 65 if necessary.

5. Select fonts to convey an upbeat mood consistent with the theme that healthy employees are happy, productive, and satisfied with the company.
   - **Slide title:** Select an informal sans serif font such as **Berlin Sans FB Demi**.
   - **Text for bulleted list:** Select an informal serif font such as **Lucida Bright**.

6. Select a bullet associated with the wellness theme, such as the figure lifting the barbell (select Webdings font, symbol #134, after selecting **Format, Bullet**).

7. Format the motto **Getting on the Right Track** using a WordArt style that is easy to read and fill and line colors with high contrast to the slide background (e.g., yellow, gray, etc.).
   *Note:* This short phrase, positioned in the bottom right corner of the slide, will keep the audience focused on the purpose of the presentation throughout the delivery.

8. Add a clip art image to the right of the motto that conveys the intended message of happy, healthy employees (e.g., diverse group of people working out or participating in other types of wellness programs).

9. Add a narrow border around the slide to add unity to the motto and clip art as it gives the sense of a "track" for these employees and the company.
   a) Use the rectangle AutoShape to draw the border.
   b) Change the line color to white and line width to 6 points (Click the Line Style button on the Draw toolbar.)

## Create Slides

1. Design a title page for the slide assuming you are the consultant making the presentation.

2. Build the slide shown in the model that presents the presentation objectives and thus serves as an agenda to preview the major points in the presentation. Key the following bulleted text on this slide:
   - **Consider issues related to a corporate wellness program that affect employees and the company**
   - **Examine the components of an effective corporate wellness program**
   - **Outline a feasible implementation plan for XYZ Company**

## Save and Print the Slide Show

3. Save the file as **Wellnesstemplate**.

4. Print the slide show as an audience handout if directed by your instructor.

## Reflecting a Company's Image

A speaker representing a company in competitive business presentations must develop a strong custom presentation design (template) that clearly reflects the company's professional image and unique corporate identity and the topic being discussed.

*Directions:* Follow instructions to create a custom template for a company of your choice or one designated by your instructor.

## Research the Company and Prepare a Sketch

1. Obtain copies of the company's printed materials (letterhead, brochures, annual report) and visit the company's Web site. Identify graphical elements, approved company colors, and logos the company is already using to create the company's identify.

2. Review the Designer's Pointers in this project to be sure you understand design principles related to font and color selection.

3. Sketch a draft of your design.

4. Reproduce or download from the company's Web site high quality images for use in the design. Keep in mind that poor reproductions will reflect negatively on the company. Be sure to clear any copyright restrictions.

## Create and Print the Slides

5. Create the title page and one bulleted list providing text of your choice (e.g., the company's major products, locations, or significant achievements). Refer to the Designer's Pointer on page 74 related to writing effective content for slides.

6. Save the file using your company name as the file name.

7. Print the slide show as an audience handout if directed by your instructor.

## Reformatting Slides for Overheads

Create professional overhead transparencies with PowerPoint. Use the default presentation design (blank) when you know in advance your output medium is overheads. If you have already developed a slide show when you learn you must deliver the presentation using overhead transparencies, you will need to make a number of modifications. These modifications are driven by the requirements of the overhead projector and the time and expense involved in color printing. You will also want to consider reducing the number of slides because of the additional time needed to display overheads over projecting slides.

*Directions:* Follow instructions to format the company template you just created for overheads.

1. Be sure the Wellnesstemplate file is open.

2. Resave the file using the file name Wellness-overhead.

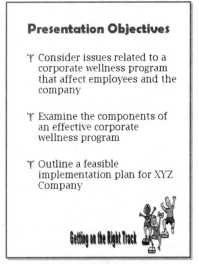

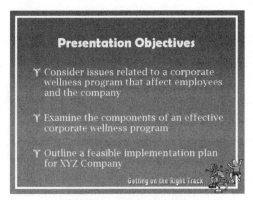

Landscape Orientation
Recommended for Slides

Portrait Orientation
Recommended for Transparencies

## Change the Slide Orientation to Portrait

3. Review the Designer's Pointer to learn more about slide orientation.

4. Click **File, Page Setup**.

# Designer's Pointer

To meet the demands of today's audiences in a fast-paced, technological environment, speakers must present highly relevant information as concisely as possible. Short attention spans and intense demand on time make it critical that slides are engaging and give audiences the gist of the slide in a glance. Well-organized, crisp slide content enhances the audience's ability to grasp the meaning and find immediate value in the information and leads to an effective delivery style. Whether you are using PowerPoint to develop a slide show for a presentation, a handout requested by a decision maker who prefers slides over an oral presentation, or posting of information on the Web for employees, customers/clients, or business partners, the following guidelines will aid you in writing concise, meaningful content. Note these principles illustrated in the original and enhanced slide.

- **Write descriptive slide titles.** The title should reflect the exact content of the slide in a way that will engage the audience's attention. In the example shown, the revised title, *Corporate Wellness Program Yields High Returns*, focuses on the key idea developed in this slide and thus prepares the audience for understanding the list of benefits included in the bulleted list.

- **Make certain that the items in a bulleted list appear together for a similar purpose.** Each item in a list must serve the same purpose. The major points should relate to the key concept revealed in the title; each subpoint should relate to its major point, and so on. Each major point in the ineffective slide is a benefit of implementing a corporate wellness program except for the first point, which seems to be a transition statement likely put on the slide as a crutch to alleviate a speaker's nervousness.

- **Limit the number of points for coherence and audience retention.** Develop a draft of the points in a list and look for overlap and repetition allowing you to collapse the content

**Benefits**

- ⵑ Happy, healthy workers yield high returns for the company
- ⵑ Lower health care costs
  — Employee sickness and injuries
- ⵑ Increase in employee productivity and efficiency
- ⵑ Reduction in employee absenteeism
- ⵑ Recruitment and retention are increased
  — Employees feel management values them and their well being, happy employees are less likely to leave
  — Can recruit more successfully when company has an innovative, "people first" image

Getting on the Right Track

Ineffective slide

**Corporate Wellness Program Yields High Returns**

- ⵑ Lowers health care costs resulting from employee sickness and injuries
- ⵑ Increases employee productivity and efficiency
- ⵑ Reduces employee turnover and absenteeism
- ⵑ Improves recruitment and retention as the company is recognized to be innovative and supportive of employees

Getting on the Right Track

Enhanced Slide: Well-organized, targeted content that an audience can understand at a glance

into a shorter list that an audience can remember more easily. The revised slide collapses the disorganized, choppy content into four precise, coherent statements. Note how combining absenteeism and medical costs and the subpoint eliminates choppiness caused by overdividing and corrects an outlining error. A point cannot be divided unless it divides into at least two parts. The final point in the revised slide is a tight, targeted summary of the final point and its subpoints.

*continued*

# Designer's Pointer

- **Write concise, to-the-point statements that you want the audience to remember.** Avoid the tendency of many speakers to clean up their notes and put them on the slide. This scripted slide becomes a crutch for a nervous or lazy speaker who reads the lines of the screen rather than prepares to deliver extemporaneously. The clarity of precise language will enable an audience to focus briefly on key points while keeping the prime focus on the speaker's explanation. Additionally, this brief, targeted slide content will be meaningful to the decision maker who today frequently asks managers to send slides rather than prepare a complete report or give a presentation. The revised slide eliminates the first major point and the final two subpoints, which are scripted text that likely would lead to poor delivery.

- **Make the items in a bulleted list parallel.** If one item is presented in a different way grammatically, it appears out of place and weakens the emphasis given to each item in the list. The inconsistency may distract the audience's attention from the message. Beginning each point in the revised slide with an action verb aids the audience in visualizing the result of implementing the speaker's recommended plan; also, a parallel list of descriptive phrases could be used (e.g., lower health care costs, increased productivity, and so on.)

- **Place ideas to be compared on the same slide when possible.** Combining ideas for comparison on the slide allows the audience to view all relevant data for easy synthesis and interpretation. Combining data in this way also guards against slide overload—bombarding the audience with too many visuals in a single presentation. The slides you created for the file Present comparing the usefulness of four types of visuals illustrates these principles of comparison and slide overload. Placing the advantages, disadvantages, and recommendations for each visual type on a single slide allows for quick, coherent delivery of a vast amount of information. Imagine the frustration of today's fast-paced audiences if the designer had created three separate slides for each visual type—twelve slides to develop one main point.

5. Change the "Slides sized for" to **Overhead** (default setting is on-screen show).

6. Change the orientation for the slides to Portrait (default setting is landscape). Retain the default to print notes, handouts, and outline in portrait orientation for easy reading of these slides typically printed on paper.

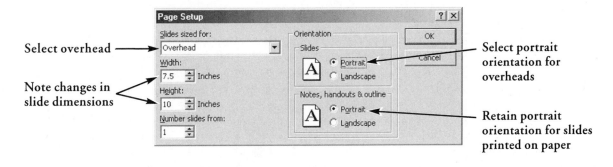

# Designer's Pointer

Slides can be formatted using either landscape (horizontal) or portrait (vertical) placement, as illustrated in the following diagram.

Choose landscape orientation for electronic slide shows because the wider arrangement

- Is more pleasing to the eye, much like the soothing feeling of looking at a wide horizon.

- Makes longer lines available for bulleted lists and pictures.

- Is designed to fit the typical size of the projection equipment. The bottom of a vertically arranged slide (portrait orientation) would be cut off.

Use portrait orientation for overhead transparencies because this vertical placement positions the text to be read across the shortest side of the page, which makes additional lines available for text. The sides of a horizontally arranged slide would not be visible if projected on an overhead projector.

**Landscape Orientation
Recommended for Slides**

**Portrait Orientation
Recommended for Overheads**

Slides, notes, and outlines printed using portrait orientation are more convenient for readers as we are accustomed to reading pages in a vertical format (longest side at the left rather than at the top).

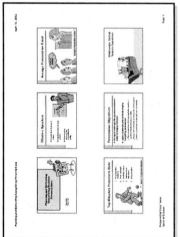

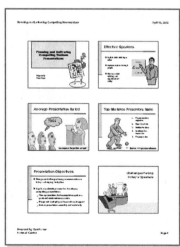

**Handouts printed in landscape orientation (left) are less convenient to read than portrait orientation (right) because they must be turned sideways to be read.**

## Modify the Color Scheme and the Format

7. Change the background to white. (Click **Format, Background**).

8. Select colors for the slide title and the bulleted list that have high contrast with the white background.

9. Modify the objects on the slide master to remove large areas of color and large logos that would require an inordinate amount of color. Your goal is to include "splashes of color" that clearly reflect the tone of the presentation.

## Critique and Edit Slides

10. Redesign the slides with animated layers (e.g., overlapping objects that hide after animation). Create a separate overhead for each layer or develop a simple bulleted list with appealing enhancements that require small amounts of color. You will learn to create these layered effects in Project 5.

11. Check each slide for changes needed in the size and the position of objects because of the reduced width.

## Print the Slide Show

12. Print the slide show as an audience handout if directed by your instructor.

# Reinforcement Activities

Add the following slides for added reinforcement of the PowerPoint features you learned in this project.

## Activity 1

Use an online database to locate the following article that compares effective speaking to the successful ski jump:

Wilson, A. B. (1996, June/July). Ache for the Impact: Four steps to powerful oratory. *Executive Speeches*, 6–7.

Design a custom template to reinforce the ski analogy that adheres to the presentation design guidelines presented in this project. Create a title slide and at least one slide that illustrates a key point made in the speech and displays the standard slide elements. Be prepared to share with your instructor and the class the rationale for your design choices. Print the slides as an audience handout.

## Activity 2

Use an online database to locate an actual speech made by a company executive. Specify "speech" as the publication type or search only in periodicals that publish speeches, such as *Executive Speeches* or *Vital Speeches of the Day*. Design a custom template that reflects the company's corporate identity and the speaker's topic based on your knowledge of the company and information gleaned from your review of the company's home page. Create a title slide and at least one slide that illustrates a key point made in the speech and displays the standard slide elements. Be prepared to share with your instructor and the class the rationale for your design choices. Print the slides as an audience handout.

## Activity 3

Design a custom template to reinforce the topic of a presentation you are currently developing following the presentation design guidelines presented in this project. Create a title slide and at least one bulleted list that illustrates a point in the speech and displays the standard slide elements. Be prepared to share with your instructor and the class your rationale for your design choices. Print the slides as an audience handout.

## Activity 4

In small groups, brainstorm to identify a creative analogy for presenting the main points of a presentation on a topic of your choice or one assigned by your instructor. For example, sports images and terminology could be used in a speech on team presentations (the winning game plan, organizing a committed team, practicing important plays, exhibiting appropriate sideline behavior, etc.). Compare the sport of surfing to "surfing the Web" to complete electronic job searches, or compare handling stress to diffusing a bomb. Create a title slide and at least one bulleted list that illustrates a key point and displays the standard slide elements. Be prepared to share with your instructor and the class the rationale for your design choices. Print the slides as an audience handout. Be creative and have fun with this activity.

## Activity 5

Develop a custom template for your college or university to be used in a recruitment or orientation presentation to new or prospective students. Create a title slide and at least one bulleted list that illustrates a key point and displays the standard slide elements. Be prepared to share with your instructor and the class the rationale for your design choices. Print the slides as an audience handout.

# PROJECT 5

## Learning Objectives

- Enhance the overall coherence of the presentation by incorporating agenda, divider, and summary slides to preview content and to transition the audience through the organizational structure of a presentation.

- Use the speller and style checker to ensure accuracy in spelling and grammar and consistency in style.

- Use the Rehearse Timings feature to identify improvements while practicing delivery of a presentation.

## Designing Coherence Devices

Showcasing the organizational structure of a presentation will assist you in delivering a presentation that an audience perceives to be coherent—a logical, smooth progression of ideas. In this project you will create (a) an agenda slide to preview major divisions of a presentation, (b) divider slides to mark the beginning of the major points in a presentation, and (c) a summary slide to preview several content slides related to one major idea. Refer to the Designer's Pointer for additional information about the value of planning coherence devices.

### Creating an Agenda Slide

You can develop a simple bulleted list to give the audience a concise preview of the main points in your presentation and the order in which you plan to cover them. Other, more creative techniques will help you capture the audience's attention and set the stage for a dynamic presentation. You will see both approaches as you complete the activities in this project.

*Directions:* Follow the directions to create the agenda slide as shown.

**Presentation Objectives**

- Recognize challenges facing communicators in today's changing workplace.

- Apply a systematic process for developing compelling presentations:
  - Plan a presentation that accomplishes speaker's goals and meets audience's needs
  - Design and use highly professional visual support
  - Deliver presentations smoothly and confidently

1. Be sure the file Present is open.

2. Create a new slide using the Title layout from Text Layouts category and position it after the slide "Top Mistakes Presenters Make."

3. Add the patterned background you used on the enhanced title slide. Alternately, you may wish to choose a background with a different fill effect (gradient, texture, or pattern) of your choice. The point is that the background should have a distinctive look different from other slides, yet be complementary.

4. Add a slide transition effect that is slightly more dramatic than the Wipe from Left used in other slides, and a subtle sound effect if desired (e.g., chime, jingle).

5. Add custom animation consistent with other bulleted lists in the presentation.

# Designer's Pointer

A clear, logical organizational pattern for the content of a presentation is fundamental to an effective presentation. A writer includes headings to serve as signposts to mark the major and minor divisions of a report. Likewise, a speaker uses verbal cues to transition an audience through a presentation smoothly. These cues include a preview of the main points to be covered prior to moving into the body of the presentation and transition words such as *first*, *next*, and *finally*. These cues can be incorporated into slides that aid in developing a smooth, coherent presentation.

## Creating Divider Slides

A divider slide is positioned at the beginning of each major point of a presentation to remind the audience where the speaker is in the organization structure and to target attention to this new discussion. Study the Designer's Pointer on page 81 before creating divider slides for the file Present.

### Create a Master Divider Slide

*Directions:* Follow the instructions to create the master divider slide design for the file Present as shown.

1. Make a copy of the agenda slide, "Presentation Objectives," that you created in the previous section. Refer to Project 1 for instructions for copying slides, if necessary.

2. Delete the bulleted list and input the title text **Challenges Facing Today's Speakers**.

3. Resize and position the text as shown in the model.

4. Select a relevant image of your choice or insert the clip art border from the Microsoft Clip Gallery. Search "Borders and Frames" using the key term "presenters."

5. Ungroup the image and delete all segments except those shown in the model. Resize and position to create the desired effect.

6. Add custom animation as desired to bring added attention to this divider slide signaling the beginning of the first major point in the presentation.

7. Edit the slide transition and add a subtle sound effect if desired (e.g., chime, jingle).

## Designer's Pointer

To achieve the goal of transitioning the audience logically and smoothly from one point to another in a presentation, you must design divider slides that are dramatic and distinctly different from content slides. A few basic suggestions follow:

- Include a descriptive title that engages the audience's attention and perhaps an image that reinforces the major idea on each divider slide.

- Select a slightly different color scheme and perhaps a different fill effect (e.g., pattern, texture) that is complementary with the presentation template, but that the audience will clearly identify as the signpost marking a new section.

- Consider selecting a subtle, relevant sound effect to bring added emphasis to this pivotal point in your presentation. A subtle sound will not be distracting since the presentation will have only a few divider slides.

If your time for designing slides is limited, you might use the Title layout for the divider slide. The positioning of the slide title and the slide master object will signal a divider between major points. For instance, the narrow tie on the Dad's tie presentation design is horizontal in the Title layout and vertical in all other layouts, and the slide title placeholder is positioned lower.

## Copy the Master to Create Each Divider Slide

*Directions:* Follow the instructions to use the master slide to create an additional divider slide for the file Present.

1. Copy the master divider slide, "Challenges Facing Today's Speakers," that you created in the previous section. Refer to Project 1 for instructions for copying slides, if necessary.

2. Edit the title **Systematic Process Is Key**.

3. Add the bulleted list:

   a) Insert a text box, click the **Bullets** button, and key the text.
   b) Highlight the bulleted list and click **Format**, **Bullets and Numbering**.
   c) Click **Customize**, select **Webdings,** and select the key. Click **OK**.
   d) Change the size to 200 and select a color for easy readability.

Select Webdings ⟶

Select the key ⟶

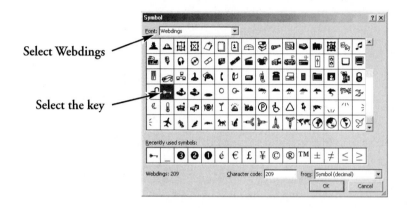
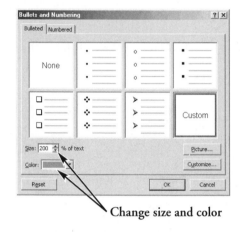

Change size and color ⟶

4. Add custom animation and sound (e.g., key jingle) to bring added attention to the bulleted list.

## Creating a Summary Slide

A summary slide, like an agenda slide, aids an audience in understanding the organizational structure and flow of a presentation. A summary slide previews the content of a series of slides related to one supporting idea for a major point. PowerPoint's summary slide feature makes creating this coherence device very simple as it compiles a simple bulleted list containing the slide titles of any slides you select.

*Directions:* Follow the instructions to build the summary slide for four slides in the file Present. This slide will preview slides providing more detailed information about each of the four types of visuals.

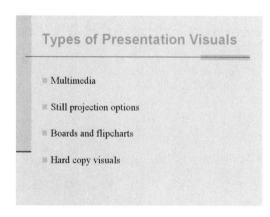

## Create the Slides to Be Included on the Summary Slide

1. Complete Project 2, Reinforcement Activity 3 on page 34 if you have not done so already. Alternately, you may create these four slides and key the slide titles only:
   **Slide 1:** Multimedia
   **Slide 2:** Still Projection Options
   **Slide 3:** Boards and Flipcharts
   **Slide 4:** Hard Copy Visuals

## Select the Slides to Be Included on the Summary Slide

2. Go to the Slide Sorter view and select the four slides to be included on the summary slide (hold down the Shift key as you click to select multiple slides). The slides are (1) Multimedia, (2) Still Projection Options, (3) Boards and Flipcharts, and (4) Hard Copy Visuals.

3. Click the **Summary Slide** button from the Slide Sorter toolbar. A new slide containing the slide title "Summary Slide" and a bulleted list of the titles of the four selected slides appears in front of the selected slides.

Summary
Slide button

Summary
Slide inserted
before the four
selected slides

Four slides
selected to
create
Summary
slide

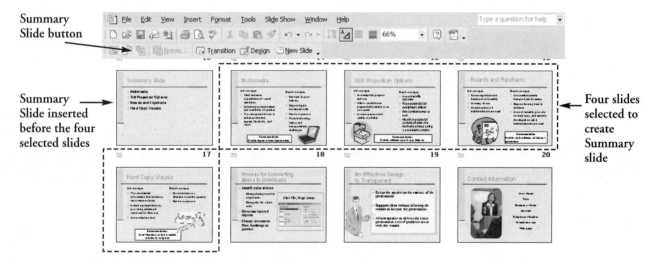

4. Display the summary slide in Normal view and edit the slide:
   a) Input the new title: **Types of Presentation Visuals**.
   b) Change the capitalization style in the bulleted list so only the first word in each bulleted item is capitalized.
   c) Increase the spacing between the lines to balance the text on the page (click **Format, Line Spacing**, select **2** for double spacing).

## Add a Slide Transition

5. Click the **Slide Transition** button on the Slide Sorter toolbar.

6. Select **Wipe from Left** as the slide transition for consistency with other slides in the presentation.

# Proofreading a Slide Show

A speaker will lose credibility instantly if slides contain spelling and grammatical errors. A systematic plan for proofreading includes using PowerPoint's Speller to locate spelling errors and the Style Checker to ensure consistency in several styles:

## Using the Speller

Follow the instructions to check the spelling in the file Present.

1. Click **Tools**, **Spelling**.

2. Select the appropriate correction from the Spelling dialog box that appears when a spelling error is detected.

   a) Click **Change** to accept a recommended spelling or select the correct spelling from the list provided and click **Change**.

   b) Click **Ignore all** instances of a word if the spelling is correct but does not appear in PowerPoint's dictionary. Click **Add** to add the word to PowerPoint's dictionary.

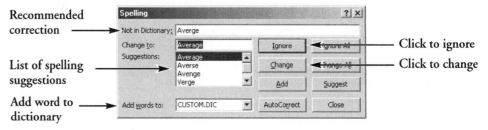

Recommended correction →    List of spelling suggestions →    Add word to dictionary →    Click to ignore ←    Click to change ←

3. Save the presentation to update the file with any corrections made while running the speller.

## Using the Style Checker

In addition to checking spelling, the Style Checker checks for visual clarity and case and end punctuation.

### Correct Detected Problems

1. Be sure the Office Assistant is turned on by clicking **Help**, **Office Assistant**.

2. Click the light bulb that appears beside a style error, and select the appropriate option for correcting the problem.

   In the illustration, PowerPoint recognizes an inconsistency in the capitalization of a bulleted list and displays several options. The designer would click **Change the text to sentence case** to capitalize the word *Reduces* and may also wish to change the style checker options to AutoCorrect this error in all other presentations.

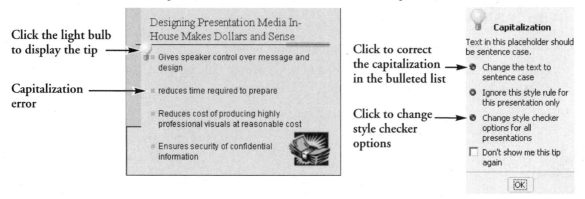

Click the light bulb to display the tip →    Capitalization error →    Click to correct the capitalization in the bulleted list →    Click to change style checker options →

PowerPoint checks the spelling regardless of the view you are in when you execute the spelling command.

# Rehearsing a Presentation

Running the Rehearse Timing feature while making a dry run of your presentation gives you a record of the actual time of the presentation and the time spent on each slide. Use this information to enhance your presentation in a variety of ways: locate errors in logical development and flow and content, develop a smooth transition from one point to the next, and enhance your delivery skills. Additional suggestions are provided in the related Presenter's Tip on page 86.

*Directions:* Follow the instructions to use the rehearsal timings to practice your delivery using the file Present.

1. Go to Slide Sorter view and click the **Rehearse Timings** button on the Slide Sorter toolbar. The slide show automatically goes into the Slide Show view.

Rehearse Timings

2. Advance through the presentation as if you were delivering the actual presentation. Use the buttons in the Rehearsal dialog box superimposed on the slide to refine your delivery:

   a) Click **Next** to move to the next slide.
   b) Click **Pause** to stop the clock as you review your notes, rethink your discussion, etc.
   c) Click **Repeat** to reset the clock so you can deliver the slide again.

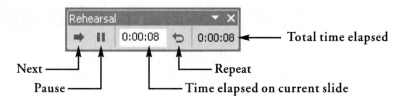

3. Continue until you have reached the last slide in the presentation and the following dialog box appears.

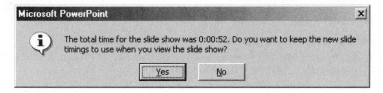

4. Click **Yes** to record the new slide timings. The slides are displayed in Slide Sorter view with the timings for individual slides displayed below each slide as shown in the following illustration. You can easily review the timings to identify areas of improvement.

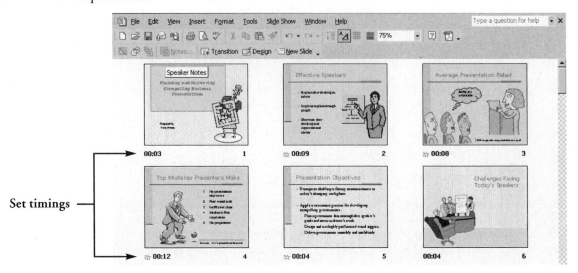

Set timings

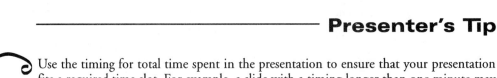

## Presenter's Tip

Use the timing for total time spent in the presentation to ensure that your presentation fits a required time slot. For example, a slide with a timing longer than one minute may contain too much information and could be divided into one or more slides. The lengthy timing could simply pinpoint difficult content that requires additional thought and deliberate practice in order to present concisely and coherently.

## Running a Slide Show with Timings

Once you have recorded timings during rehearsals (as shown in the previous illustration), you must decide each time you run the presentation whether to run it manually or with the set timings.

*Directions:* Follow the instructions to use the timings to run a presentation manually and with set timings.

1. Click **Slide Show, Set Up Show**.

2. Note the two selections in the Set Up Show dialog box:
   a) Click **Manually** to advance the slide on a mouse click.
   b) Click **Using timings, if present** to allow the slides to advance automatically using the set timings.

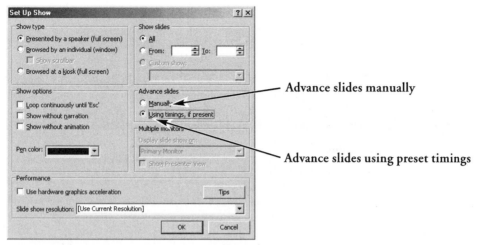

3. Run the file Present using the set timings. Run the show a second time using the manual setting.

## Presenter's Tip

Setting timings is essential when designing automated presentations that will be run at exhibit areas or sent to potential customers/clients with narration replacing a human speaker. You can use set timings as you rehearse to help you maintain the pace needed to fit a predetermined time slot. However, run the presentation manually during your actual presentation as preset timings on all slides will diminish your ability to adapt the presentation to the audience's needs and to entertain questions, manage interruptions, etc.

# Reinforcement Activities

Add the following slides to the file Present for added reinforcement of the PowerPoint features you learned in this project. Position the slides as shown at the end of the project.

## Activity 1

The original agenda slide uses a simple bulleted list to draw a clear roadmap of the three sections of a presentation that focuses on the three-part process for developing compelling presentations. A more creative approach involves using word pictures and images to make the main points memorable, as shown in the revision.

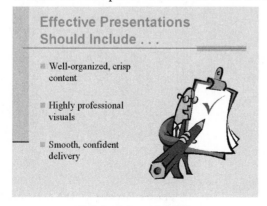

Original Agenda Slide

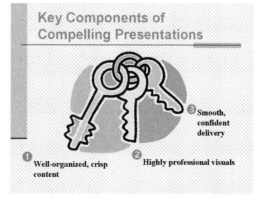

Enhanced Agenda Slide

### Instructions for Original Agenda Slide

1. Open a new presentation and create a slide using the Title, Text, and Clip Art layout from the Other Layouts category.

2. Add custom animation and a slide transition as desired.

3. Save the file as **Agendapresent**.

### Instructions for Enhanced Agenda Slide

1. Open the file Agendapresent.

2. Create a new slide using the Title Only layout from the Text Layouts category.

3. Insert relevant clip art and create the three text boxes.

4. Insert the numbered icons:

   a) Create a text box.
   b) Click **Insert**, **Symbol** and select **Wingdings**.
   c) Select the appropriate symbol.
   d) Recolor and size as desired.
   e) Group the numbered icon with the related text box and position as shown.

Select Wingdings ⟶

Select a symbol

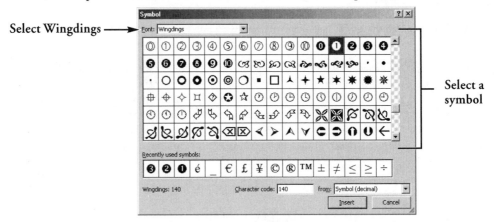

5. Add custom animation and a slide transition as desired.

## Activity 2

The agenda slide created in Activity 1 can be modified slightly to create complementary divider slides to mark the major three sections of the presentation.

1. Open the file Agendapresent that you created in Activity 1.

### Create the Master Divider Slide

2. Copy the agenda slide to create a master divider slide.

3. Emphasize the first major point by lightening the text of the other two points.

4. Add a subtle sound to the slide transition (e.g., key jingle).

5. Add custom animation to create the desired effect.

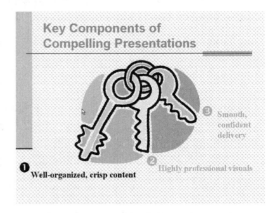

**Master Divider Slide Customized
for Major Point 1**

## Add the Divider Slides

6. Copy the master and edit to create the divider slides for the remaining sections of the presentation.

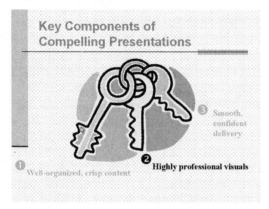

Divider Slide for Major Point II

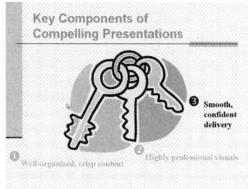

Divider Slide for Major Point III

# Activity 3

Create an agenda and divider slides using the main points of a presentation you are currently developing or the corporate wellness speech for which you created the custom design template in Project 4. Save using a file name of your choice.

# Activity 4

Locate a printed speech using an online database or the Internet (e.g., search by publication for *Executive Speeches* or *Vital Speeches of the Day*). Develop an agenda slide that you believe captures the roadmap the speaker has established for the development of the presentation and divider slides that creatively mark the beginning of each major section.

# Slide Order

Print a copy of the file Present as an audience handout with six slides per page. Resequence slides as shown. Your instructor may instruct you to print the slides created or revised in Project 5 only (highlighted slides).

1. Title Slide

2. Effective Speakers (***revised***)

3. Average Presentation Rated

4. Top Mistakes Presenters Make

5. **Presentation Objectives (*agenda slide*)**

6. **Challenges Facing Today's Speakers (*first divider slide*)**

7. Demands Changing World Places on Speakers

8. Adapting Speaking Style to Today's Fast Pace

9. Meeting the Demands of Today's Audiences

10. Personal Connection a Must

11. A Speech Is a Gift

12. **Systematic Process Is Key (*second divider slide*)**

13. Clear Presentation Objective Drives a Successful Presentation

14. Benefits of Using Presentation Visuals

15. Designing Presentation Media In-house Makes Dollars and Sense (revised)

16. Considerations Affecting Presentation Media Choice (revised)

17. **Types of Presentation Visuals**

18. Multimedia

19. Still Projection Options

20. Boards and Flipcharts

21. Hard Copy Visuals

22. Process for Converting Slides to Overheads

23. An Effective Design Is Transparent (revised)

24. Guidelines for Effective Delivery

25. Contact Information

26. Additional Resources

27. Project 3, Activity 6 (position in file will vary)

Print the slides in the file Agendapresent as an audience handout with six slides per page sequenced as shown below.

1. Reinforcement Activity 1—Original Agenda Slide or Enhanced Agenda Slide as directed by instructor.

2. Reinforcement Activity 2—Divider Slide—Major Point I

3. Reinforcement Activity 2—Divider Slide—Major Point II

4. Reinforcement Activity 2—Divider Slide—Major Point III

# PROJECT 6  Adding Creative Animation Techniques

## Learning Objectives

- Use automatic timings to enhance a slide show and to allow the presenter to deliver a seamless, professional slide show.

- Create dazzling effects with Hide after Mouse Click and Hide after Animation techniques.

## Creative Animation Techniques

Animation directs the audience's eyes to a specific object as you have already seen in the simple animation used in Project 2 (e.g., building a bulleted list and bringing in objects in a specified order). Learning the three advanced animation techniques presented in this project will empower you to create effects that will reinforce important points in ways that will dazzle your audience. These techniques include (1) using automated timings, (2) using Hide after Mouse Click animation, and (3) using Hide after Animation.

## Using Automated Timings

*Directions:* Follow the instructions to enhance the original slide as shown.

Original Slide

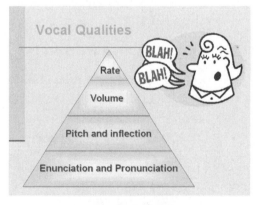

Enhanced Slide

1. Create a new slide using the Title Only layout from the Text Layouts category.

2. Insert a relevant image to reinforce the concept of sounds made by the human voice.

3. Click **AutoShapes**, **More AutoShapes** and select the pyramid chart.

4. Recolor each level using a color scheme that is complementary with your presentation design. Add a shadow to each level to add dimension to the chart.

## Ungroup the AutoShape

5. Select the pyramid chart and click **Draw, Grouping, Ungroup**. Refer to Project 3 to review grouping/ungrouping clip art if necessary.

## Create a Master for the Callout Text

6. Create a text box and key the text **Rate**

7. Format the text in the text box to include an appealing font large enough for the audience to read. Add boldface if necessary for readability.

8. Center the text box inside the top level.

## Create the Remaining Text Boxes

9. Select the text box and make a copy using the efficient drag-and-drop technique:

   a) Hold the **Ctrl** key down as you drag the grouped object. An icon with a plus sign appears as you drag the mouse.

   b) Release the mouse to "drop" a copy of the text box on the screen.

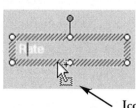

Icon with a plus sign indicates object is being copied or moved

10. Repeat the process until you have created all four text boxes.

11. Edit the text in each copied text box:

   • **Volume**
   • **Pitch and Inflection**
   • **Enunciation and Pronunciation**

12. Position the text boxes within the levels of the pyramid as shown in the model.

## Group the Text Box and the Pyramid Level

13. Select a level of the pyramid and the related text box.

14. Click **Draw, Group**, (or right-click and click Grouping, Group).

15. Repeat the process to group the pyramid levels and text boxes.

## Animate the Slide Using Automatic Timings

16. Click **Slide Show, Custom Animation**.

17. Animate each object on the slide except the slide title as follows:

   a) **Clip art:** Faded zoom → Start on Click → Fast speed
   b) **Bottom level of pyramid:** Expand → Start on Click → Medium speed
   c) **Three other pyramid levels:** Expand → Start after Previous → Medium speed

18. Extend the automatic timings on the three bottom pyramid levels to allow the audience more time to view an item before the next one is displayed:

   a) Click on the down arrow to the right of one of these objects in the Custom Animation list.

   b) Click **Timing**.

Select Timing tab

Input time of the delay

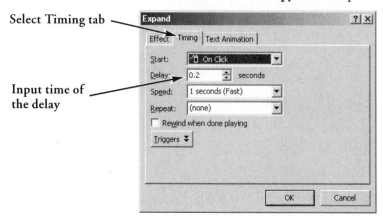

c) Input **.2** seconds in the spin box for the Delay section.

d) Repeat Steps a–c for the remaining levels.

*Note:* Refer to sections in Project 2 (enhancing with custom animation) and Project 3 (setting automatic timing), if necessary.

## Designer's Pointer ─────────────

If a slide title is longer than one line, arrange it in the inverted pyramid format. Thus, the first line of the title is the longest with each succeeding line shorter than the line preceding it.

**Unbalanced:**                           Ten Common Mistakes Made
                                                  by Presenters

**Inverted Pyramid Format:**            Ten Common Mistakes
                                                  Made by Presenters

## Using the Hide After Mouse Click Animation Technique

*Directions:* Follow the instructions to enhance the original slide as shown.

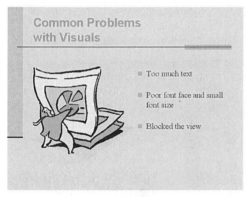

Original Slide

Enhanced Slide

1. Preview the four layers of images before you begin building the slide. A showcase box displays three separate visual effects built on one slide using the Hide after Mouse click animation effect. When the speaker advances through the slide show, the previous text disappears and the next layer is displayed in the showcase box.

Layer 1
Showcase box

Layer 2
Too Much Text

Layer 3
Poor Font Selection

Layer 4
Blocked View

2. Create a new slide using the Title Only layout from the Text layouts category.

3. Key the title **Common Problems with Visuals**.

4. Set the Zoom at 25% to provide a large desktop area to the right of the slide. (Use the Zoom button on the standard toolbar or click View, Zoom).

## Create Layer 1 (Showcase Box)

5. Use the AutoShapes rectangle to create a projection screen that serves as a backdrop or showcase box for a series of three images illustrating common problems with visuals.

6. Select a fill color and line color, width, and style, and a shadow effect to give the projection screen a realistic appearance. Refer to the instructions for creating a showcase box in Project 3 if necessary.

7. Animate the showcase box: Fade ➤ Start on Click ➤ Medium speed.

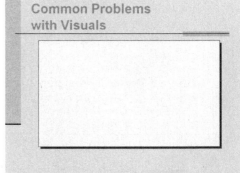

Layer 1—Showcase Box

## Create Layer 2 (Too Much Text)

8. Create a text box to fit inside the rectangle.

9. Input the title **Too Much Text**.

10. Press **Enter** and key the paragraph that appears on the Layer 2 slide.

11. Format the text:

    a) **Title:** Select a sans serif font face (e.g., Univers or Arial) with font size of 40 points.

    b) **Paragraph:** Select a serif font (e.g., Times New Roman) with a font size of 34 points.

12. Resize and reposition the text box so that the text appears to be projected on the projection screen.

13. Animate Layer 2 (Too Much Text) as follows:

    a) Wipe from Left ➤ Start on Click ➤ Medium speed.

    b) Modify the effects options to hide Layer 2 (Too Much Text) when the slide advances to the next layer:

    • Click the down arrow beside the object in the Custom Animation list.

    • Click **Effect Options**.

    • Click the down arrow beside After Animation and select **Hide on Next Mouse Click**.

Layer 2 (Too Much Text)

## Troubleshooting Tip

You cannot use the Preview option to verify the Hide after Animation effect for only one layer because the slide advances forward when the last object has been displayed regardless of the animation setting. After you have created the second layer, the Preview option can be used to verify the accuracy of the animation.

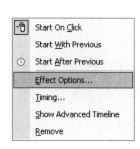

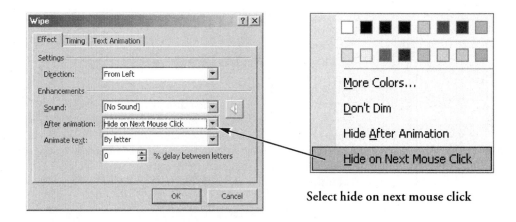

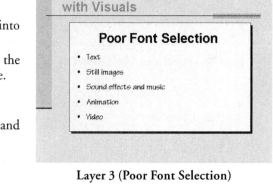

Select hide on next mouse click

## Create Layer 3 (Poor Font Selection)

14. Copy Layer 2 (Too Much Text) to save time and assure consistency in the design of each layer:

   a)  Select the text box you created for the first layer.
   b)  Hold down the **Ctrl** key as you drag the object over into the gray area outside the slide.

15. Edit the copy of Layer 2 that is positioned in front of the showcase box. Refer to the illustration below for assistance.

   a)  Input the new title **Poor Font Selection**.
   b)  Delete the unneeded paragraph.
   c)  Click the **Bullets** button on the Formatting toolbar and key the text:
   - **Text**
   - **Still images**
   - **Sound effects and music**
   - **Animation**
   - **Video**
   d)  Select a narrow, hard-to-read font face with a font size no larger than 18 points for the bulleted list.
   e)  Refer to the Troubleshooting Tip on page 96 for aligning the text in the bulleted list.

Layer 3 (Poor Font Selection)

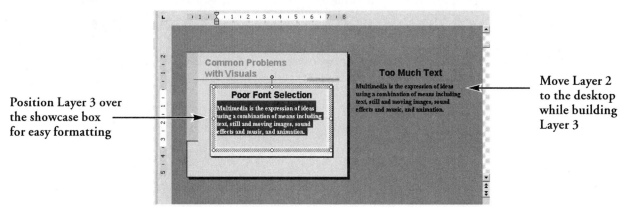

Position Layer 3 over the showcase box for easy formatting

Move Layer 2 to the desktop while building Layer 3

16. Animate Layer 3. Because you edited a copy of Layer 2, no changes are needed. Confirm the animation settings if you wish: Wipe from Left ➤ Start on Click ➤ Medium speed ➤ Hide after Mouse Click (*removes Layer 3 so the next layer can be displayed*).

# Troubleshooting Tip

Adding space between the bullet and the text will enhance the readability of the slide. To adjust the spacing, you must first display the horizontal ruler by clicking **View**, **Ruler** and then clicking **Ruler**. You can see the horizontal ruler above your slide when the slide is displayed in Slide or Normal views. To adjust the spacing, click in front of the first bulleted item to select the bulleted list placeholder and then drag the indent marker to the desired location. All bulleted items at that level change to the new position. You can repeat this process for each level of bullets.

— Drag the indent marker to a new indent setting

## Create Layer 4 (Blocked View)

17. Make a copy of Layer 2 just as you did for the previous layer. Refer to Step 14 if necessary.

18. Edit the copy of Layer 2 that is positioned in front of the showcase box. Refer to the illustration of the desktop below for assistance.

    a) Input the new title **Blocked View**
    b) Delete the paragraph.
    c) Insert a clip art image of a speaker facing forward directly in front of the projection screen.
       *Note:* If you select an image from the Microsoft Clip Gallery that contains a background such as the one illustrated, be sure to delete the background as it isn't needed with the showcase box. Refer to Project 3 (ungrouping clip art) if necessary.
    d) Group the title and the clip art so they can be animated to appear together. Alternately, animate the speaker to start with the previous event (the title of the layer).

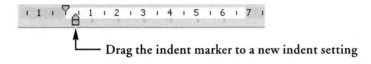

Layer 4 (Blocked View)

— Delete background

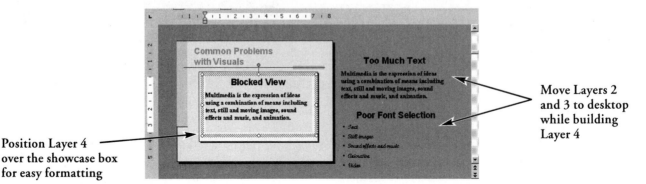

Position Layer 4 over the showcase box for easy formatting

Move Layers 2 and 3 to desktop while building Layer 4

19. Animate Layer 4 by editing the animation settings copied from Layer 2: Center Revolve ➤ Start on Click ➤ Medium speed ➤ Don't Dim. *Note:* Changing the Hide after Mouse Click effect to Don't Dim isn't necessary because the next mouse click will advance to the next slide.

## Position Layers on the Slide

20. Drag Layer 4 (Blocked View) off the slide and into the work area.

21. Position Layer 2 (Too Much Text) in front of the showcase box, making sure it is balanced attractively.

22. Position Layer 3 (Poor Font Selection) directly on top of Layer 2 (Too Much Text).

23. Position Layer 4 (Blocked View) directly on top of Layer 3 (Poor Font Selection).

## Preview Animation

It's now time to run the slide show and check the results of all these effects:

• **Slide Title:** Appear with the slide

• **Showcase Box:** Fade

• **Layer 2 (Too Much Text):** Wipe from Left ➤ Hide on Mouse Click

• **Layer 3 (Poor Font Selection):** Wipe from Left ➤ Hide on Mouse Click.

• **Layer 4 (Blocked View):** Center Revolve ➤ Don't Dim. (Next mouse click advances to the next slide.)

## Using the Hide After Animation Technique

*Directions:* Follow the instructions to enhance the original slide as shown.

1. Create a new slide using the Title Only layout from the Text layouts category.

2. Key the title and insert a clip art image of an effective speaker. Size and position as shown in the model.

3. Copy the projection screen from the slide "An Effective Design Is Transparent" to this slide. Key the text and format as shown in the model.

4. Experiment with animation effects that bring attention to the clip art (e.g., flash bulb) and diminish the importance of the showcase box (e.g., transparency). Add animation effects of your choice.

## Create a Master Star

5. Click **AutoShapes**, **Stars and Banners**.

6. Select the **5-point Star** and draw the star.

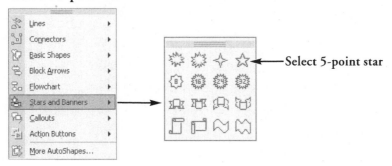

Select 5-point star

7. Create a realistic twinkling effect:

   a) Add a gradient fill effect by blending either blue, white, or yellow. Select the From Center shading style and a variant of your choice (e.g., lighter color in the center).

   b) Add a shadow effect of your choice; select a shadow color slightly darker than the fill effect.

   c) Drag on the star rotate handle in the direction you want to rotate the star.

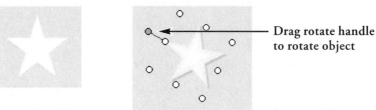

Autoshape without Enhancements                    Enhanced Star

Drag rotate handle to rotate object

8. Animate the master star: Expand ➤ Start with Previous ➤ Fast speed.

## Copy the Master Star to Create Additional Stars

9. Select the star and hold down **Ctrl** as you drag the object. An icon with a plus sign appears as you drag the slide, indicating an object is being moved.

10. Drop the star anywhere on the screen, as you will reposition it.

11. Repeat the process until you have created several stars.

12. Vary the size of the stars and reposition them to create an appealing design. (Refer to the model to view a possible placement of stars).

## Edit the Star in the Title

13. Resize and position one star directly over the word Star in the slide title. Adjust the rotation if necessary.

14. Send the star behind the title placeholder (**Draw**, **Order**, **Send to Back**).

15. Edit the animation effect: Center Revolve ➤ Start on Click ➤ Fast speed.

## Animate Selected Stars to Hide

16. Identify two or three stars that you would like to hide after they are displayed.

17. Modify the custom animation for each of these stars:

   a) Click the down arrow beside the object in the Custom Animation list.

   b) Click **Effect Options**.

   c) Click the down arrow beside After Animation and select **Hide After Animation**.

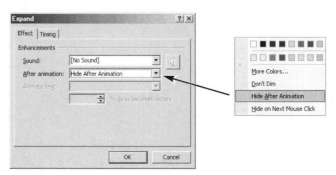

### Edit the Animation Order

18. Click **Slide Show**, **Custom Animation** and verify the animation order and effect of each object:

- **Unanimated:** Title
- **First:** Clip art with animation effect of your choice (e.g., flash bulb) and showcase box (e.g., transparency).
- **Second:** Series of stars that expand and start with the previous event. Selected stars hide after animation. Reorder the stars to display the stars in a sequence you consider appealing.
- **Third:** Star behind the slide title center revolves on mouse click.

# Reinforcement Activities

Add the following slides to the file Present for added reinforcement of the PowerPoint features you learned in this project. Position the slides as shown at the end of the project.

## Activity 1

Build the slide shown in the model.

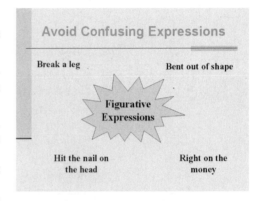

1. Choose one of the explosion shapes from AutoShapes or choose a shape of your own.

2. Animate the following objects as indicated. Extend the automatic timing to allow the audience .2 seconds to view an item before the next one is displayed.

- **First:** AutoShape: Diamond ➤ Start on Click ➤ Fast speed
- **Second:** Text box (break a leg): From Top-left ➤ Start on Click ➤ Fast speed
- **Third:** Text box (bent out of shape): From Top-right ➤ Start After Previous Event ➤ Medium speed
- **Fourth:** Text box (hit the nail on the head): From Bottom-left ➤ Start After Previous Event ➤ Medium speed
- **Fifth:** Text box (right on the money): From Bottom-right ➤ Start After Previous Event ➤ Medium speed

## Activity 2

Edit a copy of the slide created in Activity 1 to build three additional slides that illustrate other types of confusing expressions:

- **Acronyms:** FYI, ASAP, FASB, HMO or others of your choice
- **Slang:** Cool, buck, flop, dis, or others of your choice
- **Sports analogies:** Caught off guard, drop back and punt, batting a thousand, way off target, or others of your choice

*Note:* The Hide After Animation effect could be used on these four slides. However, because the timings are automatic, a "disappear" exit animation effect for the AutoShape and the four text boxes would be required to hide these objects. In this case, displaying the effects on four separate slides is a simpler design technique.

## Activity 3

Follow the instructions to build a slide that depicts a different image as each bulleted item is displayed.

1. Create a new slide using the Title, Text, and Clip Art layout from the Other Layouts category.

2. Key the first item in the bulleted list and add custom animation: Wipe from Left ➤ Start on Click ➤ Fast speed ➤ Dim effect.

3. Select a relevant image to reinforce the concept described in the first bulleted point and add custom animation: Ease In ➤ After Previous Event ➤ Medium speed ➤ Hide after Mouse Click.

4. Drag the clip art off the slide into the work area as you create the next layer.

5. Reduce the size of the bulleted list place-holder as shown.

6. Copy the text box, revise the text, and position as shown.

7. Select a relevant image to depict the content and add custom animation: Ease In ➤ After Previous Event ➤ Medium speed ➤ Hide on Mouse Click.

8. Drag this image off the slide into the work area as you create the next layer.

9. Repeat Steps 6–8 for the remaining items in the bulleted list:

   • Steady eye contact with everyone in the audience
   • Natural gestures

10. Position the first image (posture) on the slide as shown in the model making sure it is balanced attractively with the text. Layer the other three images in the order they are to be discussed.

11. Preview the animation and check for accuracy in the effects and timing and for optimal placement of the graphics.

## Activity 4

Create a slide using the Blank layout from the Contents Layout category.

1. Select three to five photos related to a topic of your choice (e.g., attractions in a city of your choice, favorite spots on your campus, highlights of an activity of one of your student groups, your latest vacation, etc.).

2. Build a creative slide using the Hide After Animation effect to showcase these photographs. You may wish to use the photo album feature for importing the photographs and developing interesting frame shapes efficiently (refer to Project 3 if necessary). Add a related slide title and photo captions and relevant sound if you wish.

3. Save in a separate file.

## Activity 5

Create a slide using the Blank layout from the Contents Layout category.

1. Design a simple slide background that depicts an image of your college/university (e.g., photo of memorable spot on campus with low contrast, wallpaper image of your logo, etc.)

2. Key the first letter of your college/university's acronym using a bold, sturdy font such as Wide Latin in a large font, at least 60 points.

3. Add custom animation: Magnify ➤ After Previous Event ➤ Fast speed ➤ Hide After Animation.

4. Copy the text box and revise it to create the remaining letters of the acronym.

5. Position the text boxes so that the letters appear in various locations across the slide spelling out the acronym of your college/university several times.

6. Add a second slide containing a series of photos related to the college/university (optional). Follow the instructions provided in Activity 4.

7. Add your college/university fight song or other music to play with the slide.

8. Save in a separate file.

## Slide Order

Print a copy of the file Present as an audience handout with six slides per page. Sequence the slides as shown. Your instructor may instruct you to print the slides created or revised in Project 6 only (highlighted slides).

1. Title Slide

2. Effective Speakers (*revised*)

3. Average Presentation Rated

4. Top Mistakes Presenters Make

5. Presentation Objectives (*agenda slide*)

6. Challenges Facing Today's Speakers (*first divider slide*)

7. Demands Changing World Places on Speakers

8. Adapting Speaking Style to Today's Fast Pace

9. Meeting the Demands of Today's Audiences

10. Personal Connection a Must

11. A Speech Is a Gift

12. Systematic Process Is Key (*second divider slide*)

13. Clear Presentation Objective Drives a Successful Presentation

14. Benefits of Using Presentation Visuals

15. Designing Presentation Media In-house Makes Dollars and Sense (*revised*)

16. Considerations Affecting Presentation Media Choice (*revised*)

17. Types of Presentation Visuals

18. Multimedia

19. Still Projection Options

20. Boards and Flipcharts

21. Hard Copy Visuals

22. Process for Converting Slides to Overheads

23. **Common Problems with Visuals**

24. An Effective Design Is Transparent (*revised*)

25. **The Speaker Is the Star**

26. Guidelines for Effective Delivery

27. **Communicate Warmth and Confidence with Body Language**
28. **Vocal Qualities**
29. **Avoid Confusing Expressions**
30. Contact Information
31. Additional Resources
32. Project 3, Activity 6 (position in file will vary)

# PROJECT 7

## Creating Compelling Tables and Charts

## Learning Objectives

- Design a compelling table, bar chart, and pie chart.
- Add creative enhancements to the chart for added clarity and appeal.

## Creating Tables

Displaying text in columnar format helps a speaker clarify large quantities of data. PowerPoint simplifies the process of creating highly professional tables.

*Directions*: Follow the instructions to enhance the original slide as shown.

**Greatest Fears**

| Speaking | 41% |
|---|---|
| Heights | 32% |
| Insects & bugs | 22% |
| Financial | 22% |
| Deep water | 22% |
| Sickness | 19% |
| Death | 19% |

**Original Slide**

**Public Speaking Tops List of People's Greatest Fears**

| Speaking | 41% |
|---|---|
| Heights | 32% |
| Insects & bugs | 22% |
| Financial | 22% |
| Deep water | 22% |
| Sickness | 19% |
| Death | 19% |

**Enhanced Slide**

1. Create a new slide using the Title and 2 Contents layout from the Content Layouts category.

2. Key the title in the Title placeholder. Note the revised title that clearly conveys the key thought presented in the data—public speaking anxiety is normal.

3. Click the clip art icon in the Left Content placeholder.

4. Select relevant clip art from the Microsoft Clip Gallery using "fear" as the search term. Resize and position as shown in the model.

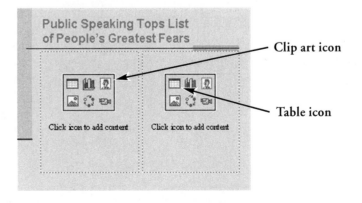

Clip art icon

Table icon

## Create the Table

5. Click the table icon in the Right Content placeholder.

6. Enter **2** for number of columns and **7** for number of rows.

7. Key the data shown in the model in the cells of the table. Use the arrow keys to move from cell to cell.

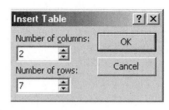

| Speaking | 41% |
| Heights | 32% |
| Insects & bugs | 22% |
| Financial | 22% |
| Deep water | 22% |
| Sickness | 19% |
| Death | 19% |

## Format the Data

8. Highlight the second column and click **Right Align** from the Formatting toolbar.

9. Highlight the first row (Speaking) and format for emphasis: Select a sturdy bold font (e.g., Abadi Condensed Extra Bold) and increase the font size to 32 points.

10. Format the remaining rows with Times New Roman font face and 28 points.

## Resize the Table and Add Source Note

11. Point to the right border until a two-headed arrow appears. Drag the mouse to the left to reduce the width of the table. Reduce the height of the table and the space between the columns until the table is positioned as shown in the model.

| **Speaking** | **41%** |
| Heights | 32% |
| Insects & bugs | 22% |
| Financial | 22% |
| Deep water | 22% |
| Sickness | 19% |
| Death | 19% |

← Drag left to reduce size of table

## Format the Table

12. Highlight the first row (Speaking) and click **Format**, **Table** (or right click and click Border and Fills).

13. Select the Fill tab, click **Fill Effects**, and select a gradient fill blending two colors complementary with the design template. Select the From Center shading style and the variant that places the lighter color in the center.

14. Highlight the remaining rows and apply the same gradient fill you applied to the first row, except lighten the colors to create a receding effect on these rows.

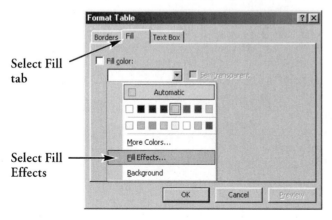

Select Fill tab

Select Fill Effects

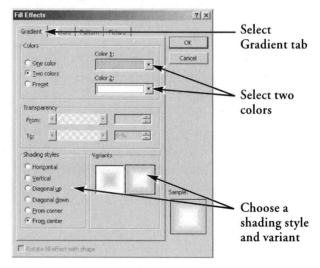

Select Gradient tab

Select two colors

Choose a shading style and variant

15. Highlight the entire table and click **Format**, **Table** (or right click and click Border and Fills).

16. Select the **Borders** tab and click on the diagram or use the buttons to eliminate all borders (outside and inside) in the table.

Select Borders tab → 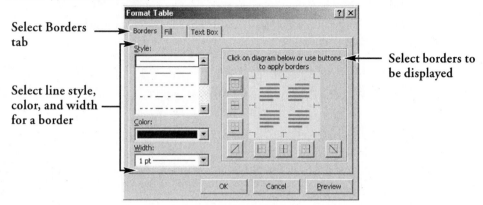 ← Select borders to be displayed

Select line style, color, and width for a border →

## Add a Showcase Box Behind the Table

An AutoShape will be used to add dimension since shadowing effects cannot be added to a table.

17. Use the rectangle AutoShape to create a showcase box slightly larger than the table.

18. Format the rectangle: Select a fill color complementary with the design template and slightly darker than the table fill colors. Select a line color, width, and style of your choice and add a shadow.

19. Send the rectangle behind the table (**Draw**, **Order**, **Send to Back**) and position with even borders on all sides of the table.

## Animate the Slide

20. Click **Slide Show, Custom Animation**.

21. Animate the slide as follows:
    • **First**: Clip art: Crawl from Left ➤ Start on Click ➤ Medium speed
    • **Second**: Rectangle: Appear ➤ Start on Click ➤ Fast speed
    • **Third**: Table: Vertical Out ➤ Start with Previous ➤ Fast speed
    • **Fourth**: Source note: Dissolve ➤ Start After Previous with .2 second delay ➤ Fast speed

# Creating Charts

Well-designed, appealing charts help the speaker convey quantitative information without overwhelming the audience. You will learn to enhance PowerPoint's basic default charts to create a bar chart and a pie chart that reflect good rules for formation of graphic aids. You will also learn to change the chart type to be certain you have depicted the data in a logical manner for the decision maker.

## Creating a Column Chart

A bar chart is effective for comparing quantities at a specific time while a line chart is effective for comparing quantities over time and illustrating trends. The bar chart is referred to as a column or vertical chart when the bars are presented vertically, as shown in the following slide, and a horizontal bar chart when the bars are presented horizontally. The chart must be labeled clearly so the audience understands key points; however, how the audience will use the data determines the extent of labeling (e.g., inclusion or omission of specific values and gridlines, etc.). To avoid visual distortion, the quantitative axis should begin at zero.

*Directions*: Follow the instructions to enhance the original slide by editing PowerPoint's default values.

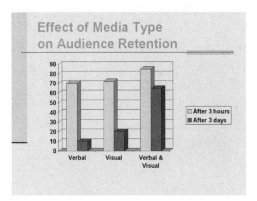

| Original Slide: Chart Built with | Enhanced Chart: Optimal |
| Software Default Values | Appeal and Readability |

1. Create a new slide using the Title and Chart layout from the Other Layouts category.

2. Key the title in the Title placeholder. Note the revised title reveals the interpretation of the data and allows the audience to grasp immediately the meaningfulness of the data as they relate to the point being developed—perceived worth of presentation visuals.

3. Consider whether the background object should be deleted to allow more space for the chart and eliminate unnecessary clutter. (To remove the graphics, click **Format**, **Background** and click to place a check in front of "Omit background graphics from master.")

## Designer's Pointer

Powerful software programs such as PowerPoint produce highly professional graphics for oral presentations and written reports. However, selecting the chart type that will depict data in the most effective manner is the first important decision you must make. Begin by identifying the primary idea you want the audience to understand related to your data. Then, choose an appropriate chart type using these general guidelines:

| Chart Type | Objective |
| --- | --- |
| Table | Shows exact figures |
| Bar chart (column or horizontal) | Compares one quantity with another quantity |
| Line chart | Illustrates changes in quantities over time |
| Pie chart | Shows how the parts of a whole are distributed |

Input your data into the datasheet. Then view your data in several chart types until you identify the chart type that communicates your primary idea most effectively.

## Select a Chart Type

4. Double-click the chart placeholder.

5. Click **Chart, Chart Type**.

6. Be sure the Standard Types tab is selected and note the various types of charts that can be built. Review the Designer's Pointer on page 106 that provides guidelines for selecting an appropriate graphic type for depicting data effectively.

7. Click **Column** and select the first option—the clustered chart. Note the various types of column charts displayed in the gallery.

Select Standard Types tab

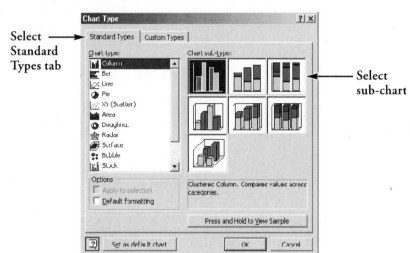

Select sub-chart

To view the data in a different chart type, click **Chart, Chart Type**, and select a different chart type and sub-type.

## Edit the Sample Datasheet to Build the Column Chart

8. Click in the first cell of the sample datasheet and input the data. Use the arrow keys to move to the next cell.

9. Input all remaining data and delete any sample data that remain (Column D and Row 3). Refer to the Troubleshooting Tip on page 109 if the structure of your column chart still reflects the extra row and column.

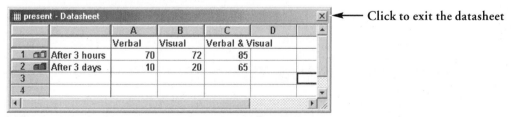

Click to exit the datasheet

| | | A | B | C | D |
|---|---|---|---|---|---|
| | | Verbal | Visual | Verbal & Visual | |
| 1 | After 3 hours | 70 | 72 | 85 | |
| 2 | After 3 days | 10 | 20 | 65 | |
| 3 | | | | | |
| 4 | | | | | |

10. Exit the datasheet to allow more space for formatting the column chart. To redisplay the datasheet for later revisions, click **View, Datasheet**.

### Input Labels

11. Click **Chart**, **Chart Options** and select the **Titles** tab.

12. Input the x-axis label: **Media Used**.

13. Input the z-axis (or y-axis) label: **Percentage**.

*Note*: No chart title is provided as the title appears in the Slide Title placeholder.

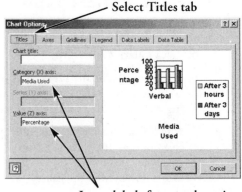

Select Titles tab

Input labels for x- and y-axis

### Format the Legend

14. Click **Chart**, **Chart Options** and select the **Legend** tab.

15. Click **Bottom**. Positioning the legend below the chart allows space for increasing the size of the chart for easy readability on a projected visual.

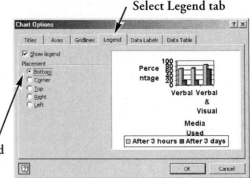

Select Legend tab

Move legend below chart

You used the menu command (**Chart**, **Chart Options**) to move the legend below the chart. An alternate method is to use the convenient right-click method. The Format Legend dialog box appears with three tabs for formatting the patterns, font, and placement. You can also right-click to access Chart Type and Chart Options (commands on the Chart Menu). Experiment and choose the method that works best for you.

### Size the Chart

16. Hold down the **Shift** key, point to a corner handle and drag the chart. Enlarge the chart to occupy the space below the slide title, allowing adequate even margins on all four sides. Use the model as a guide.

## Troubleshooting Tip

If you accidentally click off the chart and return to the slide, double-click the chart to return to the Chart Mode. To verify that you are working in Chart Mode, look for **Chart** as an option on the Menu toolbar and a diagonal border surrounding the chart.

# Troubleshooting Tip

If your chart has extra space to the right of the third column and a blank entry in the leg-end key as shown in the illustration, you likely deleted the data in Column D and Row 3 but not the column and row. Follow these commands:

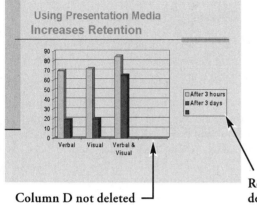

**Column D not deleted**

**Row 3 not deleted**

1. Select the unneeded column(s) (Column D) and click **Edit, Delete, Entire Column** (or right-click and click Delete).

2. Select the unneeded row(s) (Row 3) and click **Edit, Delete, Entire Row** (or right-click and click Delete).

## Animate the Chart

17. Click **Slide Show, Custom Animation**.

18. Select **Wipe from Bottom** in the Entry Animation box. This upward effect rein-forces the concept that the use of multimedia (verbal and visual) increases retention both short-term and long-term.

19. Click the down arrow to the right of the chart object in the Custom Animation list.

20. Click **Effect Options** and select the **Chart Animation** tab.

21. Select **By series**. Click **Play** and note the "after 3 hours" bars are displayed first, fol-lowed by the "after 3 days" bars.

22. Add a sound effect if you wish.

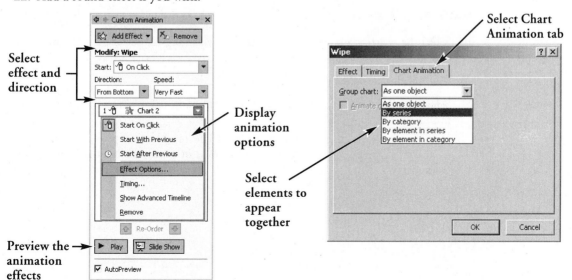

Select effect and direction

Display animation options

Select elements to appear together

Preview the animation effects

Select Chart Animation tab

## Enhance the Chart Format

You will now make four changes to enhance the appearance of the default column chart: (a) add a fill behind the chart area to add dimension to the slide, (b) increase the size of the labels for easier readability of text on a projected visual, (c) change the alignment of the y-axis label, and (d) change the bar colors. As you edit the chart, take note of other ways you can modify a column chart to increase appeal.

## Get Acquainted with the Chart Edit Technique

23. Be sure you are in the Chart Mode that allows you to modify a chart. Refer to the Troubleshooting Tip on page 108 if you are not sure.

24. Experiment with the use of the right mouse click to identify areas to be formatted.

   a) Move the mouse near the part of the chart you wish to format until a prompt identifying the selected section of the chart (e.g., Format _____ Area) appears. For example, pointing slightly below the top border of the chart selects the chart area (the entire chart including the bars, labels, legend, etc.) and the Format Chart Area prompt appears.

   b) Right-click, click **Format** _____, and input any changes in the dialog box that appears.

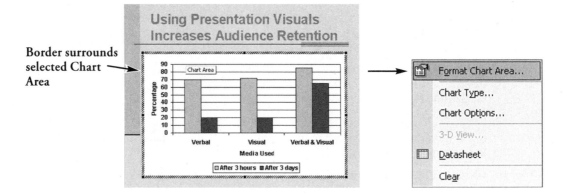

Border surrounds selected Chart Area →

## Add a Fill Behind the Chart

25. Select the chart area by pointing slightly below the top border of the chart until the Chart Area prompt appears.

26. Right-click and click **Format Chart Area**.

27. Select the Patterns tab and create appealing fill and border effects for the area surrounding the chart (chart area).

   a) Select a fill color complementary with the template. Experiment with creative fill effects (gradient, texture, pattern, or picture). Refer to Project 3 if necessary.

b) Select a line style, color, and weight complementary with the fill color.

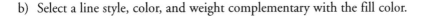

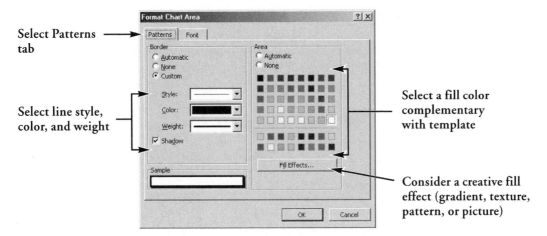

Select Patterns tab

Select line style, color, and weight

Select a fill color complementary with template

Consider a creative fill effect (gradient, texture, pattern, or picture)

# Designer's Pointer

If your presentation will include a number of charts, take the time to modify the slide color scheme to reflect the fill colors of the elements on the chart (bars, slices, levels of an organization chart, etc.). Devoting time to planning a standard chart design will assure a consistent look for all charts in a presentation, and will save you valuable production time that can be spent more wisely developing and practicing the presentation.

You can see in the sample slide in the Edit Color Scheme dialog box that the last four scheme colors in the list control the colors used in a chart. For example, the Fill color (fifth in the list at the left) is the fill color in any AutoShape drawn on a slide in this presentation, but is also the fill color for the first value in a bar chart, and so on. Refer to Project 4 to review the procedure for modifying a color scheme.

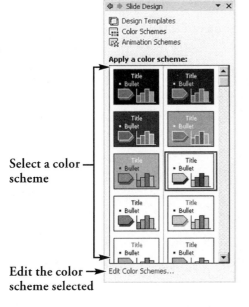

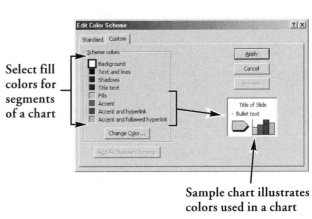

Select a color scheme

Edit the color scheme selected

Select fill colors for segments of a chart

Sample chart illustrates colors used in a chart

## Adjust the Font Size and Color of Text

28. Select the **Font** tab to specify the font face and font size of the labels (x- and y-axis) and the legend.

   a) Select an interesting, yet readable font (e.g., Arial) and select **Bold** as the font style and **20** points for front size to ensure readability.

   b) Select a font color that has high contrast with the fill effect and is complementary with the design template.

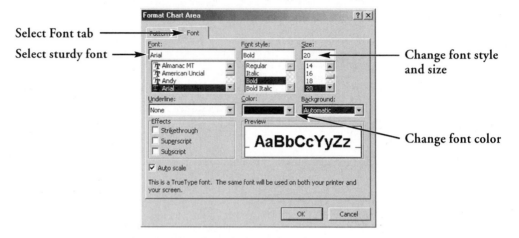

*Note:* Editing the chart area allows you to edit the font attributes of all three labels with one command. To modify one of these labels (the x- or the y-axis, or the legend), select the label you wish to edit, click the **Font** tab, and input changes.

## Change the Alignment of the Y-axis Label

29. Select the Value Axis Title area by clicking near the label *Percentage*. Refer to Steps 23–24 for selecting a specific section of the chart for editing if necessary.

30. Right-click and click **Format Axis Title**.

31. Select the **Alignment** tab.

32. Point to the red arrow controlling the orientation of the text and drag to the 12:00 position (from 0 to 90 degrees).

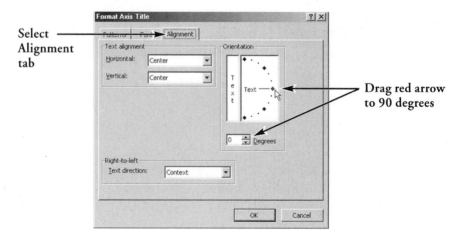

## Change the Scale for the Y-axis

To improve the readability and appeal of the y-axis scale, increase the size of the scale interval and change the maximum value to reflect the percentages depicted in the chart.

33. Select the Value Axis by pointing near the y-axis values.

34. Right-click and click **Format Value Axis**.

35. Input the following changes to the scale:

- Maximum value: 100
- Minimum value: 0
- Major unit: 20

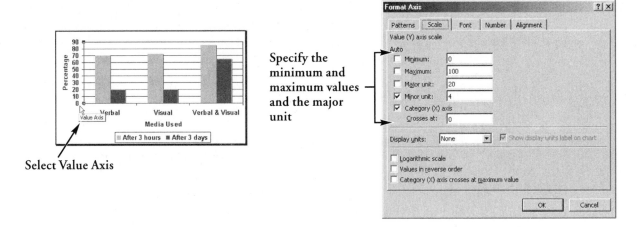

Select Value Axis

Specify the minimum and maximum values and the major unit

## Change the Bar Colors

Recolor the bars striving for high contrast with the fill effect behind the column chart (chart area) and an appealing color scheme consistent with other filled objects in the file Present.

36. Select the first series (after 3 hours) by pointing to and clicking one of these bars. Selection handles will appear on the "after 3 hours" bars at each point along the x-axis.

37. Right-click and click **Format Data Series**.

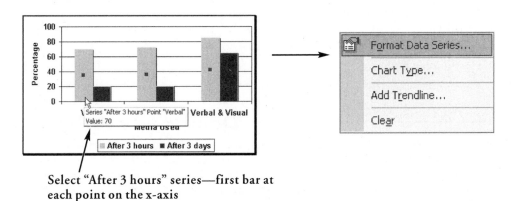

Select "After 3 hours" series—first bar at each point on the x-axis

38. Select the **Patterns** tab and select a fill color for the bars. Choose a color complementary with the design template that has high contrast with the fill behind the column chart (chart area). Experiment with creative fill effects (gradient, texture, pattern, or picture).

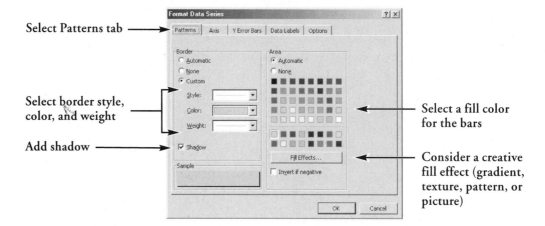

Select Patterns tab ⟶

Select border style, color, and weight ⟶

Add shadow ⟶

Select a fill color for the bars ⟵

Consider a creative fill effect (gradient, texture, pattern, or picture) ⟵

39. Repeat the process to recolor the "After 3 days" data series. The contrast between the colors you select for the two data series should be high so that the audience can easily distinguish between the two values. The Designer's Pointer highlights another important consideration for color components in a chart.

40. Get acquainted with other ways you can modify the format of the data series by clicking the other tabs: axis, y-error bars, data labels, and options.

## Enhance the Labels

41. Select the legend. Right-click and click **Format Legend**.

42. Select the Patterns tab and create appealing fill and border effects for the area surrounding the legend.

    a) Click **Fill Effects**, **Gradient** and blend two colors complementary with the template. Select the From Center shading style and the variant with the darker of the two colors in the center.

    b) Omit the border surrounding the legend to eliminate unnecessary clutter.

43. Create the same gradient fill on the y-axis label.

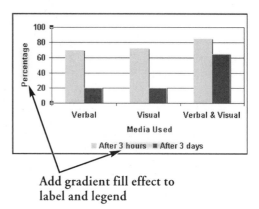

Add gradient fill effect to label and legend

## Designer's Pointer

Almost 10 percent of the population is color impaired and cannot distinguish between the colors red and green. Therefore, avoid using red and green as the colors of adjacent bars or pie slices. Additionally, avoid the use of red and green to differentiate between important points (green text on a red background or red text on a green background).

## Creating a Pie Chart

A pie chart is effective for showing how the parts of a whole are distributed. The whole is represented as a pie, with the parts becoming slices of the pie. Limit a pie chart to no more than six slices to avoid problems with complex, dense labeling. The largest slice or the slice to be emphasized should be placed at the twelve o'clock position and can be exploded for added emphasis. Preferably, place the label and value inside or just outside each slice to ease the audience's burden of interpreting the graph. A legend is a less effective method for identifying slices.

*Directions*: Follow the instructions to enhance the original slide by editing PowerPoint's default values.

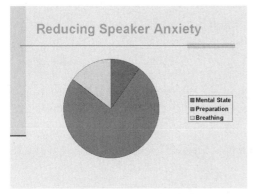

Original Slide: Chart Built with
Software Default Values

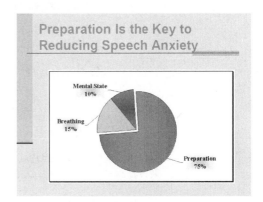

Enhanced Chart: Optimal
Appeal and Readability

1. Create a new slide using the Title and Chart layout from the Other Layouts category.

2. Key the title in the Title placeholder. Note that the revised title directs the audience's attention to the meaningfulness of the data in an engaging manner. The title communicates clearly how the data relates to the speaker's main point—research-based strategies for overcoming speech anxiety.

3. Consider whether the background object should be deleted to allow more space for the chart and eliminate any unnecessary clutter. (To remove the graphics, click **Format**, **Background** and click to place a check in front of "Omit background graphics from master.")

## Select a Chart Type

4. Double-click the Chart placeholder.

5. Click **Chart**, **Chart Type**.

6. Be sure the Standard Types tab is selected.

7. Click **Pie** from the Chart Type dialog box and select the first pie chart. Note the various types of pie charts displayed in the gallery.

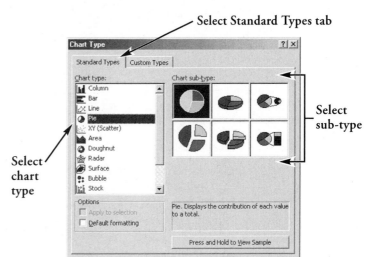

## Edit the Sample Datasheet

8.  Click in the first cell and input the data. Use the arrow keys to move to the next cell.

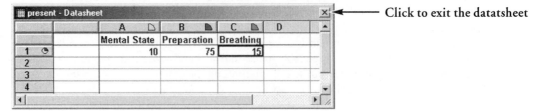

Click to exit the datatsheet

9.  Input the remaining data and exit the datasheet. To redisplay the datasheet for other revisions, click **View, Datasheet**.

10. Delete any unneeded rows and columns.  Refer to the Troubleshooting Tip on page 109 if necessary.

## Input the Chart Title

11. Do not include a title in the chart because the title will appear in the Title place-holder. If you wish to include the title in a chart, click **Chart, Chart Options**, select the **Titles** tab, and input the title.

## Format the Labels beside the Pie Slice for Improved Readability

12. Click **Chart, Chart Options** and select the **Data Labels** tab.

13. Click **Category name** to display the labels with the pie slide (e.g., Preparation).

14. Click **Percentage** to display the value and a percent sign beside the pie slice (e.g., 75%).

15. Be sure the Legend key option is not checked. If it is selected, the color-coded squares for each value in the legend will appear with the value beside the pie slice.

16. Be sure a check appears before the Show leader lines option. Lines that direct the audience's eyes from the pie slice to the related value will appear when you later drag the label away from the pie.

Select Data Labels tab

Select category name and percentage

Show leader lines but not legend key

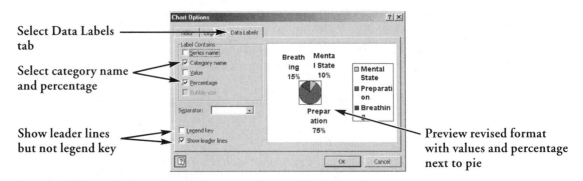

Preview revised format with values and percentage next to pie

## Omit Legend

The legend is displayed by default in the Chart layout, but is unnecessary when the value is displayed with the pie slice.

17. Click **Chart, Chart Options** and select the **Legend** tab.

18. Click to remove the check in front of the "Show Legend" box.

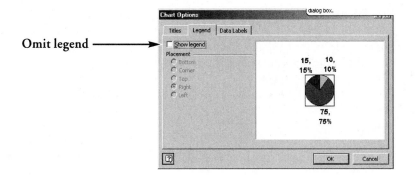

## Animate the Chart

19. Click **Slide Show, Custom Animation.**

20. Add a Wipe from Top animation effect or an effect of your choice.

21. Click the down arrow to the right of the chart object in the Custom Animation list.

22. Click **Effect Options** and select the **Chart Animation** tab.

23. Select **By category.**

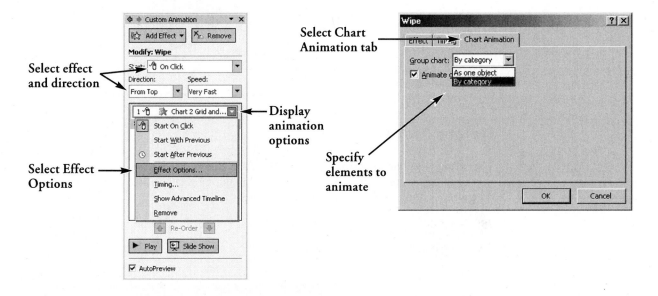

## Enhance the Chart Format

You will make the following changes to enhance the appearance of the default pie chart: (a) increase the size of the chart for added readability on a projected visual, (b) change the angle of the pie slices to adhere to guidelines for constructing pie charts, (c) change the slice colors for optimal contrast, and (d) explode the largest slice for added emphasis. As you proceed through the menus, take the time to acquaint yourself with other ways pie charts can be modified for added appeal.

## Get Acquainted with the Chart Edit Technique

24. Be sure you are in the Chart Mode and not in your slide. Refer to the Troubleshooting Tip on page 108 if necessary.

25. Experiment with the use of the right mouse click to identify areas to be formatted.

a) Move the mouse near the part of the chart you wish to format until a prompt appears identifying the selected section of the chart (e.g., Format _____ Area). For example, pointing slightly below the top border of the chart selects the chart area (the entire chart including the slices, labels, legend, etc.) and the Format Chart Area prompt appears.

b) Right-click, click **Format** _____ and input any changes in the dialog box that appears.

## Size Chart

26. Point near the pie to select the Plot Area. Right click and click **Format Plot Area**.

27. Hold down the **Shift** key as you drag a corner handle to enlarge the chart to occupy the space below the slide title.

28. Point to the border between the sizing handles and position the pie so that is balanced on the slide.

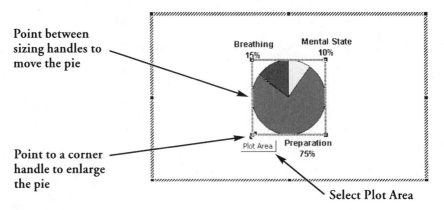

Point between sizing handles to move the pie

Point to a corner handle to enlarge the pie

Select Plot Area

## Delete Plot Marker

The rectangular border surrounding the Plot Area allows you to easily identify this section of the chart for enlarging the pie size and making other modifications. This useful design tool must be deleted once the pie chart has been built.

29. Select the Plot Area and right-click and click **Format Plot Area**.

30. Click **None** to specify no border around the plot area.

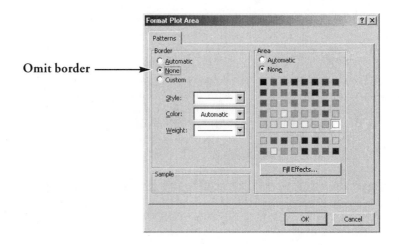

Omit border

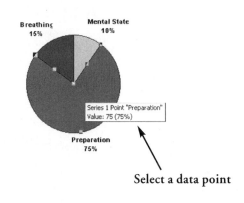

Select a data point

## Change the Angle of the Slices

PowerPoint's default setting must be adjusted to position the largest slice or the slice to be emphasized at the twelve o'clock position, a generally used guideline for constructing pie charts.

31. Point near one of the pie slices to select a Data Point area. Right-click and click **Format Data Point**.

*Note*: The angle can be changed if all data points are selected.

32. Select the **Options** tab.

33. Change the angle of the slice by clicking the spin arrow until the largest slice rotates to the 12:00 position.

Select Options tab

Click to change angle of slice

Largest slice is at the 12:00 position

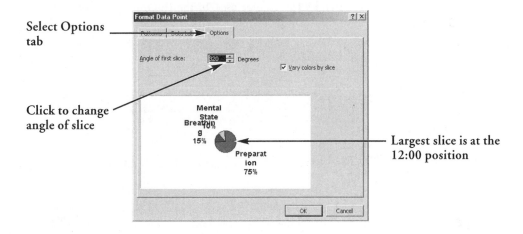

## Increase Font Size of Data Labels

34. Select the Data Labels area. Right-click and click **Format Data Labels**.

35. Select the **Font** tab and change the font size to 20 points to increase the readability of the labels.

## Position the Data Labels and Add Leader Lines

36. Point to one of the data labels and click until the sizing handles appear.

37. Drag the label away from the pie slice to display the leader lines. Position the label for balance and appeal.

38. Reposition the other labels following the same process. Use the model as a guide.

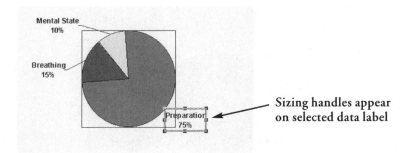

Sizing handles appear on selected data label

## Add a Fill Behind the Chart

39. Select the Chart Area. Right-click and click **Format Chart Area**.

40. Select the **Patterns** tab.

41. Apply the same fill and border effects that you applied to the column chart to ensure a consistency in the Present file. Reference the instructions for adding a fill effect to the column chart if necessary.

## Change the Slice Colors

You will recolor the pie slices striving for high contrast with the fill effect behind the pie chart (chart area) and an appealing color scheme consistent with the column chart in the file Present.

42. Select the largest slice (Preparation). Right-click and click **Format Data Series (Preparation)**.

43. Select the **Patterns** tab and select a color used in the column chart that will bring maximum attention to this most important slice in the pie.

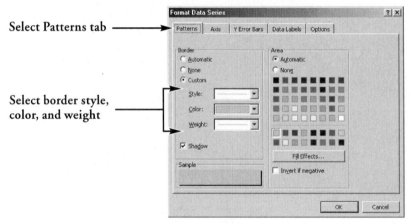

## Explode a Slice for Emphasis

44. Select the largest slice (Preparation). Right-click and click **Format Data Series (Preparation)**.

45. Drag to move the slice away from the pie slightly—just enough to provide added emphasis to this important relationship. Use the model as a guide.

## Enhance the Labels

46. Select the Data Series. Right-click and click **Format Data Series**.

47. Select the **Patterns** tab and apply the same gradient fill that you applied to the legend and y-axis label of the column chart. Omit the border surrounding the labels to eliminate unnecessary clutter.

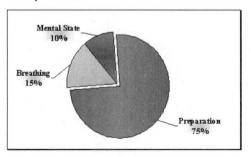

# Adding Creative Enhancements

Today's audiences (decision makers) look to effective speakers who can assist them in extracting needed information and meaning from the immense quantity of information available as a result of today's information explosion. The fundamental techniques you've already learned—selecting an appropriate chart for the data, using an engaging title that tells the audience exactly what should be taken away from the chart, and using a simple design that clarifies key data—are critical to controlling and managing information for your audiences. Depending on your audience's use of the information, you can further simplify the design to emphasize the key idea and to eliminate "chartjunk," decorative distractions that bury relevant data. Business presenters are also incorporating techniques that result in powerful, creative graphics that live up to a new standard of information graphics design set by news programs, *USA Today, Newsweek,* and other professional publications.

## Eliminating Chartjunk

*Directions*: Follow the instructions to build the slide as shown.

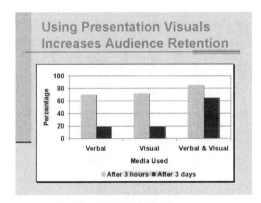

Original Slide                Simplified Chart

1. Make a copy of the column chart ("Using Presentation Visuals Increases Audience Retention") that you built earlier in this project. Refer to Project 1 for copying instructions if necessary.

2. Revise the slide title to reflect that percentages are being depicted; this addition is essential because the axes labels are not displayed in the simplified chart.

## Remove Labels

3. Double-click on the chart to edit the chart in Chart Mode.

4. Click **Chart, Chart Options** and select the **Titles** tab.

5. Delete the titles you input previously for the x-axis (Media Used) and the y-axis (Percentage).

## Add Values and Remove Gridlines

6. Click **Chart**, **Chart Options** and select the **Data Labels** tab.

7. Click **Value** to add the exact value above each bar.

Select Data Labels tab ⟶

Display value ⟶

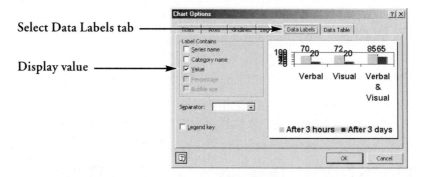

8. Click **Chart**, **Chart Options** and select the **Gridlines** tab.

9. Deselect the major and minor gridlines for the x- and y-axis.

Select Gridlines tab ⟶

Deselect major and minor gridlines ⟶

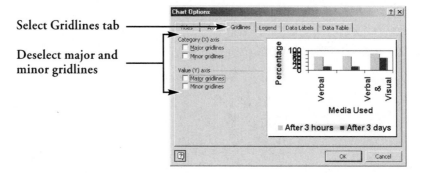

## Remove the X- and Y-Axes and the Plot Area

10. Click **Chart**, **Chart Options** and select the **Axes** tab.

11. Deselect the x- and y-axes by removing the check for Category (x) axis and Value (y) axis.

Select Axes tab ⟶

Deselect the x- and y-axes ⟶

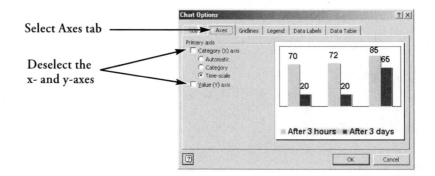

12. Select the Plot Area and right-click and click **Format Plot Area**.

13. Click **None** as the border.

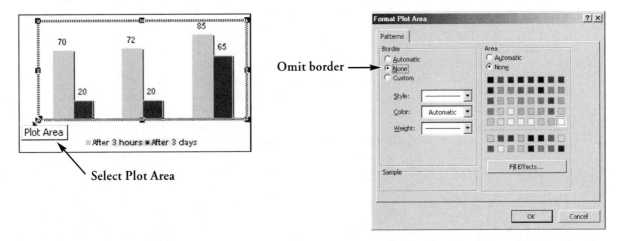

## Adding Eye-catching Fill Effects

*Directions*: Follow the instruction to build the slide as shown.

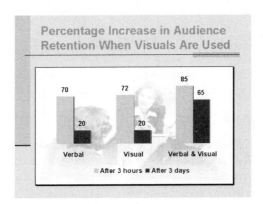

1. Make a copy of the column chart ("Percentage Increase in Audience Retention When Visuals Are Used") that you built earlier in this project.

2. Select a digital photograph obtained from the Microsoft Clip Gallery, a scanner, or digital camera.

3. Open the photograph file in a photo editing software (e.g., Microsoft Photo Editor or Microsoft Picture It) and create a transparent effect that will allow easy readability of the chart that will be superimposed over the photograph (e.g., decrease the brightness/contrast, soften the edges, etc.). Save the changes.

4. Add the photograph in the Chart Area.
   a) Select the Chart Area. Right-click and click **Format Chart Area**.
   b) Select the Patterns tab and click **Fill Effects**, **Picture**.
   c) Browse to insert your photograph.

## Designer's Pointer

Pictures also can be added as fill effects for bars and slices. It is important that you choose photographs carefully as the picture elements tend to distort as they attempt to fill the object area. Also, experiment with integrating clip art images outside or overlapping charts to aid the audience in visualizing your key point.

Recall the use of the clip art of the nervous speaker beside the table of top fears to highlight the anxiety associated with public speaking. Two side-by-side pie charts showing changes in the age demographics of the workforce could be enhanced by adding simple clip art images of workers of different ages (e.g., a younger worker overlapping the pie chart in an earlier time span, and an older worker overlapping the pie chart for the present or projected time spans). Notice other creative enhancements applied to graphics in printed or electronic sources.

# Inserting Slide Transitions

Add the Wipe from Left slide transition to the slides created in this project. Refer to Project 2 if necessary.

# Reinforcement Activities

Add the following slides for added reinforcement of the PowerPoint features you learned in this project. Position the slides as shown at the end of the project.

## Activity 1

Prepare a line chart showing earnings per share for the past five years for a company of your choice. Obtain the data from either a printed or online copy of the company's annual report. Provide an engaging title that interprets the data depicted in the chart and animate to emphasize the most important data.

## Activity 2

Select a chart from a corporate annual report or other leading publication and evaluate its effectiveness in clarifying or reinforcing major points (e.g., appropriate chart type; accurate labeling; engaging title that reveals key; simple, uncluttered design; honest representation of the data, etc.). Build the chart incorporating your suggestions for improvement. Animate to emphasize the most important data. Be prepared to discuss your improvements with your instructor or the class.

## Activity 3

Build a chart that presents compelling data to support a key point in a presentation you are currently developing. Alternatively, depict key data related to a timely issue (e.g., legal and ethical implications of technology, e-commerce, work/family balance, computer usage policies including Internet filtering, disaster recovery planning, violence in schools and the workplace, etc.). Select a chart type that will convey the data in the most effective manner. Refer to the Designer's Pointer related to chart types on page 106 if necessary. Strive for a simple, uncluttered design that presents the data clearly and honestly. Provide an engaging title that interprets the data depicted in the chart, and animate to emphasize the most important data.

# Slide Order

Print a copy of the file Present as an audience handout with six slides per page. Sequence the slides as shown. Your instructor may instruct you to print only the slides created or revised in Project 7 only (highlighted slides).

1. Title Slide
2. Effective Speakers (*revised*)
3. Average Presentation Rated
4. Top Mistakes Presenters Make
5. Presentation Objectives (*agenda slide*)
6. Challenges Facing Today's Speakers (*first divider slide*)
7. Demands Changing World Places on Speakers
8. Adapting Speaking Style to Today's Fast Pace
9. Meeting the Demands of Today's Audiences
10. Personal Connection a Must
11. A Speech Is a Gift
12. Systematic Process Is Key (*second divider slide*)
13. Clear Presentation Objective Drives a Successful Presentation
14. Benefits of Using Presentation Visuals
15. **Using Presentation Visuals Increases Audience Retention**
16. **Percentage Increase in Audience Retention When Visuals Are Used**
17. Designing Presentation Media In-house Makes Dollars and Sense (*revised*)
18. Considerations Affecting Presentation Media Choice (*revised*)
19. Types of Presentation Visuals
20. Multimedia
21. Still Projection Options
22. Boards and Flipcharts
23. Hard Copy Visuals
24. Process for Converting Slides to Overheads
25. Common Problems with Visuals
26. An Effective Design Is Transparent (*revised*)
27. The Speaker Is the Star
28. Guidelines for Effective Delivery
29. **Preparation Is the Key to Reducing Speech Anxiety**
30. Communicate Warmth and Confidence with Body Language

31. Vocal Qualities

32. Avoid Confusing Expressions

33. Contact Information

34. Additional Resources

35. Project 3, Activity 6 (position in file will vary)

# PROJECT 8

## Developing Useful Speaker's Notes and Professional Audience Handouts

## Learning Objectives

- Create speaker's notes designed to aid a speaker during delivery.
- Create professional audience handouts that extend the presentation and enhance the credibility of the speaker.

## Constructing Useful Speaker's Notes Pages

PowerPoint can be used to construct useful notes pages that aid the speaker in delivering a smooth, professional presentation. Notes pages can be created by (1) adding speaker notes while running the presentation for practice purposes and (2) inserting notes directly in the Notes pane of the Normal view.

### Adding Speaker's Notes While Rehearsing

*Directions:* Follow the instructions to create speaker's notes for one slide in the file Present. Print a copy to submit to your instructor.

1. Begin running the file Present in Slide Show view.

2. Right-click when you have advanced to the "Effective Speakers" slide, where you will input text.

3. Click **Speaker's Notes** from the menu.

4. Key the text shown in the illustration in the Speaker Notes dialog box.

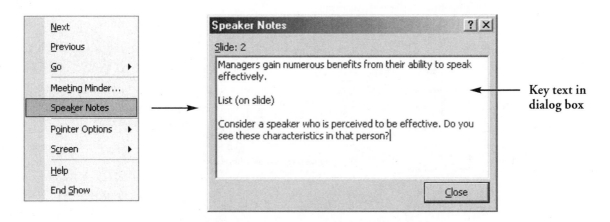

Key text in dialog box

# Presenter's Tip

Surprisingly, speakers frequently rely on notes less than they should. Under speaking pressure, speakers panic at the sight of dense, poorly prepared notes, and thus attempt to deliver the presentation without notes or they read a complete script. Preparing useful speaker's notes will reduce speaker anxiety and enhance a speaker's ability to deliver the presentation extemporaneously. Follow these guidelines for developing the content and format of useful speaker's notes to support your next presentation:

## Content

Use trigger statements that prompt you to remember the next point and highlight the logical flow of the slide. Include additional detail for content that demands precision and accuracy; for example, the introduction and conclusion, statistics, quotations, or a joke or humorous story with a punch line.

## Format

Develop an uncluttered, easy-to-read design for the notes page following these suggestions:

- Allow plenty of white space and a uniform structure (bulleted list, outline).

- Print in a large, easy-to-read font.

- Print on full-size pages that can be turned without distraction and numbered so they can be reordered quickly if they are dropped or mishandled.

- Keep notes neat with no last-minute confusing revisions, such as arrows denoting major reordering of ideas that likely won't be understood under pressure of speaking.

## Edit Notes in the Notes Pane

5. Press **Escape** and display Slide 2 in the Normal view. The text you keyed while running the presentation in Slide Show view appears in the Notes pane as illustrated below.

6. Select all the text in the placeholder by holding **Ctrl** and pressing **A (Ctrl-A)**.

7. Increase the font size to at least 14 points so the notes can be read easily in a darkened room (adjust the size of the print to a speaker's needs for a specific presentation).

8. Revise the notes if necessary. Add emphasis where needed (boldface, bulleted lists).

9. Continue to the next section.

Drag borders between panes for more space in Notes pane

Click in Notes pane to edit notes

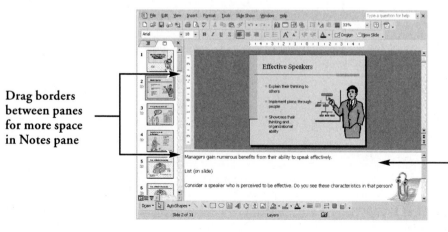

## Adding Speaker's Notes in the Notes Pane

*Directions:* Create speaker's notes for one slide in the file Present following the guidelines for writing and formatting useful speaker's notes provided in the Presenter's Tip. Print a copy to submit to your instructor.

1. Display a slide of your choice in Normal view and set the Zoom at 66% so that the text can be read easily.

2. Key the text—a few trigger statements to prompt your thoughts and remind you of the logical flow of the discussion for this slide.

3. Select all the text in the placeholder by holding **Ctrl** and pressing **A** (**Ctrl-A**).

4. Increase the font size to at least 14 points so that the notes can be read easily in a darkened room (adjust the size to fit a speaker's needs for a specific presentation).

5. Add emphasis where needed using boldface, bulleted lists, etc.

6. Continue to the next section.

## Adding a Header and a Footer to the Notes Pages

Add informative headers/footers to notes pages to identify them clearly for later use. Adding page numbers is especially helpful for keeping pages ordered correctly.

*Directions:* Add a header and a footer to the notes pages of the file Present. Print a copy to present to your instructor.

1. Click **View**, **Header and Footer**.

2. Be sure the Notes and Handouts tab is selected and edit the Header and Footer dialog box:

   a) Click to select Date and time box if you wish to print this information on each slide and click **Update automatically** to update the date. Key the date in the dialog box.
   b) Click to select the Header box and, in the dialog box, input the title of the presentation **Planning and Delivering Compelling Presentations**.
   c) Click to select the Page number box to print a page number on each notes page.
   d) Click to select the Footer box and, in the dialog box, key **Presented by** *Your Name*.
   e) Click **Apply to All**.

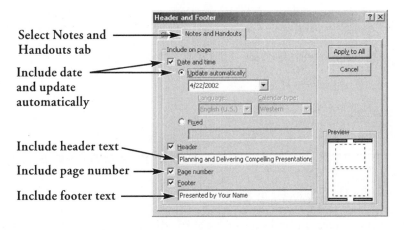

## Print Notes Page for Selected Slides

3. Click **File**, **Print** and edit the Print dialog box:

a) Select **Slides** in the Print Range box, input **2**, then the slide number of the slide of your choice.

b) Select **Notes Pages** in the Print what box.

c) Click **OK**.

Select slides to be printed ⟶

Specify notes pages format ⟶

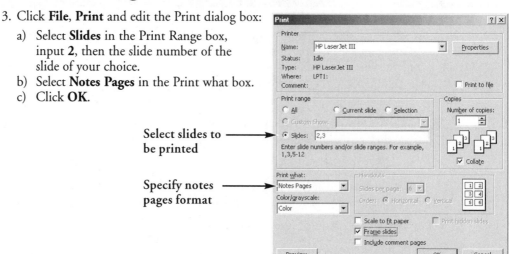

# Creating Professional Audience Handouts

Audience handouts must reflect the same degree of professionalism as the slide show and the speaker's delivery. Create professional handouts that increase a speaker's credibility by editing the Handout Master and exporting presentation slides to Microsoft Word for more elaborate formatting.

## Editing the Handout Master

*Directions:* Follow the instructions to change the format of the handout master for the file Present. Print a copy to present to your instructor.

1. Click **View**, **Master**, **Handout Master**. You will add text to the four placeholders on the handout master (shown in the illustrations).

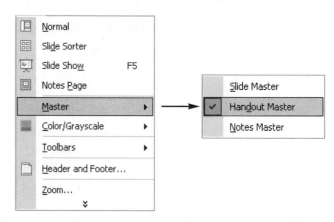

# Presenter's Tip

Adding an appealing header/footer to a top-notch handout increases a speaker's credibility as a competent person in the specific area being discussed. Also, the complete identification (name, company, and date) serves as an advertisement for a presenter and his/her company.

2. Edit the header placeholder:

   a) Click in the header placeholder and input the title of the presentation **Planning and Delivering Compelling Presentations**.

   b) Select a font face of your choice and set the font size to 9 points and bold face.

   c) Resize the placeholder so the text appears on one line.

3. Edit the date placeholder:

   a) Click in the date area.

   b) Highlight the text that appears in the placeholder (Date/Time) and key the date.

   c) Format the text to match the text in the header area using the shortcut illustrated in the FYI feature box on page 132.

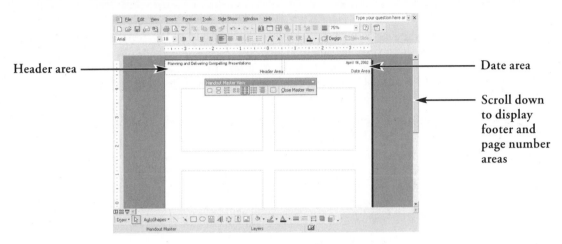

4. Edit the footer placeholder:

   a) Click in the footer placeholder and input **Prepared by Your Name**.

   b) Press **Enter** and key the title of the course you are taking that requires you to complete this presentation.

   c) Format the text to match the text in the other placeholders using the shortcut illustrated in the FYI feature box on page 132.

5. Edit the page number placeholder:

   a) Click in the page number placeholder.

   b) Input the word **Page** before the text that appears in the placeholder (#). Highlight the text and format it to match the text in the other placeholders using the shortcut illustrated in the FYI feature box on page 132.

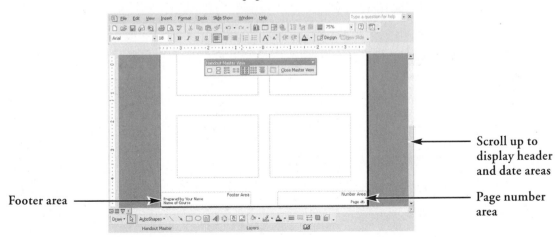

## Print Handouts for Slides 1–3

6. Click **File**, **Print**.

7. Edit the Print dialog box:

   a) Select **Slides** in the Print range box and input **1–3**.
   b) Select **Handouts** in the Print what box and select **3 per page**.

8. Click **OK**.

## Creating Audience Handouts Using the Send-to-Word Feature

Editing the Handout Master enhances the appeal of slides created using the PowerPoint print option. Exporting slides to Microsoft Word provides additional template layouts as well as the power of Word to create a custom format that works best for your presentation. Refer to the Designer's Pointers on pages 134–135 for additional advice on preparing these custom handouts.

*Directions:* Follow the instructions to export the presentation file Present to Word and then input notes in the available space.

1. Click the **Color/Grayscale** button on the Standard toolbar and select the **Pure Black and White** button to convert the slides to black and white. Omit this step if you intend to print using a color printer.

Select Pure Black and White →

Color/Grayscale

**FYI**

The Format Painter is a fast, convenient way to format text for consistency between similar design elements. This shortcut is especially helpful when the format to be copied contains multiple commands (e.g., change of font face and font size and a print attribute such as bold). To use the Format Painter,

1. Select the text that is already formatted (e.g., header area).

2. Click the **Format Painter** button. The mouse pointer turns to a paint brush.

**Format Painter**

3. Click and drag the paint brush over the area to be reformatted (Date Area).

4. Select the Format Painter again and repeat to format other text.

2. Click **File**, **Send to**, **Microsoft Word**.

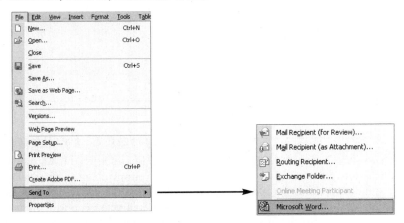

3. Take a moment to study the five available layouts: Notes next to slides, Blank lines next to slides, Notes below slides, Blank lines below slides, and Outline only. Each of these formats can be accomplished through the PowerPoint print option except for adding "Notes next to slides" and printing "Blank lines below slides."

4. Select **Notes next to slides**. The Notes pane will appear in a notes column beside the slide.

5. Wait as your presentation is exported to Microsoft Word and formatted into a three-column table. The notes you keyed in a previous activity will appear beside two slides. Refer to the Designer's Pointer on page 135 for an explanation of the text shown beside Slide 1.

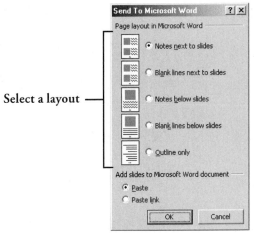

Select a layout

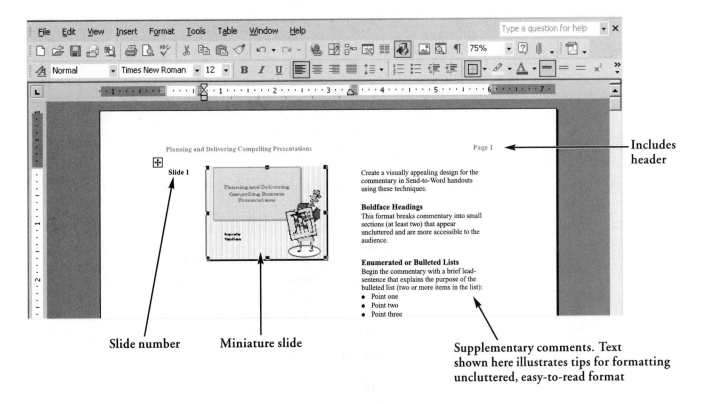

Includes header

Slide number

Miniature slide

Supplementary comments. Text shown here illustrates tips for formatting uncluttered, easy-to-read format

6. Save this Word document as **Present.doc**. Note the file size is extremely large because of the graphic intensity of the content.

---

## Designer's Pointer

The notes next-to-slides format automatically creates a highly professional handout with a handy column inserted to the right of the slide for adding supplementary notes related to the slide content or questions for consideration. The "take home package" is especially useful for an audience who will be responsible for the material covered in the presentation, such as seminar participants in required training programs. Additionally, the commentary will aid persons who cannot attend the presentation but are responsible for the material or who simply wish to benefit from the presentation.

The commentary shown for selected slides in the file Present on page 135 includes brief, precise statements that help the audience immediately grasp the relevance of the slide. Repetition of information included on the slide is not needed as the slide appears with the commentary; examples provided during the presentation but not included on the slide might be summarized here.

---

## Delete Unneeded Slides

7. Select the row containing the slide "A Speech Is a Gift" by clicking in the first column and dragging across to highlight the entire column.

8. Click **Table**, **Delete** and select **Rows**. The row is deleted and the other slides move up to fill the space. Alternatively, highlight the row, right-click, and click Delete Cells, Delete entire row.

**Delete selected → row(s)**

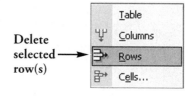

9. Repeat the procedure to delete any other slides you believe should not be included in a formal handout.

## Input Supplementary Notes in the Send-to-Word Handout

*Directions:* Follow the instructions to input supplementary notes to one slide.

1. Click in the Notes column (third column) to the right of a slide of your choice. Key notes that will aid even a person who was not present in understanding the slide. Follow the format tips described in the Designer's Pointer on page 135 and shown in the illustration on page 133 to avoid dense, unappealing text.

2. Scroll to display the text for the two slides you added earlier. Change the format to match the format of the notes you input directly in the Word document if necessary.

3. Continue to the next section to complete the Send to Word handout.

## Designer's Pointer

Create a visually appealing format that will entice the audience to read rather than discard your handout. Use the design to help the audience quickly comprehend your content and highlight important information for maximum attention. The statements in the model are simply keyed as a paragraph in a 10- or 11-point font but are visually appealing because of their brevity. To avoid a cluttered, unorganized look for longer commentary, consider using the following:

- Headings to partition the commentary into short sections the audience can access more easily.

- Enumerated or bulleted lists to bring greater impact to items in a series. A brief lead-in sentence that clearly clarifies the purpose of the bulleted list will help the audience find immediate meaning.

You can see these techniques applied in the illustration on page 133.

Include in a formal audience handout only the slides you anticipate the audience will need for later reference. For example, exclude dramatic opening or closing slides used to capture the audience's attention and any graphic-intensive slides that may not have meaning outside the presentation. Evaluate the usefulness of each slide closely if you have one slide printed on the last page so you can minimize reproduction and distribution costs.

**Planning and Delivering Compelling Presentations**    **Page 1**

**Slide 1**

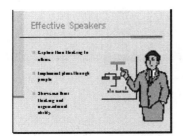

Managers gain numerous benefits from their ability to speak effectively. Do you see these characteristics in a person perceived to be an effective speaker?

**Slide 2**

Low ratings of average presentations given in business today support the need for managerial training in public speaking skills.

**Slide 3**

While delivery techniques are vital to an effective presentation, most of the top mistakes made by presenters can be eliminated by careful planning and practice (e.g., clear objectives, preparation, effective opening and close, strong visual support, etc.).

## Adding a Header and a Footer to a Send-to-Word Handout

*Directions:* Follow the instructions to add a header and a footer to the presentation Present. Print a copy to present to your instructor.

### Insert a Header

1. Click **View, Header and Footer.**

2. Click in the header placeholder and input the title of the presentation **Planning and Delivering Compelling Presentations**.

3. Press **Tab** until the cursor reaches the end of the placeholder. Key the text **Page** and space once.

4. Click **Insert Page Number** in the Header and Footer dialog box. The number *1* appears to the right of the word *Page*. This number will change as you move through the pages of the document. You can change the beginning page number to a value other than 1 by clicking the Format Page Number button.

5. Highlight all text in the header placeholder. Format with a font face of your choice, a font size of 9 points, and bold face.

6. Click **Switch between Header and Footer** to move to the footer placeholder at the bottom of the page.

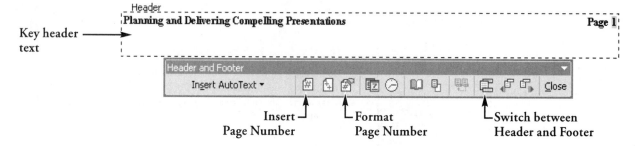

Key header text

Insert Page Number   Format Page Number   Switch between Header and Footer

### Insert a Footer

7. Click in the footer placeholder and input the text **Prepared by your name**.

8. Press **Enter** and key the text **Name of your university/company.**

9. Press the **Tab** key until the cursor reaches the end of the placeholder. Key the current date.

10. Highlight all text in the footer placeholder. Format this text to match the header using the Format Painter feature to ensure consistency. (Review the FYI feature box on page 132 if necessary.)

11. Click **Close** to exit the header and footer area and return to the document.

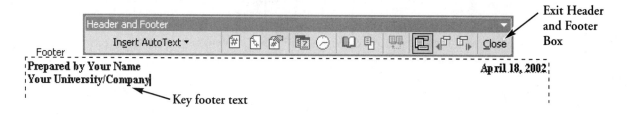

Exit Header and Footer Box

Key footer text

**Print Send-to-Word Handout**

12.  Click **File**, **Print** and **OK**.

# Reinforcement Activities

Complete the following activities for added reinforcement of the PowerPoint features you learned in this project.

## Activity 1

Create the speaker's notes for a presentation you are currently developing using both techniques presented in this project: (a) adding notes as you complete an actual dry run of your presentation or (2) inserting notes in the Notes pane. Be prepared to share with your instructor your opinion of the specific usefulness of each method. Print the notes pages to submit to your instructor.

## Activity 2

Edit the Handout Master for a presentation you are currently developing to include complete identification of the presentation (title of presentation, date, preparer, and page number). Print the slides six to a page to submit to your instructor.

## Activity 3

Create a Send-to-Word handout for a presentation you are currently developing. To the right of each slide, add precise commentary that will increase the usefulness of the handout following the presentation. Develop a visually appealing format for the commentary, and include complete identification for the presentation in a header/footer. Print the file to submit to your instructor.

# Slide Order

Slides are sequenced in the order shown in Project 7, page 125.

# PROJECT 9

## Learning Objectives

- Hide a slide that can be accessed conveniently should the information be needed during a presentation.

- Create hyperlinks to the Internet and to slides within a presentation using the mouse click and mouse over techniques.

- Create a series of hyperlinks accessed from a summary slide to provide increased flexibility over the sequence in which the slides are displayed.

- Link a PowerPoint chart to a Microsoft Excel notebook to update data in the chart automatically when changes are made in the notebook file.

## Adding Interactivity to Slides

Experienced speakers recognize the importance of adapting a presentation in response to feedback received from an audience during an actual presentation. Hidden slides and hyperlinks build flexibility and convenience into an electronic presentation by allowing the speaker to move through a presentation in sequences other than the typical linear pattern from the first slide to the last, and launch other applications automatically (e.g., notebook file or an Internet browser).

### Hiding a Slide

A hidden slide allows you to customize a slide show for a particular audience. You simply mark slides you don't want to project unless the information on the slide is needed during a presentation. For example, you may want to include on a hidden slide detailed data needed to substantiate a point in case an audience asks for further explanation.

*Directions:* Follow the instructions to hide specific slides and to project the hidden slides during the presentation.

1. Display the file Present in the Slide Sorter view.

### Hide a Slide

2. Select two slides of your choice and click the **Hide Slide** button on the Slide Sorter toolbar. A diagonal line appears over the slide number to indicate the slide is hidden.

Hide Slide
button

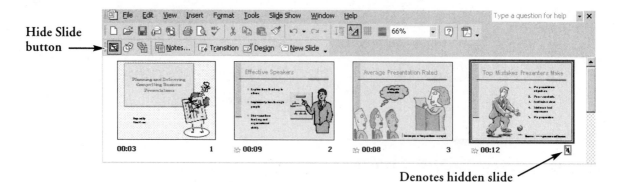

Denotes hidden slide

3. Select the slide that immediately precedes the hidden slide.

4. Click the **Slide Show View** button to begin running the presentation.

5. Click the mouse once. Note that the slide following the hidden slide is displayed, bypassing the hidden slide.

## View a Hidden Slide

6. Select the slide that immediately precedes the hidden slide.

7. Click the **Slide Show View** button to begin running the presentation.

8. Press the letter **H** to advance to the hidden slide.

## Unhide a Slide

9. Select the hidden slide in the Slide Sorter view.

10. Click the **Hide Slide** button on the Slide Sorter toolbar (or click Slide Show, Hide). The diagonal line over the slide number is removed. Alternatively, right click the Slide icon in the Outline pane and click Hide.

## Presenter's Tip

Another way to view a hidden slide is to right-click and click **Go**, **Slide Navigator**. The slide number of a hidden slide is enclosed in parentheses in the list of titles. Using the keyboard command presented in the previous activity (Steps 6–8) is preferable because of the seamless delivery. The effort spent completing these mouse clicks and the display of several unattractive drop-down menus draw attention away from the speaker and toward the technology.

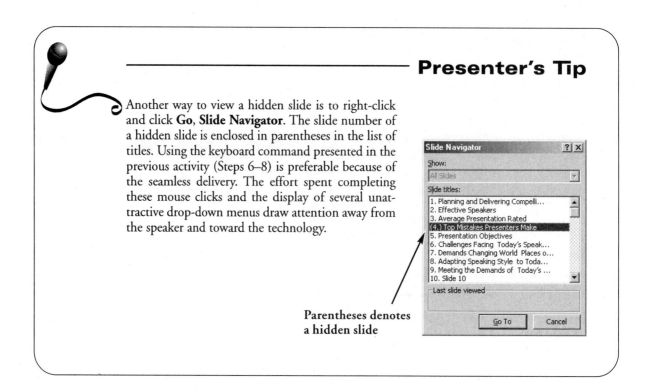

Parentheses denotes
a hidden slide

# Creating Hyperlinks

A *hyperlink* is an area of the screen the speaker clicks to move to a variety of locations automatically. In this project you will create hyperlinks to (1) access a Web site, (2) move to a specific slide within a presentation, and (3) open a Microsoft Excel notebook. Hyperlinks can also be added to move to a different PowerPoint presentation and numerous other locations.

## Adding a Hyperlink to a Web Site

*Directions:* Follow the instructions to create a hyperlink to a Web site.

### Insert Hyperlink

1. Display the "Top Mistakes Presenters Make" slide in Normal view.

2. Highlight the source note text: **http://www.presentersonline.com**

3. Click **Insert**, **Hyperlink**.

4. Input the URL address for the source **http://www.presentersonline.com**. The text you highlighted in Step 2 is now displayed on the slide in a different color—the color of the hyperlink before it is accessed.

Add hyperlink to source note

Input URL address

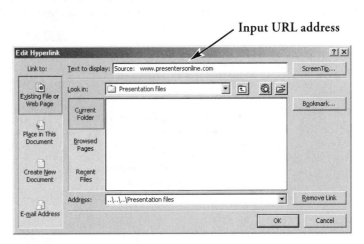

### Access the Hyperlink to Verify Accuracy

5. Display the slide in Slide Show view.

6. Move the mouse over the hyperlinked text (words accented in a different color) until the hand pointer appears.

A hyperlink can be created from any object on the slide—text, clip art, photograph, AutoShape, table, graph, diagram, etc.

7. Click the text to access the hyperlink, which opens the default Internet browser and connects to the appropriate Web site.

8. Click the **Exit** or **Minimize** button in the Internet browser to return to the presentation still running in Slide Show view.

Click the hyperlink when the hand pointer appears

## Edit the Color Scheme for the Hyperlink

You will need to specify colors for the hyperlink before and after it has been accessed. Select colors with high contrast to the background to ensure that the audience can read the text. Review editing color schemes in Project 4 if necessary.

9. Click **Format**, **Slide Design**.

10. Click **Color Schemes** and **Edit Color Schemes**.

11. Change the color of the hyperlink before it is accessed.
    a) Select the color thumbnail for "Accent and hyperlink."
    b) Click **Change Color** and select a color from the Standard or Custom tab.

12. Repeat the process in Steps 9–11 to select a color for the "Accent and followed hyperlink" color thumbnail, which controls the color of hyperlink after it has been accessed.

Select color for hyperlink before it is accessed

Select color for hyperlink after it is accessed

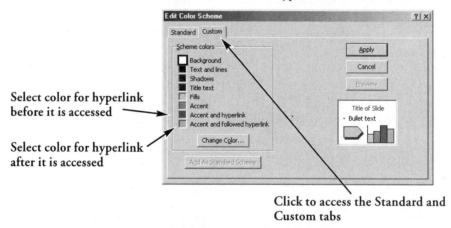

Click to access the Standard and Custom tabs

## Hyperlinking Using the Mouse Over Technique

*Directions:* Follow the instructions to create a hyperlink to a specific slide that you will access by moving the mouse over the hyperlinked object rather than pointing to the object and clicking the mouse.

### Insert a Hyperlink

1. Display the "Adapting Speaking Style to Today's Fast Pace" slide in Normal view.

2. Select the photograph and click **Slide Show**, **Action Settings**.

3. Select the **Mouse Over** tab. Note the mouse click is the default method for accessing a hyperlink.

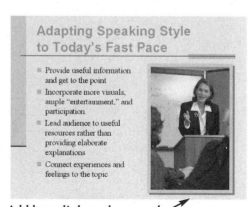

Add hyperlink to photograph

4. Click the **Hyperlink to** option.

5. Click the list arrow and select **Next Slide**.

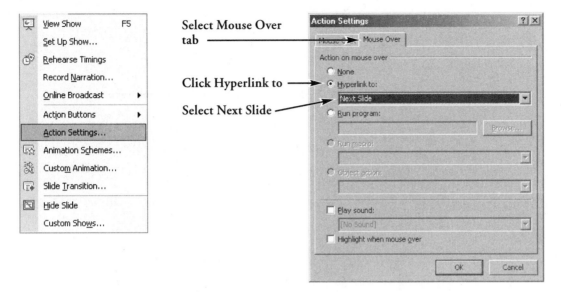

## Access the Hyperlink

6. Display the slide in Slide Show view.

7. Move the mouse across the photo without clicking, and the slide advances to the next slide ("Meeting the Demands of Today's Audiences").

# Troubleshooting Tip

A hyperlink cannot be applied to a grouped object. Thus, if you add a showcase box (AutoShape with enhancements) behind the photo in the activity, do not group the two objects. Instead, animate the objects to be displayed together. Refer to Project 3, "Enhancing with Custom Animation" if necessary.

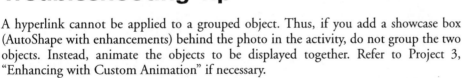

## Creating Hyperlinks on a Summary Slide

Hyperlink buttons created with AutoShapes create a subtle, virtually transparent design. Attention remains directed toward the speaker and the message—unlike with the obvious underlined hyperlinks illustrated in the original slide. Hyperlink buttons are dynamic and appealing, and the audience is unaware of the presence of a hyperlink until the speaker accesses it.

*Directions:* Follow the instructions to enhance the original slide and create four hyperlinks that will allow you to jump to specific slides in the file Present. You will create (a) a hyperlink from each button to a specific slide in the presentation and (2) return hyperlinks to jump back to the summary slide, where you can draw attention to the summary list before transitioning into the discussion of the next point hyperlinked.

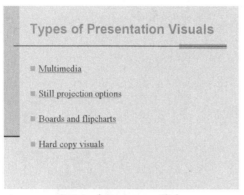

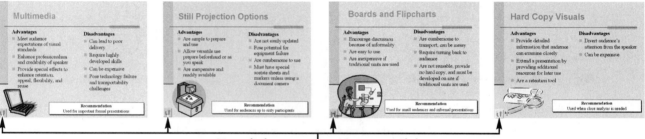

Hyperlinks to return to Summary Slide

1. Display the "Types of Presentation Visuals" slide in Normal view.

2. Delete the bulleted list placeholder.

## Create a Master Design for the Hyperlink Buttons

3. Click **AutoShapes**, **Basic Shapes**, **Bevel**.

4. Drag to draw the button.

5. Release the mouse and key the text describing the first hyperlink in the text box in front of the button **Multimedia**.

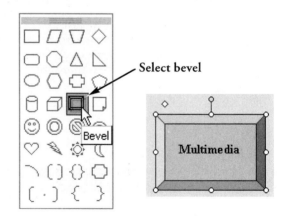

6. Format the button and the text allowing space for the four buttons to appear attractively on the slide as shown in the model.

   a) Center the text in the button.

   b) Select an appealing font face and size that fits in the button but is large enough to be read easily. Add effects such as bold or shadow to create the appearance of your choice.

**FYI**

A shortcut for editing an AutoShape is to right-click and click **Format, AutoShape**. The tabs allow you to conveniently edit (a) colors and lines, (b) size, and (c) position. Specific techniques that can be applied from these menus follow:

## Size Tab

1. Input an exact dimension and then compare these values with other AutoShapes to ensure consistency.

2. Input a percentage in the scale section. Click **Lock aspect ratio** to change the height and width proportionally.

Input exact dimensions

Resize proportionally

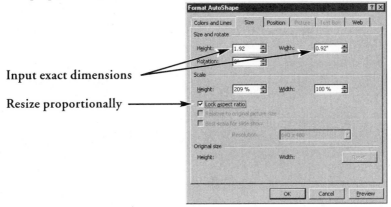

## Position Tab

Increase or decrease the horizontal or vertical placement to align an object in a precise location.

Input specific value

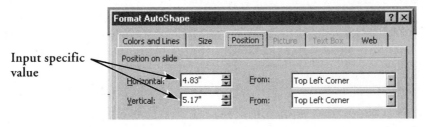

## Create the Remaining Buttons Using the Copy Feature to Ensure Consistency

7. Select the completed button and hold down the **Ctrl** key as you drag the button. An icon with a plus sign appears as you drag the slide, indicating an object is being moved.

8. Release the mouse to drop the button in a new location on the slide.

9. Repeat steps 7–8 to create two additional buttons. Position the four buttons attractively on the slide.

10. Edit the text in each copied button to create the following four buttons:
   - **Top left:** Multimedia (already keyed)
   - **Top right:** Still projection options
   - **Bottom left:** Boards and flipcharts
   - **Bottom right:** Hard copy visuals

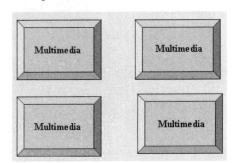

## Insert the Hyperlinks

11. Click to select the first button (Multimedia).

12. Click **Slide Show**, **Action Settings**.

13. Be sure the Mouse Click tab is selected.

14. Click the **Hyperlink to** option.

15. Click the list arrow and select **Slide**.

16. Scroll down and select the "Multimedia" slide as the destination of the hyperlink—the slide where the hyperlink will jump when it is accessed.

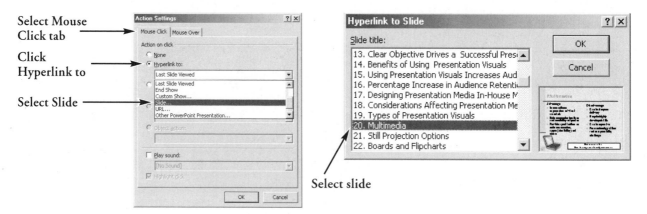

Select Mouse Click tab

Click Hyperlink to

Select Slide

Select slide

17. Repeat Steps 12–16 to insert the hyperlinks from each of the other three buttons on the summary slide to its related slide describing the advantages and disadvantages of each visual type.

## Create the Return Hyperlinks

18. Display the "Multimedia" slide in Slide view.

19. Click **Slide Show**, **Action Buttons** (or click AutoShapes, Action Buttons).

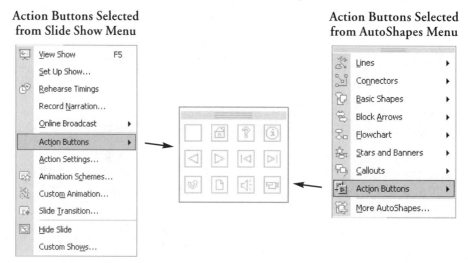

**Action Buttons Selected from Slide Show Menu**

**Action Buttons Selected from AutoShapes Menu**

20. Note the variety of return buttons available. You can use ready-made action buttons that depict commonly understood symbols (arrows that refer to next, previous, first and last slide; information, help; sound; and movies) or create a custom button using your own text or graphics.

21. Select the return arrow 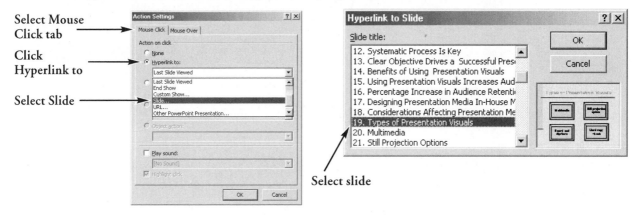 or create a custom button **Menu** that will remind you to go back to the summary slide "Types of Presentation Visuals."

22. Drag to draw the button and release the mouse to display the Action Settings dialog box.

23. Be sure the Mouse Click tab is selected.

24. Click the **Hyperlink to** option.

25. Click the drop-down list and select **Slide**.

26. Scroll down and select the "Types of Presentation Visuals" slide as the destination of the hyperlink—the slide where the hyperlink will jump when it is accessed.

Select Mouse Click tab

Click Hyperlink to

Select Slide

Select slide

## Edit the AutoShape (the Button)

27. Select a fill color, line color, and line style. Consider using a design similar to the button on the summary slide as a reminder of the destination.

28. Size the button to achieve a subtle look but large enough to click conveniently while running the presentation.

## Create the Remaining Buttons Using the Copy Feature to Ensure Consistency

29. Select the hyperlink button and click **Copy**.

30. Display the "Still Projection Options" slide in Normal view.

31. Click **Paste** to insert the hyperlink button on this slide. Note that the copied button already includes the correct action setting to jump to the summary slide "Types of Presentation Visuals."

32. Paste the hyperlink button on the "Boards and Flipcharts" and the "Hard Copy Visuals" slides.

## Access the Hyperlinks to Verify Accuracy

33. Display the "Types of Presentation Visuals" slide in the Slide Show view.

34. Click the first hyperlink button (Multimedia) and verify that the slide show advances to the "Multimedia" slide.

35. Click the return hyperlink on the "Multimedia" slide and verify that the slide returns to the summary slide "Types of Presentation Visuals."

36. Verify the accuracy of the other three hyperlink buttons on the summary slide and each return hyperlink to the summary slide. Follow this procedure for editing an action setting if the hyperlink does not jump to the correct slide:

   a) Right-click and click **Edit Hyperlink**.
   b) Edit the Action Setting Box by selecting the correct slide from the list of slide titles.

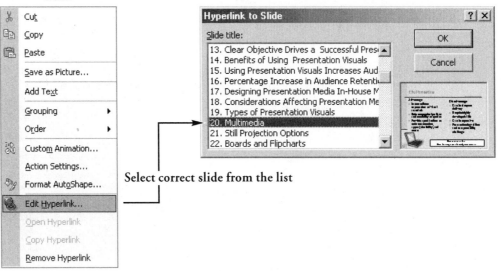

Select correct slide from the list

---

 ## Designer's Pointer

A return hyperlink can be omitted on the last slide ("Hard Copy Visuals") if the speaker plans to access the hyperlinks in the order presented on the slide. The speaker advances to the next slide rather than return to the summary slide ("Types of Presentation Visuals"). However, adding the hyperlink to each button gives the speaker flexibility to adapt the presentation order to meet the audience's needs or to omit sections, if necessary, to fit the time slot. Also, an individual viewing a presentation posted on the Web could access the hyperlinks in any order and return conveniently to the summary slide, as you will see in Project 10.

# Linking a Chart Created in Excel to a PowerPoint Slide

Linking documents allows managers to update timely information in a source document with automatic updates to any linked object. For example, current values input into a notebook file are reflected in other documents linked to this notebook file; e.g., charts in a written report prepared in word processing software and slides prepared in PowerPoint.

## Presenter's Tip

A speaker can use the linking feature to facilitate an audience's analysis of various viable solutions to a problem. Using a spreadsheet linked to a chart in PowerPoint, the speaker inputs the values for a specific "what if" analysis and then switches to project the results on a PowerPoint slide.

## Creating a Notebook File

*Directions:* To complete this project, you will create a column chart using Microsoft Excel, link the Excel chart to a slide in the PowerPoint file Present, and revise the source document noting the automatic update of the chart on the PowerPoint slide.

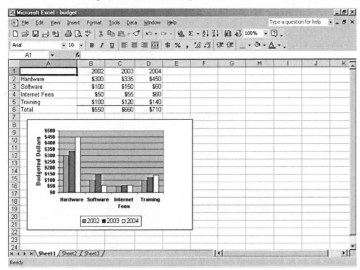

Chart Created in Microsoft Excel
(Source document)

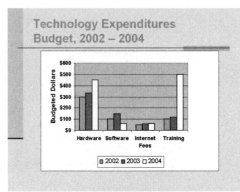

Slide with Chart Linked to the
Microsoft Excel File

## Create the Notebook File

1. Open Microsoft Excel (Click **Start**, **Programs**, **Office 2002**, **Excel**).

2. Enter the labels and amounts (including the $ signs) shown for each cell.

|   | A | B | C | D |
|---|---|---|---|---|
| 1 |   | 2002 | 2003 | 2004 |
| 2 | Hardware | $300 | $335 | $450 |
| 3 | Software | $100 | $150 | $60 |
| 4 | Internet Fees | $50 | $55 | $60 |
| 5 | Training | $100 | $120 | $140 |
| 6 | Total | $550 | $660 | $710 |

3. Increase the width of column A:
   a)  Position the cell pointer on any cell in column A.
   b)  Click **Format**, **Column**, **Width**. Enter **18** and press **Enter**.

4. Highlight cells B5 to D5 and click the **Borders** button on the Formatting toolbar to insert a line above the total row.

Borders

## Create the Chart

5. Highlight cells **A1** to **D5**. Note that this range does not include the column totals.

6. Click the **Chart Wizard** button on the Standard toolbar.

Chart Wizard

## Respond to the Wizard Prompts to Build the Chart

7. Click **Column** for the chart type and **Clustered Column** for the chart sub-type.

8. Click **Next** to confirm the chart type.

9. Click **Next** to confirm the chart source data.

10. Be sure the Titles tab is selected and input the label for the y-axis: **Budgeted Dollars**. *Note:* Because the items in the x-axis are self-explanatory, an x-axis label is omitted for a simple, uncluttered design.

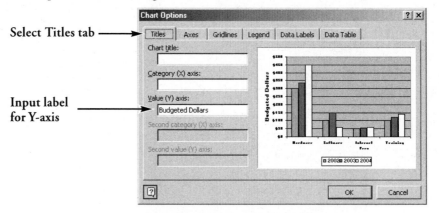

11. Make sure the As object in button is selected and click **Finish**.

## Format the Chart

12. Make the following format changes to the chart. Refer to the FYI box on page 151 for formatting tips.
    a) Move the legend below the column chart.
    b) Change the font size for the category axis to 8 points bold so that the expense categories (hardware, software, Internet fees, and training) will fit horizontally across the x-axis. Format the y-axis in the same manner for consistency with the x-axis.
    c) Save the notebook using the file name **Budget**.

Format a chart created in Excel using the right-click technique to select specific areas of the chart just as you do in PowerPoint. Refer to Project 7 to review detailed instructions for formatting charts.

## Linking the Chart to the Slide

13. Select the column chart by pointing and clicking to the outside border of the chart. Handles appear on the outside border of the chart when the chart area is selected.

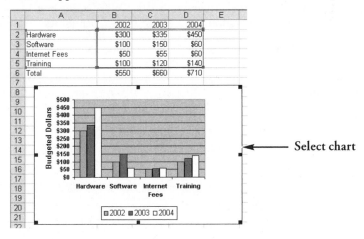

Select chart

14. Click **Copy**.

15. Minimize Excel and make PowerPoint your active application.

16. Create a new slide using the Title and Chart layout from the Other Layouts category.

17. Read the instructions for formatting special symbols in the FYI box on page 152 and then key the chart title in the slide title placeholder **Technology Expenditures Budget, 2002 – 2004**.

## Link the Notebook File to the PowerPoint Slide

18. Click one time to select the chart placeholder.

19. Click **Edit**, **Paste Special** and click **Paste Link**.

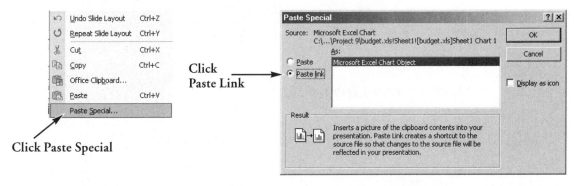

Click Paste Special

Click Paste Link

# Designer's Pointer

Special symbols often help create highly professional slides and handouts and ensure accuracy when phonetic spelling is needed. Some keystrokes, such as quotation marks and fractions, are automatically replaced with such special symbols. To insert a symbol that is not on the keyboard or replaced automatically, click **Insert**, **Symbol**, then click the appropriate category and scroll to locate the desired symbol. Following are some special symbols and their appropriate uses.

### En dash
Use instead of a hyphen to separate words indicating a duration (May–June or 2003–2004).

### Em dash
Use instead of a dash (- -) to indicate an abrupt change in thought or a title (Project 9—Hyperlinks).

### Feet/Inches or Hours/Minutes
Use the prime mark (′) instead of a single quotation mark (') for feet or hours and the double prime mark (″) instead of a quotation mark (") for inches or minutes.

### Fractions
Create common fractions ( $2/3$, $3/8$, $5/8$, and $7/8$ ) rather than key the numbers separated by a slash if the software does not replace them automatically with the symbol. Special symbols are available for common fractions only.

### Phonetic spelling
Key José rather than Jose and résumé rather than resume for accuracy.

### Other symbols
Use the symbols for ©, ®, ™, ÷, ¶, etc.

---

20. Note the chart is inserted in the presentation and linked to the Excel file Budget (source file) so that changes to the Excel file can be reflected in the chart on the slide.

21. Format the chart to fit the chart placeholder
    a) Click the list arrow beside the chart.
    b) Select **Undo Automatic Layout**. To bypass this reformatting process for other charts, select **Stop Automatic Layout of Inserted Objects**.

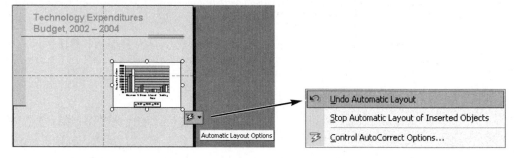

## Update the Linked Notebook

22. Click one time to select the chart on the PowerPoint slide.

23. Right-click and click **Linked Worksheet Object**.

24. Select **Edit**. The notebook file (source document) is displayed for revisions.

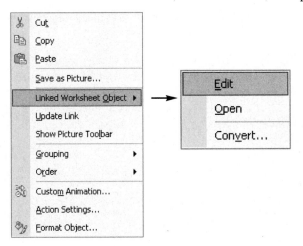

25. Change the cost of training in 2004 to **$500**. Press **Enter**.

26. Save the file and return to the PowerPoint slide. Note the revised value is reflected in the chart.

---

## Troubleshooting Tip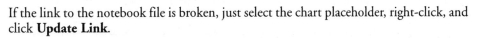

If the link to the notebook file is broken, just select the chart placeholder, right-click, and click **Update Link**.

---

# Inserting Slide Transitions

*Directions:* Follow the instructions to add slide transitions to the slides created in this project.

1. Display the presentation in Slide Sorter view and select slides without slide transitions.

2. Click the **Slide Transition** button on the Slide Sorter toolbar, and select the **Wipe from Left** effect at a Fast speed setting.

3. Click **Apply**.

# Reinforcement Activities

Add the following slides to the file Present for added reinforcement of the PowerPoint features you learned in this project. Position the slides as shown in the table at the end of the project.

## Activity 1

Add a hyperlink to your personal home page or your college/university's home page that will be accessed by clicking your name or the name of your college/university on the "Title" slide.

## Activity 2

Copy the "Types of Presentation Visuals" slide and create the enhanced design as shown in the model.

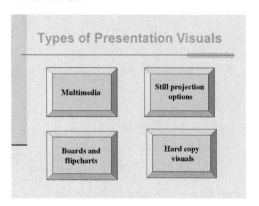

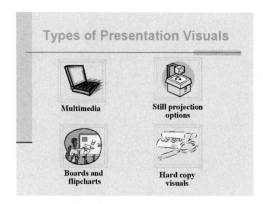

**Original Slide**                    **Enhanced Summary Slide**

1. Reposition the text box beneath the hyperlink button.

2. Copy and paste the clip art of the laptop from the "Multimedia" slide in front of the button. If the image falls behind the button, select the button and click **Draw**, **Order**, **Send to Back**.

3. Reformat the AutoShape button to create a subtle backdrop for the image as illustrated in the model or create an effect of your own:

   a) Eliminate the fill color by selecting **No Fill** as the fill color.
   b) Select a .75-point line slightly darker than the background color.
   c) Decrease the angle of the bevel by dragging the yellow rectangle away from the center of the bevel.
   d) Reformat the remaining three buttons using the format painter. Refer to the FYI box on page 132 for instructions for using this time-saving technique.

Select
No Fill  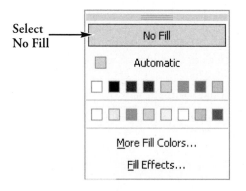          Drag to reduce
angle of bevel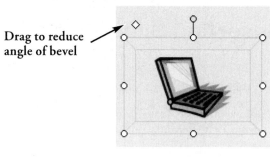

4. Group the clip art and the "Multimedia" text box.

5. Animate the grouped object to start with the hyperlink button directly above it (e.g., laptop button and text "Multimedia") and add animation effects of your choice.

   You can bypass the grouping process; simply animate the text box and the image to be displayed with the button (use the "Start with Previous" animation). The grouping process is recommended because it reduces the number of objects you must manage in the Custom Animation list.

6. Insert a hyperlink on the button **and** the text box to jump to the related slide just as you did in the project.

## Activity 3

As manager of the Human Resources Department at Becker Enterprises, you must submit a periodic written report and presentation depicting the relative attendance in the company's executive training programs. The number of managers attending the programs offered in 2003 includes the following: Electronic Presentations, 152; Internet Commerce, 142; Leadership Skills, 84; Public Speaking, 75; Conflict Resolution, 64; and Customer Service, 44.

1. Use the Chart Wizard to construct a pie chart in Microsoft Excel showing the percentage of managers participating in each program. Input the raw data as Excel will compute the percentages when the pie chart is built. Save the file as **Training**.

2. Create a new slide in the file Present using the Title and Chart layout from the Other Layouts category.

3. Input a slide title: **Management Executive Training Attendance, 2003**.

4. Link the pie chart from Excel to the PowerPoint slide.

5. Return to the Excel file Training (source document) and input revised values for 2004: Electronic Presentations, 168; Internet Commerce, 145; Leadership Skills, 96; Public Speaking, 82; Conflict Resolution, 58; and Customer Service, 84.

6. Save the Excel file and return to the PowerPoint slide to verify the changes and to revise the date in the slide title.

## Slide Order

Print a copy of the file Present as an audience handout with six slides per page. Sequence the slides as shown for Project 7, page 125, with the changes noted below. Your instructor may instruct you to print the slides created or revised in Project 9 only.

1. Title Slide *(revised with hyperlink)*

2. Top Mistakes Presenters Make *(revised)*

3. Adapting Speaking Style to Today's Fast Pace *(revised with hyperlink)*

4. Types of Presentation Visuals *(revised with hyperlink buttons)*

5. **Types of Presentation Visuals (*revised with images superimposed on hyperlink buttons*)**

6. Multimedia *(revised with hyperlink)*

7. Still Projection Options *(revised with hyperlink)*

8. Boards and Flipcharts *(revised with hyperlink)*

9. Hard Copy Visuals *(revised with hyperlink)*

10. **Technology Expenditure Budget, 2002–2004 (position after "Considerations Affecting Presentation Media Choice")**

11. **Project 9, Reinforcement Activity 3 (position at end of slide show).**

# PROJECT 10

## Designing Web Presentations to Reach Remote Audiences

### Learning Objectives

- Design a presentation specifically for viewing on the Web for the purpose of reaching remote audiences.
- Publish a PowerPoint presentation as a web page and view the Web version on an Internet browser.

## Designing Web Presentations

Publishing a presentation on the World Wide Web allows presenters to reach a broad audience in various remote locations. The process is simple, as a wizard converts a PowerPoint presentation to a series of Web pages that can be viewed by anyone with access to the Web site, but the speaker may require assistance from a systems administrator to actually post your Web presentation to a Web server. At the same time, consider options for access to your presentation. Will you give anyone on the Web access to your presentation, or restrict access to employees at various company locations or to business partners (vendors, supplies, or customers)? Technology also allows for delivering live Web presentations, where hundreds of viewers can watch presentation visuals on their Internet browsers while hearing a speaker's live presentation on a conference call or viewing it in conjunction with Internet conferencing software such as Microsoft NetMeeting.

Creating effective Web presentations is challenging because of the multitude of technical issues that affect the way a presentation loads on a viewer's monitor. These issues are explored in greater detail in the Designer's Pointer on page 158.

### Creating the Web Pages

*Directions:* Follow these instructions to create a presentation to be posted to the company intranet to inform employees about the company's wellness program—complete with text and engaging photographs illustrating the benefits of this company-sponsored program. The Web presentation consists of (a) an Opening Page that identifies the company, reveals the purpose of the page, and provides a legend for navigating through the presentation, and (b) a series of pages related to the three components of the wellness program accessed from the legend on the Opening Page. Your instructor may require you to customize the design for a company of your choice and adapt the design to fit your company and your own style.

**Opening Screen**

# Designer's Pointer

Presenting a presentation on the Web gives you access to many more people than you could gather in a conference room, especially when many of these people are located in numerous remote locations. Simply posting an existing presentation is an ineffective practice that could sabotage your success in achieving the goals set for the presentation. Rather, follow these basic guidelines for designing a presentation specifically for the Web:

- **Design a unified look and feel for the presentation.** Begin with a tightly organized Opening Screen that clearly identifies the company and reveals the purpose of the presentation. Consider repeating certain elements from the Opening Screen to other pages within the presentation to tie the sections of the presentation together.

- **Design your presentation for easy navigation.** Give viewers control over the order in which they will view the presentation. The Opening Page may include a simple legend that lays out the viewers' options for creating their own experiences within your presentation.

- **Consider selecting a Web template until you gain experience designing Web content.** A Web template will assist you in selecting simple light backgrounds with spots of color using a Web-safe palette of colors. You can be confident that these presentation slides will be clear and easy to read and will load on the screen in a minimal amount of wait time. Likewise, attempt to keep animation and sound effects to a minimum. While these effects may be dazzling on your laptop computer, not all viewers may be able to download them because of vast differences in technical setup.

- **Use graphics effectively.** Include only graphics that serve a specific function in the presentation and limit the total size of the graphic to reduce the time it takes for the image to download.

Now note how these guidelines are illustrated in the Web presentation you will build for this project.

## Create the Opening Screen

1. Open a new presentation using the default (blank) presentation design. Select a color scheme following the guidelines presented in the Designer's Pointer.

2. Create a new slide using the Title Only layout in the Text Layouts category.

3. Input the title in the Title placeholder using a 32-point Arial Black font. Position as shown on the model on page 157.

4. Insert and format the company's name and address attractively: **American Insurance Agency, 7346 Executive Park Drive, Chicago, IL 74957.**

5. Insert an image or company logo that portrays the company's corporate identity and professional image.

6. Create the legend users will use to navigate through the presentation:
   a) Create the buttons for the three items in the legend using the bevel AutoShape or an image of your choice.
   b) Add the text identifying each item in the legend.
   c) Format the hyperlink button and the text box attractively using colors complementary with your color scheme.

7. Position relevant photos in front of each button. If the image falls behind the button, select the button and click **Draw, Order, Send to Back.**

8. Save the file as **Webpresent.**

## Create Linked Pages from the Legend—Health Testing

You will create two pages that provide more specific information about the health testing component of the wellness program. Employees access the first of these two pages by clicking the Health Testing button on the Opening screen.

**Page 1—Health Testing Component**

**Health Testing**

You can receive health testing every quarter at absolutely no charge to you. Tests available at this time include:

- blood pressure monitoring
- cholesterol testing
- variety of cancer screenings

Each test is performed by a physician from a local hospital. Click here for more information about scheduling an appointment.

**Page 2—Health Testing Component**

**Schedule for Health Testing**

January 6 – 10
April 3 – 7
July 5 – 9
October 1 – 5

Please call Diane Heath at Extension 2398 to schedule an appointment.

9. Create page 1 as shown in the model.
    a) Create a new slide using the Title & Text layout in the Text Layouts category.
    b) Input the title in the Title placeholder using a 40-point Arial Black font.
    c) Key the text using a 24-point Arial font; use a bulleted list to highlight the types of tests.
    d) Copy the company image/logo and the photo associated with the Health Testing legend button from the Opening Screen. Resize and reposition for appeal. Adding these elements on the link pages creates unity with the Opening Screen and assures users they have not inadvertently followed a link out of the presentation.

10. Create page 2 as shown in the model.
    e) Create a new slide using the Title & Text layout in the Text Layouts category.
    f) Input the title in the Title placeholder using a 28-point Arial Black font.
    g) Key the text using a 24-point Arial font and position as shown on the model.
    h) Insert a photo that conveys the key idea of scheduling an appointment and has a tone consistent with the other photos in the Web presentation.

## Link the Legend and Related Pages

11. Insert a hyperlink from the legend button on the Opening Screen to page 1 ("Health Testing"). Review the process of creating hyperlinked text and objects in Project 9 if necessary.
    a) Select the photo **and** the AutoShape. Sizing handles will appear on both the photo and the AutoShape if both objects are selected.
    b) Click **Slide Show, Action Settings.**
    c) Select the Mouse Click tab to require viewers to click the hyperlink to access the first link page or the Mouse Over tab to simply pass the mouse over the hyperlinked image to activate the hyperlink.
    d) Click **Hyperlink to** and select **Next Slide** (or click Slide and select the desired slide title.

12. Insert a hyperlink from the text box ("Health testing") on the Opening Screen to page 1 ("Health Testing").

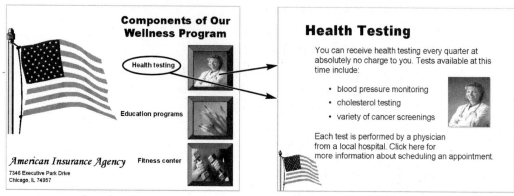

Opening Screen                     Page 1—Health Testing Component

**Link legend button and text box to page 1—Health Testing Component**

13. Insert a hyperlink from the word *here* on page 1 to additional information provided on page 2.

   a) Display page 1 ("Health Testing") in Slide view.
   b) Select the Mouse Click tab to require viewers to use a mouse click to access the hyperlink.
   c) Highlight the word *here*, click **Insert**, **Hyperlink**, and select page 2 ("Schedule for Health Testing").

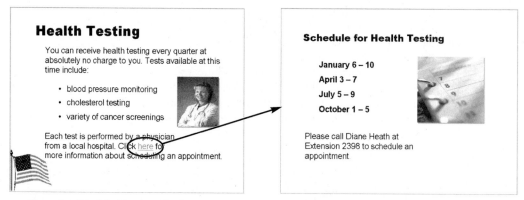

Page 1—Health Testing Component        Page 2—Health Testing Component

**Link *here* on page 1 to access page 2**

14. Insert hyperlinks on the two pages related to Health Testing to return viewers to the Opening Screen. From the Opening Screen, viewers can link to other legend buttons ("Education programs" or "Fitness Center").

   a) Display page 1 in Slide view.
   b) Draw and format an attractive, but subtle hyperlink button such as the one shown in the model. This custom hyperlink includes the text *Home* inside a Rounded Rectangle (found in AutoShapes, Basic Shapes) to denote clearly that the link returns to the Opening Screen.
   c) Select the AutoShape and click **Slide Show**, **Action Settings**. If this command results in underlined text, refer to the Troubleshooting Tip on page 162.
   d) Select the Mouse Click tab to require viewers to use a mouse click to access the hyperlink.
   e) Click **Hyperlink to**, select **Slide**, and select the Opening Screen from the list of slides.

f) Copy the "Home" hyperlink button to page 2. The hyperlink requires no editing because it is already set to return to the Opening Screen.

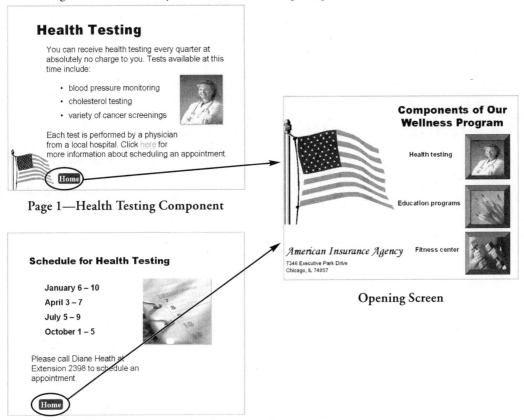

Page 1—Health Testing Component

Page 2—Health Testing Component

Opening Screen

**Link from pages 1 and 2 back to the Opening Screen**

15. Create a hyperlink on page 2 to return to page 1.

a) Display page 2 in Slide view.

b) Create an attractive, subtle hyperlink button using the left arrow from AutoShapes, Block Arrows. The arrow pointing to the left communicates clearly that the hyperlink will move backward in the presentation. A custom hyperlink with the text *Previous* would achieve the same results.

c) Select the Mouse Click tab to require the viewer to use a mouse click to access the hyperlink.

d) Click **Hyperlink to**, select **Previous** (or click Slide and select the desired slide title from the list of slides).

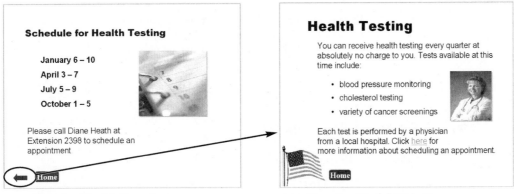

Page 2—Health Test Component

Page 1—Health Test Component

**Link from page 2 back to page 1**

16. Run the presentation in Slide Show view to check the accuracy of all hyperlinks.

17. Continue to Reinforcement Activity 2 to build the remaining slides in this Web presentation.

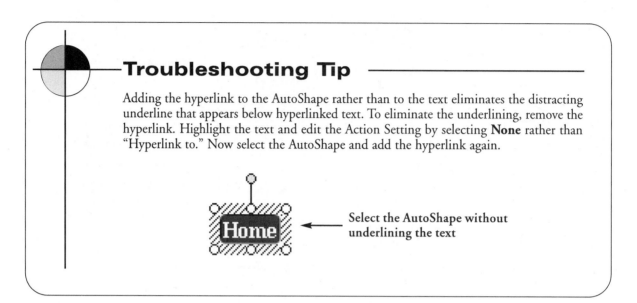

## Troubleshooting Tip

Adding the hyperlink to the AutoShape rather than to the text eliminates the distracting underline that appears below hyperlinked text. To eliminate the underlining, remove the hyperlink. Highlight the text and edit the Action Setting by selecting **None** rather than "Hyperlink to." Now select the AutoShape and add the hyperlink again.

Select the AutoShape without underlining the text

---

## Adding Voice Narration to a Presentation

Adding voice narration to a PowerPoint presentation can enhance your Web-based PowerPoint presentation or self-running slide show presentation at a kiosk or booth. Also, recording audience comments, notes, and action taken during a presentation can allow you to create a record of the presentation for later review. To record a voice narration, you need a sound card, microphone, and speakers. You may choose to provide notes with your narration for the benefit of those without the appropriate computer equipment or anyone having difficulty hearing. Any notes keyed in the Notes pane of the PowerPoint window will appear beneath the slide as it is displayed as a Web page.

1. Display the Opening Screen of the Webpresent file in Normal view.

### Create Narration Notes

2. Click in the Notes pane and key a couple of sentences you will later record to introduce employees to the company's corporate wellness center. This text will appear below the slide when it is displayed in the browser.

3. Key brief notes for both pages of the Health Testing component.

### Prepare Narration Settings

4. Click **Slide Show**, **Record Narration**.

5. Click **Set Microphone Level** and follow the directions to set your microphone level, and then click **OK**.

6. Click **OK** to begin recording the narration and to embed the narration sound so that it becomes a part of the presentation and travels with the presentation.

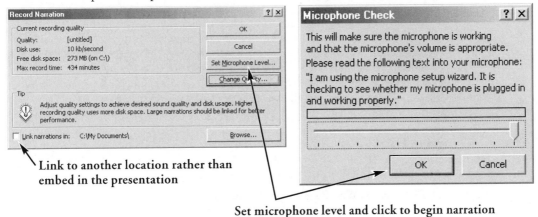

Link to another location rather than embed in the presentation

Set microphone level and click to begin narration

You can link, rather than embed, the narration sound in a presentation file. A linked file is stored where you specify and plays with the presentation. The file size is smaller and the sound will play faster, but you must remember to move the linked narration file if you move your presentation to another computer.

7. Designate the slide where the recording will begin. If you begin recording on a slide other than the first slide, you will receive the following prompt.

   Click **Current Slide**, to start the narration on the currently selected slide. Click **First Slide**, to start the narration on the first slide in the presentation.

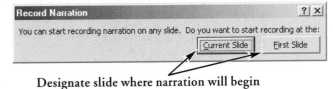

Designate slide where narration will begin

## Record the Narration

8. Display the Opening Screen in Slide Show view and speak the narrative text for the first slide into the microphone. Click to advance to the next slide and speak the narrative text for that slide, advance to the next slide, and so on. To pause and resume the narration, right-click the slide, and on the shortcut menu click **Pause Narration** or **Resume Narration**.

9. Click **Exit** when you are ready to stop recording and save the narration.

10. Determine the timings you will use to advance the show. Click **Save** to save the timings resulting from the narration or click **Cancel** to set timings separately. Refer to using rehearsal timings in Project 5, page 85, if necessary.

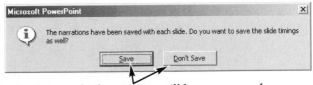

11. Run the Webpresent file in Slide Show view and listen to the narration.

Designate whether timings will be set separately

## Publishing a PowerPoint Presentation to a Web Site

Rather than save your presentation in the default format as a PowerPoint presentation, you will convert the presentation to an HTML document using a PowerPoint wizard. Your Web browser (such as Internet Explorer® or Netscape®) interprets instructions and taglines written in HTML (hypertext markup language) and displays the page on the viewer's screen. You will view your Web presentation in your browser to see how it looks as a series of Web pages but post the presentation to an actual Web server only if directed by your instructor.

### Create the Web Pages

1. Be sure that the file Webpresent is open.

2. Click **File, Save as Web Page** and click **Publish**.

Click Publish

3. Edit the Publish dialog box as follows:
   a) Click **Complete presentation** to publish all slides in the file.
   b) Specify support for both Netscape and Internet Explorer by selecting **All browsers listed above** to ensure greater support to your viewers.
   c) Specify the drive location you want to use for saving your Web files.

4. Click **Publish**. PowerPoint creates an HTML, or Web page, version of your presentation and saves it in the specified location.

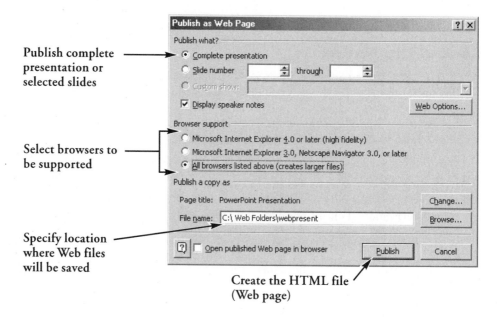

Publish complete presentation or selected slides

Select browsers to be supported

Specify location where Web files will be saved

Create the HTML file (Web page)

## View the PowerPoint Web Pages

You will open in your Internet browser the page or HTML document that you created so you can see exactly how it will look after it has been published as a Web page.

1. Open your Internet browser (Internet Explorer or Netscape).

2. Click, **File**, **Open** and browse to locate the Web file.
   Note the browser window shown in the model is divided into two vertical frames, similar to the Normal view in PowerPoint. You can navigate through the presentation by clicking (a) the title of each slide displayed in the left frame, (b) the previous and next slide buttons at the bottom of the slide, or (c) the legend buttons you designed earlier. The address in the browser indicates that the presentation is stored on a local drive and not a Web server.

3. Consult your instructor for directions related to publishing the Web presentation to a Web server for others to view.

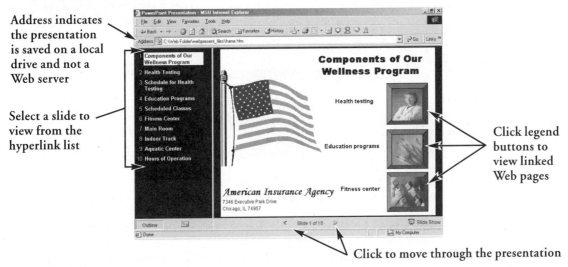

**Address indicates the presentation is saved on a local drive and not a Web server**

**Select a slide to view from the hyperlink list**

**Click legend buttons to view linked Web pages**

**Click to move through the presentation**

# Reinforcement Activities

Add the following slides to the file Webpresent for added reinforcement of the PowerPoint features you learned in this project. Position the slides as shown in the table at the end of the project.

## Activity 1

Create the remaining slides in the Web presentation related to the corporate wellness program: (a) two linked pages from the Education Programs button and (b) one linked page from the Fitness Center button, and (c) slides of your own design to complete the Fitness Center component of the Web presentation.

### Create the Linked Pages from the Education Programs Component

1. Create the two pages related to Education Programs that will be linked to the legend on the Opening Screen. To increase your efficiency and to ensure consistency in the design, copy the pages created for the Health Testing component (page 159). Revise as shown in the models.

Page 1—Education Programs Component     Page 2—Education Programs Component

2. Insert the hyperlinks to link these pages. Refer to the instructions for linking the pages in the Health Testing component if necessary.

   a) Link the Legend Button ("Education programs") and the text box on the Opening Screen to access page 1.
   b) Hyperlink the word *here* on page 1 to access page 2.
   c) Add a hyperlink on page 1 and page 2 that takes the viewer back to the Opening Screen.
   d) Add a hyperlink on page 2 that takes the viewer back to page 1.

### Create the Linked Pages from the Fitness Center Component

3. Create the page related to the Fitness Center that will be linked to the legend on the Opening Screen. Edit a copy of another first page for optimal efficiency, just as you did in Step 1 of this activity.

Page 1—Fitness Center Component

4. Insert the hyperlinks to link these pages.

   a) Link the Legend Button ("Fitness center") and the text box on the Opening Screen to access page 1.
   b) Add the hyperlink on page 1 to return the viewer to the Opening Screen.

5. Design the linked page containing the Fitness Center's hours of operation using your own information. Add a hyperlink to the word *here* on page 1 to access your page ("Hours of Operations") and add a hyperlink on your page to return the viewer to page 1.

6. Design a page of your own for the links to the three areas in the Fitness Center ("main exercise room," "indoor track," and "aquatic center"). Add a photograph depicting each of these areas and brief information describing what the employee could expect to experience there. Add the hyperlinks needed to (a) move from Fitness Center, page 1 to your three pages and (b) return from each of your pages to Fitness Center, page 1.

7. Run the presentation in Slide Show view to check the accuracy of all hyperlinks.

## Activity 2

Add voice narration to the new slides you created in the Wellpresent file in Reinforcement Activity 1.

## Activity 3

Publish the updated file Wellpresent as a Web page and view the Web version of your presentation in your Internet browser. Publish the Web presentation to a Web server if directed by your instructor.

## Slide Order

Print the slides in the file Wellpresent as an audience handout with six slides per page sequenced as shown below.

1. Components of Our Wellness Program (Opening Screen)

2. Health Testing

3. Schedule for Health Testing

4. Education Programs

5. Scheduled Classes

6. Fitness Center

7. Main Exercise Room (student's design)

8. Indoor Track (student's design)

9. Aquatic Center (student's design)